Bon Voyage

ECCENTRIC

OXFORD

a Practical Guide

Bradt Travel Guides Ltd, UK
The Globe Pequot Press Inc, USA

Bradt

The Bumps rowing races in Oxford are sometimes literally that, the aim being to bump the boat in front without being bumped by the boat behind. No-one hurt this time, but could be painful if you catch your rowlocks on something (BH) page 275

WEIRD CUSTOMS

Oxford has more strange traditions than you can shake an old stick of a professor at. Some may be daily but others are rarer, even once every hundred years

That's the way to do it: Elegant travel in a punt. But next time, why not have a wicker hamper with canapes, champers on ice, blazers, boaters, floaty dresses and a wind-up gramophone?
(PA/P) pages 203–10

e dining hall at Magdalen showing High Table
d (below) lunch at Christ Church with Latin
ce on the lectern. All you need is Dumbledore
d a few floating candles – *Homenum Revelio* –
d it's pure Hogwarts. Mind you, if it's anything
e boarding school, the food will be vile. And
ouldn't they have learned the grace off by
eart? Poor show... (JM) page 279

An undergrad wearing sub fusc gets totally
trashed with pies, cakes and shaving foam hurled
at him to mark his finishing finals. Posh bubbly to
hand too – all good training to be a top banker in
the City of London (RB/A) page 282

STRANGE SCULPTURES

Look up as you walk round Oxford and you'll be rewarded with superb sights. Mind you, not all pleasant. They say the devil is in the detail. Literally, sometimes, in this city

Antony Gormley may be Britain's greatest living sculptor, but in Oxford his statues are often dressed up by students with football shirts, academic gowns and ball dresses. Well done, chaps. How about an enormous pair of straight wings? (DG)

Unbelievable: It looks as if a shark just fell out of an aircraft into this terrace house in Headington. The most eccentric sculpture in Oxford – and in Britain (RS/A) page 71

One of the Emperors outside the Sheldonian. The photographer, Ethan Tucker, captioned this rather well: 'Wait! Did I leave the gas on?' They all go to the pub on Christmas Eve, apparently (ET) page 161

What is she up to? This grotesque looks like she could have been in the film *Shrek*. (AC)

... while this moustachioed chap has ears bigger than Andrew Marr's (AC)

Split personality? Or Siamese twins? Perhaps they are merely modelled on real students (AC)

CARTOONS IN STONE

Gargoyles and grotesques, creatures that form a significant part of Oxford's population, are a deeply eccentric part of the architecture – subversive, mocking and counter-culture.

One of my favourites is this bishop facing Magdalen Bridge blessing people as they cross the Cherwell at the end of the High. If you're heading for Cowley Road you might need it! (AC)

You'll love the details hiding in corners, such as this not-very-grim reaper gathering the harvest in (AC)

This evil little devil at Brasenose looks like he was carved less than 20 years ago. Indeed, the date translates as 2003 (MJ)

grotesque, to be found at College, is modelled on ern don: after all, did they alf-moon glasses in medieval (MJ) page 138

Shouldn't have had that kebab after 16 pints of Old Disgusting. Well, he wouldn't be the first to lean out of an Oxford building for a technicolour yawn... (NH)

May morning in the High:
Only in Oxford would
streets be packed before
dawn to have the remote
chance of hearing a Latin
hymn wafting down from a
tower (SO'R) pages 8–11

May-
The outfi
eccentric
hankies and
on trous
distraction
Morris dan
is approp
for a city
saved Eng
folk music
pag

May morning: If you do catch a glimpse of the choristers atop
Magdalen tower, they are not always angelic. They have clearly
outraged the stone chap just below them (DJ) page 149

May Day: Well, thank God
that's over for another
year. Fancy a quick gapser
down by the bridge?
(DG) pages 8–11

You just have to squeeze in the Oxford Folk Festival. Well, accordion to their fans! (BR/A)

Cowley Road Carnival, contrary to the outfits, clearly appeals to middle-of-the-road types (S/A) page 16

TOWN & GOWN FESTIVITIES

Few cities of this size on earth have so many eccentric events, oddball, intensely intellectual or inexplicable, as Oxford ...

xford's annual Santa Run, held on a mid-December Sunday, is a bit bonkers, particularly when the sea f red and white breaks into a flash dance. Surreal. More than 1,000 people take part to raise cash for he local children and young people's hospice (BC/A)

This St Giles pub, called 'the Bird and Bastard' by some, was the crucible for the 20th century's greatest fantasies: *The Lion, the Witch and the Wardrobe* and *The Lord of the Rings*. Might do it for you too (TT) page 188

Literary importance? Well, the Bodleian Library is simply the most beautiful library in the world, the biggest and the best, and the statue outside is of William Herbert, third Earl of Pembroke, Chancellor of the University (1616–30), who paid for Shakespeare's plays to be first printed and thus saved for us. And he featured in the sonnets. And had an utterly amazing sex life (JH) pages 157–8

LITERARY OXFORD

You can hardly walk a few paces in Oxford without coming across spots linked to inspiring books, hit movies, great TV series and purest poetry. There's something in the air (and we don't mean wacky backy, Bill)

Bill Clinton

IT IS ALLEGED THAT IT WAS HERE AT THE TURF TAVERN THAT BILL CLINTON, WHILE HERE AT OXFORD UNIVERSITY, DURING THE SIXTIES, 'DID NOT INHALE' WHILST SMOKING ILLEGAL SUBSTANCES. (WHAT HE DOES WITH CIGARS IN HIS OWN TIME IS HIS BUSINESS)

You don't have to be young to enjoy the Turf, as Colin Dexter's Inspector Morse found out in the detective series often filmed here (PG) page 154

Shelley's Monument in University College sometimes has a certain appendage painted bright blue by students. Once the surrounding basin was even filled with water, complete with goldfish (RH) page 140

Ben le Vay's
ECCENTRIC
OXFORD
a Practical Guide

Bradt

Second edition published October 2011
First published 2004

Bradt Travel Guides Ltd
IDC House, The Vale, Chalfont St Peter, Bucks SL9 9RZ, England
www.bradtguides.com
Published in the USA by The Globe Pequot Press Inc,
PO Box 480, Guilford, Connecticut 06437-0480

ISBN: 978 1 84162 426 6

British Library Cataloguing in Publication Data
A catalogue record for this book is available from the British Library

Photographs
Alamy (A): Richard Baker (RB), Barry Clack (BC), Ben Ramos (BR), Robert
Stainforth (RS), Septemberlegs (S); Photolibrary (P): Peter Arkell (PA); Alan
Coleman (AC); Darrell Godliman (DG); Pedro Guzman (PG); Rex Harris (RH);
Becca Hayes (BH); Skye Hohman (SH); Nick Holloway (NH); James Head (JH);
Maggie Jones (MJ); Donald Judge (DJ); Jon M Myers (JM); Shamus O'Reilly
(SO'R); Thorskegga Thorn (TT); Ethan Tucker (ET)

Illustrations
Cover artwork & in-text silhouettes Neil Gower (www.neilgower.com)
In-text cartoons Rowan Barnes-Murphy (www.rowanbarnes-murphy.com)

Maps
Map data © OpenStreetMap contributors, CC-BY-SA
Cartography by David McCutcheon (www.dvdmaps.co.uk)
Otmoor Bike Ride map by Alan Whitaker

Typeset from the author's disc by D & N Publishing, Baydon, Wiltshire
Production managed by Jellyfish Print Solutions; printed in India

DEDICATION

For Martin, born in Oxford, who saw from his pram at Wolvercote the sky black with planes and gliders heading for D-day, was later at Pembroke College, was married in this city, who endured illnesses in its hospitals, a sometime denizen of Old Marston, a long-term eccentric habitué of Cowley Road, and who vowed to die within the Oxford ring road and did so in 2010. For him, his beloved Oxford was the world, and he could hardly walk ten yards down the High without meeting an old friend, from roadsweeper to professor, whom he treated, and was treated by, with equal courtesy. A great gentleman, a hugely supportive elder brother, an inspiration and a help with this book.

ACKNOWLEDGEMENTS

With thanks to: Andy Simpson, Rita Ricketts, Robert Popham, John Price, Alan Whitaker, Julian Le Vay, Jo Dobry. Plus the brilliant editors, mapmaker, illustrator and photographers. Any mistakes, however, are all my own work.

CONTENTS

Key to Maps

INTRODUCTION

WHY OXFORD?

Most guidebooks at this point would say something like this: 'Oxford, a unique gem of dreaming spires, a treasure house of precious honeyed stone set in a bowl of green velvet hills.' Totally true – and totally trite touristy guff that you know already.

This book aims to offer you more – such as the deeply eccentric people in *Chapter 4* – while covering the basics too. And, after all is said and done, just because something has the ring of a cliché doesn't stop it being true, worthwhile and important.

Take it instead from a real, first-time visitor I was showing round. The visitor, walking into Radcliffe Square from Brasenose Lane, said: 'Wow. Look at that.'

A period of silence letting the beautiful shapes in sunlit golden stone sink in, the Gothic of St Mary the Virgin contrasting hugely with the circular classical discipline of the Radcliffe Camera, and everywhere the backdrop of ancient richly decorated seats of learning. Century upon century of a strange mix of scholarship and youthful excess.

The visitor recovered his speech and went on: 'It's like a wonderful film set, except it's real. There's nothing to spoil the view, nothing. It's so English, so calm, so sombre. Everywhere the detail is fabulous.'

Of course, it *has* been a film set, many times from *Accident* to *Inspector Morse*. But if you are a first-time visitor, that moment of discovery awaits you too, and I envy you that.

What else would a regular guidebook say? That it's central to Britain, on the way to anywhere (unlike a supposed rival establishment that rots gently in some remote East Anglian bog), easy to reach from London and Stratford-upon-Avon, reachable from all the main motorways, handy for Heathrow (see *Chapter 14*), central to the national rail system, and that it's compact and flat so ideal for exploring on foot. Yes, we know that, dearie, talk about stating the obvious. We didn't think it was in Florida or a mountain skiing holiday.

No, what you, the intelligent, educated, humorous and curious guidebook reader, want is a look at the eccentricities of Oxford, its secrets and foibles, its nooks and crannies, the oddballs, the laughable, the brilliant and the daft. This book will provide that, together with all the key information you need to explore this city, small enough to be seen in one sweep from Elsfield churchyard or Boar's Hill, but rich enough to yield up surprises for a lifetime of visits.

WHY IS OXFORD UNIVERSITY DIFFERENT?

An odd thing about Oxford is the things that are invisible. Just as there is no very visible cathedral (only an overgrown college chapel, really, hidden away) there is no university, in the sense that you can't ask to be taken there by a taxi driver. Where on earth would the cabbie take you?

It is a collection of colleges, each with its own character and strength, a loose federation that sometimes reminds me of an airman's wry definition of the Lancaster bomber ('20,000 rivets flying in loose formation'). Like the regimental system of the British Army, herein lies its strength, for each unit generates intense loyalty and rivalry, striving for academic and sporting success.

One applies for admission to one of the several dozen colleges, each with its own idiosyncratic ways and special areas of excellence. Admissions tutors have famously employed tactics such as apparently being bored and opening a newspaper and saying 'Impress me'. The applicant who set fire to the paper got through. Or seemingly absurd examination questions such as 'Is this a question?' (best answer: 'If this is an answer, yes'). Exams may be enough for other universities, but not, it seems, for eccentric Oxford. Recent questions have included 'Do worms think?' and 'Name all Santa's reindeer' or 'Why do you read *Cosmopolitan*?' Or 'If you had to write a book on 18th-century teaspoons, how would you make it interesting and relevant to a reader today?'

Other tutors lie on the floor, or feed live chicks to a ravenous bird of prey perching at their elbow. It can be disconcerting, but they are not there to be pleasant. It is a test of character, a search for initiative and excellence.

While the lectures, medical facilities, nuclear laboratories or whatever are provided by the university, it is in the weekly one-to-one tutorials on a college level that an undergraduate's mind is tempered and sharpened. Here last week's essay is analysed and read out, next week's discussed. The tutor, unless you are extremely unlucky, will be one of the best in the world at his or her subject.

At other universities you can fool around and miss most of the teaching until the exams at the end. Not at Oxford, where the intense pressure is on from the start. Some of the students crack, and the suicide rates and mental hospital admissions have always been high – although this could be a corollary of the quest for individuals of original genius rather than the academic pressure. Most, it must be said, thrive and shine.

The exams themselves give rise to eccentric stories, such as Oscar Wilde's at Magdalen (see page 150). One, possibly apocryphal, concerns a student who refused to start writing because an ancient statute said each 'clerk' should have a flagon of ale for the examination. The authorities checked, rushed out and bought the beer. On the way out the student was arrested for not wearing a sword.

But it is not mere snobbery for an employer's eyes to light up when he or she sees a good Oxford degree on a CV. In a world of shifting standards, compromised admissions criteria and political correctness, Oxford still stands for something.

WHY ECCENTRIC?

As detailed at more length in my book *Eccentric Britain*, this country's tolerance of, and love of, eccentrics has paid off handsomely in making what could otherwise be a rather bleak, wintry, windswept Atlantic island more bearable. Whereas other countries have frowned on and shunned mad professors, idiosyncratic inventors, eccentric explorers, mad marquesses and dotty dukes, we have always rather liked them. If somebody is weird enough, for example, to instal a giant shark plunging into their roof, as has happened at Oxford (see page 70), in the end, when we get over the shock, we rather like it and give them a regular slot on Radio Oxford. Eccentricity has paid off with extreme explorers from Oxford, with brilliant writers creating many weird worlds right here, crackpot to merely curious inventors and, above all, real characters. We meet many of them in this book.

BAD THINGS, AND GOOD THINGS, ABOUT OXFORD

The bad things include the swarms of visitors on summer weekends, although anyone with this guidebook or a map can soon find hidden city lanes, riverside walks and paths to peaceful villages that escape the madding crowd. Traffic has been a real headache, too, and this has been dealt with by making it almost impossible to drive through the city centre. Parking is a nightmare or non-existent, so for these two reasons the car-borne visitor must stop short of the city and take a bus. How to survive that, and some insider tips are detailed in the last chapter of this book.

But the real gems in this absolute jewel of a city are unspoiled and lie to the east of the north–south axis defined by St Giles, Cornmarket Street and St Aldate's. In *Chapter 8* we take a look at a collection of wonderful buildings unparalleled anywhere on earth, and also delve into the back streets away from the hubbub of tourist honey-pots to find the quiet flavour of ancient Oxford in peaceful cobbled lanes and secretive pubs with hardly a soul to be seen.

The essence of Oxford, then, is a pleasing blend of almost mystical mellow crumbliness with a surprisingly youthful brilliant buzz. Old genius and young genius paraded before you. So it is never, ever boring.

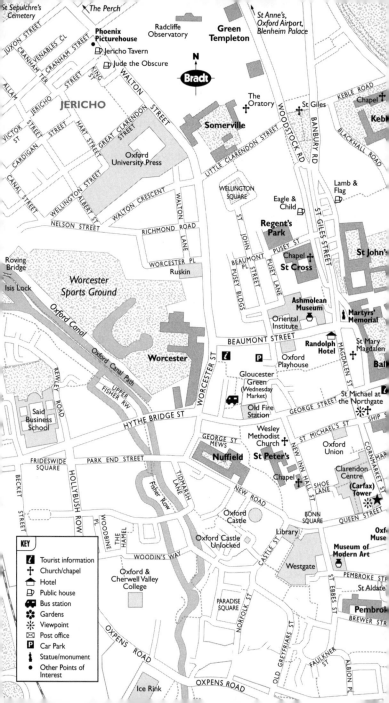

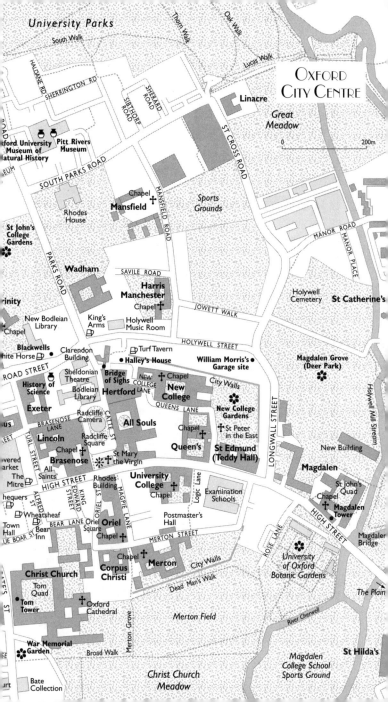

OXFORD CITY CENTRE

0   200m

University Parks

South Walk

Thorn Walk   Oak Walk

Lucas Walk

Linacre

Great Meadow

HALDANE RD   SHERRINGTON RD

SIBTHORP ROAD

SHEBARD ROAD

MANSFIELD ROAD

ST CROSS ROAD

...ford University Museum of ...atural History

Pitt Rivers Museum

SOUTH PARKS ROAD

Rhodes House

Chapel   **Mansfield** †

Sports Grounds

MANOR ROAD

MANOR PLACE

St John's College Gardens

PARKS ROAD

Wadham

SAVILE ROAD

Harris Manchester

Chapel †

JOWETT WALK

Holywell Cemetery

St Catherine's

...inity

New Bodleian Library

Chapel

King's Arms

Holywell Music Room

HOLYWELL STREET

Holywell Mill Stream

Magdalen Grove (Deer Park)

Blackwells
...hite Horse

Clarendon Building

Turf Tavern

Halley's House

William Morris's Garage site

City Walls

Sheldonian Theatre

History of Science

Bodleian Library

Bridge of Sighs

NEW COLLEGE LANE

† Chapel

New College

New College Gardens

LONGWALL STREET

ROAD STREET

Exeter

Hertford

CATTE STREET

QUEENS LANE

New Building

...us

BRASENOSE LANE

Radcliffe Camera

All Souls

† St Peter in the East

Lincoln

Radcliffe Square

Chapel †

Queen's

St Edmund (Teddy Hall)

Magdalen

...vered ...arket

Chapel †

Brasenose

All Saints

† St Mary the Virgin

University College

St John's Quad

The Mitre

HIGH STREET

Rhodes Building

† Chapel

MAGPIE LANE

Logic Lane

Chapel †

Magdalen Tower

...hequers

TURL STREET

ALFRED STREET

KING EDWARD STREET

Examination Schools

Magdalen Bridge

Wheatsheaf

Bear Inn

BEAR LANE

ORIEL STREET

Oriel

Oriel Square

Rhodes Building

Postmaster's Hall

ROSE LANE

Magdalen College School Sports Ground

Town Hall

...UE BOAR ST

Chapel †

MERTON STREET

University of Oxford Botanic Gardens

The Plain

Christ Church

Chapel †

Corpus Christi

Merton

City Walls

Dead Man's Walk

Tom Quad

† Oxford Cathedral

Tom Tower

Merton Grove

Merton Field

River Cherwell

War Memorial Garden

Broad Walk

St Hilda's

...urt

Bate Collection

Christ Church Meadow

THE
ECCENTRIC
YEAR

The full story of Oxford's oddest events, with brief mentions of some other possibly more boringly sensible ones. For an up-to-date listing of Oxford events such as plays and films, see *www.visitoxford.org or the Tourist Information Centre, Broad Street, Oxford.*

Even better, go online and see *www.dailyinfo.co.uk* – I guarantee you will be astonished at how much goes on in this pulsating city. As the website itself puts it, 'The creative energy of Oxford event organisers is something frightening. As a city, we never sleep. There's always something going on, from charity festivals to professional and student theatre, world class opera, local film screenings, dozens of yoga, dance and fitness classes, political rallies, mind-expanding lectures, many dozens of gigs and concerts each week, a hundred or so churches and weird and wonderful meetings and exhibitions.' That's for daily one-offs. What we can do here, by contrast, is list some of the extraordinary and eccentric traditions.

Note: events change, so the listings don't guarantee that they are happening or will happen. Check nearer the time. Events are included here because they are eccentric – that is, curious, amusing or fascinating – not always because they are open to the public, which will become clear.

JANUARY

HUNTING THE MALLARD Some eccentric British customs, such as the Dunmow Flitch, happen every four years. Some, such as the Corby Pole Fair, every 20 years. But it would seem beyond belief that a richly complicated ritual should survive if it were only happening every 100 years. After all, how would anyone remember the special songs and dances?

But All Souls College, Oxford, achieves this seemingly impossible feat with its truly ancient and suitably bizarre ceremony, Hunting the Mallard.

It all started in 1437 when the foundations of the college were being built. A mallard was found by workmen in a great drain, and it was of prodigious size. The custom grew up of feasting on this anniversary, called Mallard or Gaudy Night, and then searching the college for this legendary duck.

This has traditionally involved the Fellows of the college led by a Lord Mallard elected for the night and six officers, all wearing special mallard medals depicting the duck (to help them recognise him, I suppose). At midnight the whole procession starts off bearing lanterns,

white staffs and flaming torches, and singing loudly the 'Mallard Song'. The search goes through every cellar, every room and over the rooftops and is not ended until daylight (unless they really meet the giant duck, I suppose, which would give them a shock).

The special 'Mallard Song' has several verses, of which this is just the first:

> *The Griffin, Bustard, Turkey, Capon,*
> *Let others hungry mortals gape on,*
> *And on their bones with stomaches fall hard,*
> *But let All Souls' men have their Mallard.*

The rather odd chorus being:

> *O, by the blood of King Edward,*
> *O, by the blood of King Edward,*
> *It was a swapping, swapping Mallard!*

Presumably 'swapping' meant not that the duck was a great stamp collector, but that it was 'whopping', ie: very big indeed.

3

The hunt has at times degenerated into unseemly Mallard malarky, and it was in the 17th century that Archbishop Abbot complained bitterly in a letter to the college:

Civil men should never so far forget themselves under pretence of a foolish mallard, as to do things barbarously unbecoming.

Apparently the Mallard hunt had extended around the city, with the doors of sleeping citizens being beaten down in the middle of the night to search for the great bird.

Another bishop, in 1801, watched with astonishment as he recorded: 'I had a full view from my garret of the Lord Mallard and about 40 fellows in a kind of procession on the library roof, with immense lighted torches... all those within half a mile must have been awakened by the manner in which they thundered their chorus.'

So if you are in Oxford and are woken up by a procession of mallardy singing weirdos with torches and staves coming through your house, possibly having smashed the door down, looking for a giant bird that doesn't exist, don't worry (if the year ends in 01 and it is 14 January, that is). They won't be back for another 100 years... *14 January, only if the year ends in 01.*

MARCH

OXFORD LITERARY FESTIVAL A bookworm's bonanza in March or April. Top-notch novelists, historians, biographers, crime writers, scientists, economists, cookery writers, commentators, artists, art writers, critics, and travel writers visit to speak, answer questions and, of course, sign books. Names you would know and names you should know. *Date varies.*

☎ 0870 343 1001 (may change in future years)

🖳 www.oxfordliteraryfestival.com.

TORPIDS College rowing races held on the River Isis (Thames). As 'torpid' means slow, sluggish, as in 'torpor', these may take longer than you expect. I think it means relatively slow compared to the faster eights, but perhaps I'm just being torpid. Apparently college hearties call them 'toggers', as rugby becomes 'rugger', the Radcliffe becomes 'Radders'. At this rate, I don't want to know what they call that other set of races, the Bumps.

POOH STICKS WORLD CHAMPIONSHIPS Held at Day's Lock, Little Wittenham, near Oxford (well, nearer Didcot), usually at noon. This could be seen by some as slightly silly (that is, making a world event of a fictional sport of a talking bear, Winnie the Pooh, and his chums, an event which supposedly anyway happened in deepest Sussex and was in fact written by a Cambridge man). That would be to miss the point, which is that pooh sticks is a surprisingly pleasant occupation, and for a country which holds the world championships in sports taken as seriously as snail racing, toe wrestling and black pudding throwing, why not? If you haven't read *Eccentric Britain*, the sport consists of more than one person simultaneously dropping sticks into a river on the upstream side of the bridge over a river or stream, then racing or strolling, depending on the rate of flow of said watercourse, to the other side of the bridge to see whose stick comes out first. Throwing the sticks is not allowed, nor are carbon-fibre computer-designed racing sticks. They must be natural sticks and they must be dropped. Surely it's just local sticklers, not a real world championship? Well, one recent event was won by the Czech Republic with Latin America taking the silver, and Iceland not making it to the medal podium. The event, which attracts up to 2,000 serious contestants, benefits the Royal National Lifeboat Institution, which may be a good thing given the possible effects of the deluge of sticks from this event on the next one, further downriver, often on the same day. *Late Saturday.*

Days Lock, Little Wittenham OX14 8RB
☎ 01235 522711 🖳 www.pooh-sticks.com
🚗 M4 J13 or M40 J9, to Didcot via A34, stay on A4130 round north side of town, take B4016 then lane to Long Wittenham first. Parking in narrow lanes a problem; get there early. 🚂 Appleford, just north of Didcot on London Paddington-Oxford line. A nice walk east two miles, or taxi from Didcot station.

MARCH/APRIL

THE OXFORD AND CAMBRIDGE BOAT RACE Odd really, in that it isn't in Oxford or Cambridge; up to a quarter of a million people turn out to watch, even though most of them know little about rowing, are not supporters or graduates of either Oxford or Cambridge, and will be able to see only a small part of it. Around another nine million watch on TV. But in eccentric England things have become much-loved traditions for much less reason. It takes place on the Thames in London, from Putney to Mortlake. But as one Londoner said: 'It's the first day out beside the river in the year, and it's free, so why not if it's a nice day?' The course goes upriver from the University Stone, just upstream of Putney Bridge, to Chiswick Bridge. The pubs such as the Dove, the Rutland and Blue Anchor on the north side just west of Hammersmith Bridge (itself eccentrically ornamental but for some reason not open that day) would be good vantage points, but crowded, ditto the White Hart on the south side a little upriver in Barnes, which has more room and a generous sweep of the river. So well ingrained is the event that in Cockney rhyming slang, 'Nice girl, pity about the boat' means she's ugly, but otherwise charming. Held since 1829, when a Cambridge student challenged an Oxford former school friend, that challenge is still to be settled, because each year the loser challenges the winner to a rematch. It started at Henley and then Westminster, but settled on the current course in 1845. The score at the start of 2012 was 80–76 to Cambridge, with one dead heat. Favourite year: 1912, both boats sank (so it was rerun in more clement weather), and 2003 when two rowers in each boat had a brother in the opposite boat, making it a particularly close-fought race. *Last Saturday in March or first in April.*

🖥 www.theboatrace.org
🚇 Putney Bridge 🚂 Mortlake from Waterloo

EGG ROLLING, SHOTOVER COUNTRY PARK Easter for many British children nowadays sadly means just stuffing your face with too many chocolate eggs, with little religious significance, except that Lent is over. Had the podgy blighters abstained from anything during that period, it might mean something. But here in Oxford the older idea of rolling or hiding brightly decorated hard-boiled eggs is not forgotten. At Shotover Country Park, Headington, there are competitions for rolling painted hard-boiled eggs. It reminds me of an Oxford-educated charity worker in Nepal hiding coloured eggs in her garden. She then told the local children they had to find them. They looked puzzled. 'But you know where they are, we don't.' Hard-boiled, those kids. *Easter Monday.*

APRIL

OXFORD CITY BUMPING RACES Sounds like something very silly indeed, but is another set of rowing races on the Isis, for coxed fours. *Mid-April.*

MAY

MAY MORNING At 5.30am on 1 May each year, come rain or warm weather, small knots of people are seen scurrying through the lanes and alleyways of Oxford, heading east towards the rising sun (or in the barely light gloaming if it is overcast). As they converge on the High, the crowd becomes a determined stream heading towards Magdalen Bridge, joined by more people from every side street at a time of day when there should be barely a soul astir, until a torrent of people is washing down the High. Some are families carrying children, some are town youths in anoraks or shell suits with base-ball caps on backwards, joshing with policemen who line the route. Many are undergraduates, dressed in black tie and ballgowns, late revellers still out from the night before. There are those with silly headdresses, flags and balloons too, plus bookish dons and curious intellectuals from around the country joining what has become a flood moving down the street. It has that cup-tie feeling of a huge crowd intent on one great thing, and yet what is it they seek, what has dragged perhaps 10,000 people from their beds or kept them up all night in anticipation? Merely the chance of hearing Latin medieval madrigals float down from the top of Magdalen Tower, where already the white vestments of the choir can be glimpsed above the parapet. At the appointed hour, the 10,000 babbling voices in the hubbub jammed shoulder to shoulder down below grow silent without being bidden to do so, and that ethereal sound floats down on the damp morning air, hanging like May morn magic, a dim memory of that old pagan beginning of spring, but now with a Christian prayer for Oxford inserted firmly between the hymns. Very little else happens. There is no great funfair of burger bars and fire jugglers. True, as the bells of the tower peal out in celebration afterwards, students often jump into the Cherwell thanks perhaps to inebriation, but this is ill-advised. The bridge is relatively high and the river only about 4ft deep. Many a serious injury has been caused, and many a ballgown spoiled. The latter problem was spectacularly avoided by one buxom student who stripped off and jumped in naked in 1996. I remember the pictures causing quite a stir on a Fleet Street picture desk when they arrived, and also when they appeared in the paper with her black hair miraculously lengthened in just the right places to make the picture seem more 'decent'. Don't believe everything you see in the papers.

Morris dancers form up in side streets with their eccentric outfits of bells, sticks, hankies and pigs' bladders. I saw one such bunch of morris men line up in Rose Lane beside the Botanic Garden facing towards Magdalen College. Ahead of them was a wall of people jammed in like vertical sardines. Indeed a crowbar and some olive oil would have seemed necessary to remove any one of them, and we had given up trying to make progress towards the bridge. The order went out to the morris men and the hankies started waving, the bells jangling, the squeezebox squawking and the drum booming as the well-rehearsed machine started dancing towards this immovable human wall. It was insane, like the Light Brigade charging the Russian guns at Balaclava. Nothing could save this from being another Valley of Death, yet the disciplined morris men kept going in perfect time like a clockwork machine and the wall of humanity stood impassively, completely blocking the end of the road. Disaster surely beckoned. I stood transfixed, muttering: 'C'est magnifique, mais…'

Yet then a miracle took place. The crowd somehow parted just enough to let the morris men into its ranks and they passed in without missing a step. The wall reclosed and now only the flying hankies, the jingling bells and the boom of the drum showed their progress through the sea of people. It wasn't the Charge of the Light Brigade after all – it was Moses and the Red Sea. A morris minor miracle.

The city pubs and some on the Cowley Road side are open from 6am for pots of ale and cider and hearty breakfasts for those who want to continue celebrating this the first day of Oxford's spring. Others go punting with hampers and champers. The morris men spread throughout the city, livened up by characters such as the Fool and the Hobby Horse (or 'Obby 'Oss). Broad Street is a good place to catch them later. But most people just go on home, or to work, for it is the *real* 1 May, not the one on the nearest Monday that the rest of the country is forced to observe. As one Oxford celebrant put it strongly to me: 'We're not having some bloody bureaucrat in London telling us in Oxford when it is May morning, and that's an end to it.' For a few years at the end of the 20th century the road was partly closed because the authorities feared the Magdalen Bridge parapet was about to give way, but when it became clear the crowd wanted to stand on it, the parapet was strengthened to cope with the modern-day throng. So that's May morning in Oxford. Thousands of people getting up very early, from far and wide, on the chance of hearing a little Latin and then, by and large, quietly going home. Very Oxford, very English, and very eccentric. Be there at 5am if you want to be near the base of the tower, and know that you won't be able to move until after 6am. Oddly, it's worth it. *May Day, 1 May.*

OXFORD PRIDE Celebration of Oxford's gay community. Oxpens Recreation Ground. Music, food, cabaret. *1 May or nearest Saturday.*

🖳 www.oxfordpride.org.uk

MAYFLY Live bands, South Park, Oxford. *May Day Bank Holiday (nearest Monday to 1 May).*

EXAMINATIONS Only in Oxford, surely, do students dress formally for examinations and wear white carnations on the first day and red ones on the last. *Throughout May.*

OXFORD BALLOON FESTIVAL Cutteslow Park, Oxford. Typically, mass balloon launches, parachute jumps, camel races, etc, plus music in the evening. *Mid-May weekend.*

OXFORD ARTISTS open their studios and often homes for the public to look around in the biggest arts event of its kind, involving 500 artists across the county, many here in Oxford. You can get a guide to where and when they all are from local libraries, tourist information or online. *Throughout May, check times.*

Oxford Artweeks, PO Box 559, OX14 9EF
☎ 01865 865596 🖳 www.artweeks.org

BEATING THE BOUNDS – THRASHING CHOIRBOYS AND CHERRY CAKE If you don't find the sight of a bunch of choirboys thrashing the floor in the ladies' underwear department of Marks & Spencer in Queen Street with long canes while a vicar looks on approvingly even slightly eccentric, then you must be born and bred in Oxford. This bizarre ritual takes place on Ascension Day and is part of the ancient ceremony called Beating the Bounds. This involves taking the youngsters of the church to the boundary stones of their parish and beating them – the stones and, formerly, the youngsters – with canes, shouting 'Mark! Mark! Mark!' to impress on the next generation where the boundaries are. In some cities the boundaries may be in a river, so boys thrash the water, or new buildings may be built higher, so the boys may be lowered head first into a hole in an office floor to knock their heads on the stones.

Here in Oxford one such procession leaves **the church of St Michael** at the North Gate after the morning service on Ascension Day for a three-hour perambulation of 30 stones, all marked with a cross, which the vicar marks with a further cross in chalk and the church's initials before the boys (or middle-aged parishioners nowadays) beat them. The reason that this church has such a large boundary (for a city parish) is that it absorbed the church of St Martin (demolished, leaving only Carfax Tower) and All Saints (the spire ringed with a cylinder of columns in the High that is now above a college library). The clergy and boys go through shops and clamber over high walls, for nothing must stop their ancient route, and the vicar, knowing that it will take at least three hours, fair powers along, with appropriate blessings at each spot.

We bash the wall of Boots the chemist and the vicar says: 'Bless those who would heal the sick', and we dive through the storerooms of Littlewoods to find a stone under some racking and he says: 'Bless those who supply our city with food and other goods.' And so it goes on, and although: 'Devil take the hindmost' isn't the best phrase to use, don't stop for a natter or you'll be left behind while the stick-bearing throng surges off through startled shoppers like a bunch of Viking invaders. At one college, St Peter's, after plunging through the undergrowth shocking students swotting in the gardens, we stop in a common room and I'm served orange juice by a professor of statistics who is also a priest. 'What are the odds against that happening?' I wanted to say. No time, we plunge onwards.

It finishes at **Lincoln College**, where the boundary beaters have lunch in hall and a special beer drunk from pewter tankards. After lunch hot pennies are traditionally thrown from the roof into the front quad for the choirboys to scramble for. This is another bizarre old custom mixing benevolence with pleasure in cruelty (or 'sport' as we English call it) whereby coins were thrown for paupers but were red-hot. Your smarter pauper put rags round his hands. A further twist at Lincoln is that some cold coins are thrown by watchers hoping to confuse the little urchins (or possibly well-fed brats) about which coins are hot. Possibly the smarter boffiny brat today carries a hand-held laser thermocouple-radar with digital read-out and can detect the cold ones in mid-air, plotting the trajectory so he merely stands in the right place with his hand, or pocket if the coin is hot, wide open.

As I say, one of the marks is appropriately in Marks (and even more appropriate that their brand name is St Michael) but you may receive, as I did, odd looks for grovelling about on the carpet in the ladies' support garments section looking for the brass plate. This marks the real spot and must be thrashed but the boundary stone has been moved to a corner where it is on display behind a glass door. An inscription tells us who put 'this sacred stone' there (being Oxford, it's Hunc Lapidem Sacrum wotshisname Posuit).

The **church of St Mary the Virgin** also goes in for this (without the ladies' knickers), but the choir goes along and sings various verses of an Ascension Day carol at preordained spots, such as Brasenose College front quad. At All Souls College coins are thrown to the choirboys in the north quad and they are served breakfast in hall, including a special cherry cake in memory of an orchard that stood here centuries ago. Oddly, their right to enter All Souls on this one day for this one purpose *cannot be denied* for it is ordained in an Act of Parliament of 1714. The procession goes on via University College and Oriel College and the other side of Brasenose and back to the church in time to sing, exhausted, the last verse of what must be a very long hymn. Still, the pay isn't bad – flying pennies and cherry cake.

Since a boundary stone by definition marks the corner of two or more parishes, it is clearly possible that troops of stick-wielding boys from opposing sides could meet, with mayhem the result. I put this amusing thought to a lady parishioner of St Michael as we sped from spot to spot on Ascension Day. She seemed shocked at the suggestion of mayhem: 'Oh no, I think we'd all join hands and celebrate our stewardship of Oxford.' I think I was being told off for being un-Christian.

You can join in for what must be one of the best, fastest, cheapest and most historic walking tours of Oxford if you are not part of a large group and if you ask nicely at the end of the service, which usually includes quite beautiful madrigals. Or just go along for the first two or three then peel off. *Ascension Day (typically late May, related to Easter).*

EIGHTS WEEK Serious inter-college rowing races. Those who are less fit like me might prefer After Eights Week. *Wednesday–Saturday of fifth week of Trinity (summer) Term.*

JUNE

ENCAENIA Sounds like a herb for nervous women, but it is the full pomp and panoply of the university on show in a procession to, among other things, confer honorary degrees on international bigshots at the beautiful Sheldonian Theatre. This is preceded by a special university occasion of utmost seriousness to which the invitations read:

> *Mr Vice-Chancellor invites Pro-Vice-Chancellors, Heads of Houses, holders of the Oxford Degrees of Doctor of Divinity, Civil Law, Medicine, Letters, Science, and Music, the Proctors, the Assessor, the Public Orator, the Professor of Poetry, and the Acting Registrar to partake of Lord Crewe's Benefaction to the University. Thence they will go in procession to the Sheldonian Theatre, where will be spoken the Oration in Commemoration of the Benefactors of the University according to the intention of the Right Honourable Nathaniel, Lord Crewe, Bishop of Durham.*

And although one may wear academic dress of 'certain other universities' to many official occasions, this is one where it is absolutely necessary to wear Oxford gowns, silly hats, fluffy bits, etc. And the event that was decreed by Lord Crewe in the 17th century? The eating of peaches and cream with champagne, difficult to do in the full robes but a necessary part of being an Oxford don. Tough, isn't it? *Noon on the first Wednesday following full Trinity Term.*

COWLEY ROAD CARNIVAL Cowley Road celebrates its multi-cultural make-up, with a colourful parade, much food and music, all strongly flavoured. The road is closed and cafés and restaurants spread their tables outside (weather permitting), while people climb on roofs to get the best view of the extraordinary and fabulous floats, dancing teams and costumes. Expect Caribbean reggae, Hindu gods, Chinese dragons, and even people from Swindon. Usually on a Sunday. At about the same time, probably the day before: **Jericho Street Fair**, in Canal Street. *Mid-June weekend.*

FEAST OF ST JOHN To mark the feast, bullrushes are spread on the ground under the open-air pulpit in St John's Quadrangle, Magdalen College, to symbolise the wilderness. The service is attended by the Chancellor or Vice-Chancellor of the university, mace-bearers and bedells. Why St John, as it's not St John's College? This quad was built on the site of the 1180-built Hospital of St John. *24 June.*

OOMF Festivally stuff, usually outdoor music/drama things and free. There was also, in 2004, the Oxford Open Water Festival. The very creative programmes evolve for each year. *Late June.*

Also runs events at different times of the year.
☎ 01865 204042 💻 www.oomf.org.uk.

JULY

HENLEY ROYAL REGATTA This isn't messing about in boats, but is *the* serious rowing event for those who aren't just good but the best in the known galaxy. Some people who row from the fabled Temple Island up the legendary straight course towards the town bridge go on to win four or even five Olympic gold medals, gaining knighthoods and other honours (such as local boy Sir Steve Redgrave, whose daughter, by the way, won a race here in 2011). There's also a famously posh if not snooty social scene, part of 'the Season' whereby the idle rich drift from Epsom to Royal Ascot to Wimbledon to Henley to Cowes to Goodwood to Cheltenham. These events are so famous that the mere mention of the names, for Brits at any rate, doesn't need the addition (respectively) of horses, more horses, tennis, boats, more boats, more horses and more horses. It doesn't mean the rest of us (idle poor, even) can't enjoy these events, however, and we do. The Royal Regatta, which has been running in this pretty little town since 1839, is followed by the Henley Festival (arts, music, books) which uses the regatta stands to good effect.

TOP PUB: the Angel on the Bridge. If the pub's full, walk across and go to the Little Angel in Berkshire. Heavenly.

ECCENTRICITIES: The warning to engine drivers at each end of the bridge, the annual pilgrimage to Dusty Springfield's grave ('the greatest white singer there ever was' – Elton John) at St Mary the Virgin, each 2 March.

☎ 01491 572153 🖾 www.hrr.co.uk
🖾 www.henley-festival.co.uk

🚗 Southwest from Oxford on the A4074 then the 4130, a very pleasant drive, or, coming from London, M4 J8.

🚂 Henley-on-Thames is on its own charming short branch line off the London-Paddington to Oxford route (change at Twyford).

AUGUST

PARTY IN THE PARK Live music in South Park.

JAZZ IN THE PARK Live Music in Cuttesloe Park. Not the most original of names. They could try… *Date varies.*

PARK IN THE PARK Doesn't exist, but the visiting motorist could certainly do with it.

PORK IN THE PARK Hog roast. Also doesn't happen. Yet. *Various Saturdays.*

CROPREDY FESTIVAL A huge annual gathering at a tiny place called Cropredy near Banbury north of Oxford of fans of a folk-rock band – you might need this explaining if born after 1965 – called **Fairport Convention**, billed as 'The rock gods of Oxfordshire' by some of their followers. In fact it claims to be Europe's largest folk festival. Wasn't it this band who were so old in the 1970s that one of the albums had a huge fold-out family tree of who had been in and out of the band? Amazingly, this is not a tribute band but the original band (re-formed a few times). Well good luck to them. If Mick Jagger can keep going for ever (and apologies if that comment is overtaken by events), why not Fairport? Hippie grandparents, dog on a piece of string, dream catchers, ethnic drums, tie-dyed T-shirts –

yes, we're still in the 1970s, but pleasant enough. The band used to convene, by the way, in a house called Fairport in Muswell Hill, London. *Mid-August weekend.*

☎ 0900 637 1644 💻 faircrop@aol.com.
As it's on the Oxford Canal, you could go by boat.

SEPTEMBER

HERITAGE OPEN DAY If you feel your family should be behind bars this is your chance, with Heritage Open Day letting you into Oxford's ancient prison and many other rarely open buildings. They might let you out again too if you're law-abiding. *Second weekend.*

💻 www.oxfordopendoors.org.uk

GREAT BRITISH CHEESE FESTIVAL Sometimes at Blenheim Palace, Woodstock, near Oxford. Eat 700 different cheeses – well not all of them in one sitting – from rampant-goat flavour to apple and garlic. But no Stilton from the village of Stilton. It's never been made there, oddly. If it's held elsewhere – tough cheddar! *Last weekend (usually).*

💻 www.thecheeseweb.com

ST GILES FAIR *Where?* St Giles, north of Oxford city centre. *What?* This genteel, wide, leafy street of academic brainboxes, and intellectual pubs frequented by such as J R R Tolkien, C S Lewis and Graham Greene becomes a cacophonous, noisy funfair with gaudy colours, music blaring, rifle ranges banging, hucksters shouting, the stink of sizzling burgers mingling with the sickly smell of candyfloss and that heady mix of generator exhaust fumes and the oily smell of Dodgem cars – the garish lights and neon tubes flashing as the rides whirl round and round – the hair-gelled youths from every village and hicktown strutting their stuff where professors wheeled their bikes a day or two before, and the well-spoken children of academics as wide-eyed as the rest. Or as Beatrice Batty put in 1888:

> Drums and fiddles accompanied the dancers in two or three dancing tents. Almost every show had its drum, organ, brass-band, gong, or instrument of some sort to bray forth its whereabouts; and those which had not were advertised by the stentorian voice of a show-man or show-woman ceaselessly inviting persons to enter and see the show 'about to begin'. And the shows were various and varied indeed!

This assault on all the senses ends after a couple of days and, miracle of miracles, there is nothing to show it ever took place the next day. Not one chip wrapper or half-sucked lollipop. Amazing.

When? This gets eccentric. It is held on the Monday and Tuesday after the feast of St Giles, which is September 1. But, if the Feast of St Giles is itself on a Sunday, it is held on the following Monday and Tuesday. Furthermore, the first Sunday being on the first doesn't count, which I think amounts to much the same thing. Any guide telling you it is the first Monday or Tuesday in September, as some do, has, therefore, two ways to be wrong. Also, any student with the name Giles can ask for free rides if the four digits of the year add up to the age of the reigning monarch.

Why? This may be merely of parish origin or one of the ancient country fairs of old England. Sometimes called charter fairs, the rights to have these go back to time immemorial, or sometimes to dated royal charters. Often these fairs were hiring fairs, sometimes called Mop Fairs (and they still are in some parts), where you could hire domestics, or, as in Thomas Hardy, farm workers such as draymen or farriers who would all carry a tool of their trade. They were hired because the harvest was over – all these great fairs are in the autumn – and the sideshows sprung up because these poorest of the poor had, for once, a few pennies in their pocket. They might be given a fasten-penny to commit them to turn up for work at the new farm. There were also Runaway Mop Fairs a week or so later for those who didn't like their new situations.

No government can interfere in any such ancient fair without a new Act of Parliament, and indeed when the powers that be tried to cancel St Giles Fair in 1914 because World War I had recently begun, the Home Secretary was told he had no such powers, so it went ahead.

Of course, in Oxford there's been controversy from time to time, not a little caused by snobby people in the big houses here unable to understand why the lower orders should invade their turf for a few days. In 1838 the gypsies were banned by the city fathers, which caused much protest as the fair was an important source of income for them.

In the 19th century it was recorded that none of the showmen was allowed to enter the city until 4am on the Monday, and no spaces were reserved, so there was a mad scramble as Old Tom rang and the showmen whipped their horses to pull their carts and wagons at breakneck speed down the streets to get the best pitches. *Monday and Tuesday after the first Sunday after the feast of St Giles (1 September).*

OCTOBER

RESTORATION DAY This day commemorates Magdalen College's finest hour in 1687 when the foolish and deeply

unpopular King James II tried to force a Roman Catholic President upon Magdalen, a Catholic bishop upon Oxford, and a Catholic council upon the city. Magdalen refused to do the hugely unpopular king's bidding, sticking to its own statutes, and after a long wrangle, including the king sending a troop of horsemen to enforce his new man upon the college (the Fellows all quit rather than have anything to do with the toady), the college and the city won. The king was soon deposed in the Glorious (and bloodless) Revolution of 1688, and later, when another unpopular king was brought over the bridge into the city, he asked what tower that was standing by the bridge. 'That is Magdalen Tower, Your Majesty, the one that King James II ran his head against.' Which all goes to show the British constitution works as long as the monarch doesn't actually do anything, in which case it is everyone's duty to resist like hell.

On this day Magdalen quite rightly congratulates itself with a special peal of bells, a special dinner and a special toast *jus suum cuique* – justice for all. *25 October.*

DECEMBER

St Thomas's Day The bell-ringer at Cowley is given a shilling (five pence in modern money, but once a week's wage) under the terms of a 17th-century shepherd's will, to mark this day of charity. Magdalen College gives the St Thomas's Day dole of bread to villagers on its land at Selborne in Hampshire, or did until recently. Clearly, a day for the upper crust to be generous to the poor. *21 December.*

ECCENTRIC HISTORY

OXFORD BAGS OF HISTORY

For a place where so much ancient history is studied and written, Oxford has surprisingly little of its own. Yes, if you come from Wagga Wagga, Vulture Gulch or Beaver Creek, more than 1,000 years is plenty, but by European standards that's not a lot. It's not an ancient place.

And the reason for that is mud, mud, glorious mud. The Romans just couldn't be bothered with muddy, sticky riverbanks. They preferred nice hard ground for building their roads over and plonking splendid temples and villas on (although they did have a pottery here because of the clay: a piece of their work marked with its local source can be seen in the city museum as proof).

The Roman love of famously straight roads meant they didn't see rivers as a way to get about but as a hindrance to be crossed where the banks were firmer than here. So Oxford (ironically today one of the few places in Europe where the Romans' language is honoured and thrives)

would not have been an ideal site for a Roman settlement.

Three hundred years after the last legions had marched away, things were very different. The Roman roads had gone to hell – rutted, thigh deep in mud and ruined – while invaders' new settlements were not on those routes anyway.

Your average Saxon, therefore, who had by now pushed the Ancient Brits off to Wales, saw the rivers as his highway. Unlike the roads, where even horses could become stuck, someone was continually refilling and levelling the rivers: Nature. Not only that, but rivers made frontiers in the more fractured politics once the Roman Empire had fallen away. Here we have the natural boundary between the kingdoms of Wessex and Mercia and this made Oxford – the Saxon name being simply where you could ford the river with oxen because of the hard gravel bottom near the junction with the Cherwell – of strategic value.

Sadly for the Saxons, the Vikings and Danes could also use rivers as highways, and would penetrate this far inland if the raping, looting and pillaging were worth it.

Of course the rivers were wider, shallower and slower in those days, the banks being marshes, so there were plenty of islands or *Seys* on which to build more defendable settlements. Hinks*ey* and Bin*sey* at Oxford. Down at London, Batter*sea*, Chel*sea* and Bermond*sey* were all Saxon-named islands along the edge of the Thames.

Then you had easily cultivated and watered meadows or *lees*, such as Cow*ley*, Iff*ley* and Rad*ley* near Oxford.

Still other parts of Oxford need no decoding at all, so close was the medieval language to our own: Littlemore and Horspath in Oxford were what the names still say to us, for example.

Given this lack of ancient history, the first recorded mention of Oxford's existence is later than many towns and cities. In AD912, say the *Anglo-Saxon Chronicles*: 'King

THE STORY OF OXFORD'S patron saint, **St Frideswide**. It is virgin on the comic, if you'll pardon the pun. Although a 7th-century virgin, she'd definitely make it on to *Woman's Hour* on today's Radio 4 because she has stuff to say about women's empowerment, getting in touch with yourself, give me space, women in control, I am not a victim, revenge and alternative cures. But Frideswide was a bit more than that, it seems.

The local sub-king is Didan in the late 7th century and he has a rather pious daughter, a fan of the new Christianity, the aforementioned Frideswide (as the name Kylie had yet to be invented). The King is wholly holy too and sets up in Oxford the church of Holy Trinity and St Mary, a forerunner of today's St Mary's.

Young Frideswide sets up a community of nuns there and becomes the abbess. So far, so pious.

Thank God it's Frideswide

However, when Didan becomes dead 'un, Frideswide and Oxford seem up for grabs. King Algar of Leicester (ghastly name, ghastly chap) arrives with his troops, determined to have his wicked way with Frideswide and grab Oxford too.

She flees to Bampton or Binsey (it isn't clear but let's say the latter). God, meanwhile, is getting fed up with all this malarky and strikes Algar the Ghastly blind for his sins. (Or maybe to prevent their having children with even more stupid names.) A pukka saint has to perform a miracle, and indeed she does. The forgiving Frideswide

(CONTINUED OVERLEAF)

25

Thank God it's Frideswide

(CONTINUED)

strikes the ground at Binsey and a spring wells up (or well springs up, whatever). The fluid from this is worth more than all the Specsavers in Wessex, for it totally restores Algar the Ghastly's sight. He repents and clears off back to the land of stinky red cheese whence he came, while she lives happily ever after, getting Frideswider and wider in her nunnery. For more on the well, which is still there to see even for those blinded by divine intervention, see page 221. For more on churches connected with Frideswide, see page 121.

Edward took possession of London and Oxford and all the lands that thereunto belonged.'

Clearly a town existed already for the King to seize, and one that could be mentioned in the same scope as London. It was part of his fortifications against the Danes in the long wars fought from the Saxon capital at Winchester, and Oxford would have been a frontier point in this struggle to keep the Danes back, who were by this time a threat overland. In the *Domesday Book* (the inventory of England famously ordered by William the Conqueror after 1066) under the county of 'Oxenefordscire', it says:

Before 1066, Oxford paid to the King £20 a year and 6 sesters of honey… In this town, within or without the wall,

are 243 houses which pay tax; apart from them, there are
500 houses less 22 so derelict and destroyed that they cannot
pay tax.

So did the other 478 pay? A millennium later, we still
haven't sorted out local government finances.

At the end of the 11th century a causeway was built
across the muddy meadows south of what is now called
Folly Bridge. Being Norman (after all, just Frenchified
Norsemen) they called it Grandpont, and although it is
today the A4144 Abingdon Road, the area on the south
bank here is still known as Grandpont.

THE UNIVERSITY GETS GOING

When the university started to function, the numbers of
students living all over the town caused friction. It was
decreed they must all live in halls. Hundreds of these
sprang up, often just a private house with a few students
living there, but sometimes with rudimentary teaching and
catering. Later – in the 13th century onwards – colleges
emerged with much better teaching provision and proper
endowments to allow them to function properly. These
supersede halls, which largely disappear, although St
Edmund Hall (now a college) remains, having been founded
in 1225.

The mid-13th century sees the oldest colleges, **University
College**, **Balliol** and **Merton** being founded (between
1249 and 1264, although I don't think anyone can state
exactly when). **Exeter** and **Oriel** followed early in the next
century. Members of colleges, by the way, are collegians;
members of halls are aularians, and St Edmund Hall
members still have that title.

Oddly, there are private halls still in Oxford associated with the university, although not quite the same thing as the mediaeval ones (the Reformation having messed things around a bit in the 16th century). But they exist and are often religious teaching institutions. This means little **Blackfriars**, a hall run by Dominicans, but descending from the original founded in 1221 – and hardly a *grand fromage* in the order of Oxford things – could be the city's oldest teaching institution. They do have a precise history – they were founded on 15 August, 1221, although that Henry VIII caused a 400-year gap in the middle. When they were refounded in 1921 (neatly 700 years after the first date) did the monks say: 'As we were saying before were interrupted…' I do hope so.

1267: North v South – chuffing 'eck, it were no joke, 'appen

Talking about racial or national divisions, North versus South battles were a big problem in the Middle Ages. Today it is a friendly rivalry, and one can imagine a *Carry On* film with flat-capped Northerners throwing black puddings and Yorkshire puds and the smock-wearing Southerners who retaliate with salvos of Cornish pasties and deadly Melton Mowbray pork pies.

(There is a deep echo even today of the North–South divide, going beyond accent into more subtle areas. Humour for example: people north of the Trent will sometimes 'not get' what amuses people south of it and vice versa. One culture isn't right and the other wrong, just slightly different. Even the place names give away deep racial divides going back to Angles and Vikings. Would a Southerner call a place Arkengarthdale, or a Northerner call one Nether Wallop? Never!)

In the 13th century there were street battles in Oxford between these two 'nations' – the Northerners (including the Scots) and the Southerners (including the Irish and the 'excitable' Welsh). Most medieval universities were divided this way (eg: Paris had four 'nations' based on origin). One has to remember Europe's nation states as unifying forces had hardly emerged as a precise definition. Great Britain as a legal entity was 500 years in the future, Italy and Germany 600.

After two bad North–South outbreaks in Oxford in 1267 and 1274 in which many were killed, a North–South Peace Treaty was made – it still exists – laying down careful mechanisms for uniting the university and selecting seven Northerners and seven Southerners as representatives, etc. Every university body had to have the same number from above the River Nene as below.

It seems comical today yet, if you replaced Northerners and Southerners with Ulster Catholics and Protestants, or Palestinians and Israelis, the tone darkens to what it must have been if they were willing to kill each other. The North–South battles diminished in regularity and the last recorded one was outside St Mary's in 1506, when 'only' three students were killed and several injured.

1355: THE ST SCHOLASTICA'S DAY RIOT, 10 FEBRUARY – AN UNHOLY MASSACRE

You may have thought ancient Town-versus-Gown rivalry fairly harmless class conflict, whereby today snooty Toby and Araminta might consider themselves above oiks Wayne and Kylie, who would in turn jeer at them in the pub for being toffee-nosed gits. Or where what the tabloid press calls heartless toffs ravish simple chambermaids. Whatever. It always seems to involve pubs. But **Town versus Gown** was not always harmless.

In 1355, on the day known appropriately as St Scholastica's (or possibly the eve of St Scholastica), two gownie students Roger and Walter were in a pub called, also rather appropriately, Swyndlestock on the corner of Carfax when a townie landlord served them bad (yet expensive) wine. In general, the rich Oxford merchants then had the upper hand economically, charging the mostly poor students what they liked for not very good victuals, poor wine and third-class cuts of meat (not at all like today then!). The town pushed around the gown. The greater privilege was the town's. This was about to change.

On this occasion Roger and Walter, even though they were technically clergymen (as were all students), were not putting up with it. They not only threw the jug of wine in the landlord's face, but beat him senseless with the quart pot. The town authorities tried to get the university to arrest the two, but a gang of 200 angry students gathered, armed with bows and arrows, as their bell at St Mary's was rung to gather them together, and attacked and wounded several townspeople, including a 14-year-old who died.

The next day it got worse, with students burning down houses and killing and wounding many more, while the town, in the person of the Mayor, appealed to the King in nearby Woodstock. The townspeople, gathered by *their* bell at St Martin's,

Carfax, being rung – you can begin to see why every inch between the two towers has had blood shed on it, according to locals – returned to the attack on that day and the next.

Although the scholars tried to shut the gates of the town, they were no good against an army of 2,000 countrymen bearing a black flag who came to help the townies, and broke into the halls of learning, killing or wounding everyone there. In one murderous attack the rioters were heard shouting: 'Havoc, havoc, give good knocks, slay, slay!'

Amazingly, the King, who was now approached for help by the gown – the Chancellor and scholars – did nothing to stop Oxford tearing itself apart. The eventual death toll was around 63. Some students were buried alive in dunghills. (Today students prefer Dunhills if they can get them.)

At one point the monks tried to calm things down by parading a crucifix and the pyx (box) of sacred relics, those touching which, by custom, were given sanctuary and protection. Shockingly, the monks were stoned and those holding on to the pyx beaten to death.

The King finally made Town and Gown surrender all their hard-won privileges, then gave back a few to the town but far more to the gown. The university could now control just about everything: the price and quality of bread and ale, weights and measures in the market (you can still see the measures issued by the university in the Museum of Oxford) and even matters such as street cleaning.

The Mayor had to swear to respect the university and every year on St Scholastica's Day 63 townspeople had to attend a service at St Mary's for the souls of those killed in the riots and bring a penny each as penance, legend having it that the Mayor had to wear a humiliating halter round his neck.

(Was this grudge long-lasting? Well, the annual service of humiliating penance by the town and subjection to the gown went on until 1825, *470 years* later! Not only that, but after the university, still annoyed, had the pub knocked down to obliterate its presence, the town in recent years had the name of the Swyndlestock pub carved in the southwest corner of Carfax, where it may still be seen. So they haven't forgotten either.)

Things had not been much better in 1298 when the worried Pope sent a cardinal to the great abbey to investigate the morals of the university. The students clamoured riotously to be let in, so an Italian cook poured boiling water on them, seriously scalding an Irish scholar. Then a Welsh scholar shot (with an arrow, of course, gunpowder not having arrived) the cook through the chest, kebabing him to death. Must have impressed the Cardinal no end.

Actually, I'm impressed that in an age when it took months to get across muddy roads in Europe with a horse, here we have such a blend of nationalities. One historian interestingly blames 'the excitable behaviour of the Italians, Irish and Welsh' as a factor. Welsh? Excitable?

1555: RELIGIOUS HATRED – CHRISTIAN KILLING CHRISTIAN

Although the **Reformation** started more in that little-known rival university, Cambridge, by the middle of the 16th century Oxford was strongly Protestant. The great abbey in Oxford had been suppressed by Henry VIII, along with all the other rich monasteries and convents. The abbey bell ended up in Tom Tower in Christ Church.

But by 1555 the Catholic Queen 'Bloody' Mary was the monarch. She ruthlessly tried to stamp out the new religion, and the radical preacher (I was going to say firebrand but that would be too close to what comes next) **Hugh Latimer** (1490–1555) and prayer-book writers **Nicholas Ridley** (1500–55) and **Thomas Cranmer** (1489–1556) were arrested and tortured near to death. Ridley and Latimer, who would not break their faith, were burned at the stake in Broad Street – the cross in the roadway marks the terrible spot (see page 183).

Dr Ridley's brother brought him a bag and tied it around his neck. Dr Ridley asked what it was and was told it was gunpowder. He said: 'I will take it to be sent of God and will receive it' and asked for some for his brother, meaning Latimer.

Then they brought a burning branch and put it in the heap at Dr Ridley's feet.

Dr Latimer said: 'Be of good courage, Master Ridley, and play the man. We shall this day light a candle, by God's grace, in England that I trust will never be put out.' Cranmer chickened out by signing a recantation. A year later, ashamed of himself, he dramatically recanted that recantation in St Mary's church and was also burned, famously thrusting his right hand into the flames to burn first, as it had sinned by signing the confession the authorities wanted. Cost of burning the bishops: 11 shillings and fourpence (57p) for good dry firewood and labour. There's an impressive monument to the martyrs at the town end of St Giles.

With Mary's death in 1558 the Catholics were again on the receiving end of persecution and a great many, such as the Jesuit Edward Campion arrested near Oxford in 1581, were taken to Tyburn (today's Marble Arch in London) and hanged, again courageous martyrs for their faith.

1640: Civil War – The siege of Oxford

After a good start to the 17th century when James I's enthusiasm meant great new buildings for Oxford, things began to go seriously pear-shaped for the Stuart kings and for Oxford. In the 1640s Oxford was at the centre of the conflict between the King and Parliament. Charles I and his Cavaliers fled from London to Oxford to make his headquarters in the battle for supremacy against the Roundheads of Parliament. He melted down the colleges' gold and silver plate to make coins to pay his troops, some of which can still be seen at the Museum of Oxford, and ripped lead from roofs to make bullets. Miles of complicated ramparts enclosed Oxford. The occasional incoming cannonball lodged in a college tower. Yet academic life continued: when the King sent for books from the Bodleian, the library sent back a note saying that the rules stated that it was not a lending library and you had to read the books there (and you still do). King or no king, war or no war, library rules were rules. A wise move, as in 1649 the King got his head chopped off so any overdue book fines wouldn't have been paid.

1681: The 'Protestant whore' and 'Popish bitch'

After the **1660 Restoration** of the monarchy, Oxford entered a golden age of building and progress, with the university's own genius, **Christopher Wren** (1630–85), and later his brilliant student **Nicholas Hawksmoor** (1661–1736) contributing greatly. The sensibly tolerant King Charles II (1630–85) had many mistresses but not a legitimate son, leaving his hated younger brother, the Roman Catholic-leaning James II (1633–1701), an extremely unpopular heir to the throne. Two incidents, one rather funny and one menacing, involving women in Oxford illustrate the fiery and unpleasant relationship between religion and politics.

In 1681 the mobs are seething around in Oxford angry at the King's refusal to bar his (Catholic) brother James from the throne (which he was to ascend in 1685 and then be thrown off in 1688). At this point word goes around that the elegant carriage that has just arrived from London contains one of Charles's many King's mistresses. The angry crowd fear it is the disliked Roman Catholic Louise de Karoualle, and rock the coach alarmingly. At this point the window goes down on the coach and another of his mistresses, much-loved orange-seller and actress Nell Gwynne (1650–87) , calls out to them: 'Pray, good people, be civil: I am the Protestant whore!' A huge cheer goes up and hats are thrown into the air.

Less funny was the plight of the city's few remaining Catholics. The Mitre pub in the High, a well-known Catholic haunt where secret masses were reputed to be conducted, was often the target of mob fury. The hostess there in 1683, Miss Lazenby, was called a 'Popish bitch' by three Fellows of the university who threatened to return to cut her throat. They didn't have to: she lay down and died of terror. In 1688 the landlord expressed Catholic opinions and every window in the pub was broken and every Roman Catholic home in Oxford sacked. For more on the Mitre, see page 143.

1768: Methodism in their madness

In an almost inevitable process of history repeating itself, by the mid-18th century many Church of England clergy seemed fat, lazy, corrupt, given to feasting not fasting and snobbishly hunting with the gentry rather than being interested in lost souls; they had kicked out the Catholics for just such sins less than three centuries before.

John Wesley (1703–91), a Lincoln College Fellow, started a movement to observe proper religious practices, which led to Methodism. In 1768 six of its followers at St Edmund Hall were kicked out for refusing the Church of England's tenets (a requirement of students until the 19th century). This led to one of those great exchanges between the famed wit and writer of the first proper dictionary **Dr Johnson** (Johnson had been a student at Pembroke; 1709–84) and his Scottish diarist and admirer **Boswell** (who filled a role rather like the unimpressive sidekicks certain radio DJs choose nowadays to make themselves seem ever more brilliant).

Johnson: *'What have they to do at an University who are not willing to be taught, but will presume to teach? Where is religion to be learnt, but at an University?'*
Boswell: *'But was it not hard, Sir, to expel them, for I am told they were good beings?'*
Johnson: *'Sir, I believe they might be good beings, but they were not fit to be in the University of Oxford. A cow is a very good animal in a field, but we turn her out of a garden.'*

It was not the last time Oxford would be at the centre of religious storms. Or Johnson would contradict Boswell.

Meanwhile the city prospered. In 1790 the **Oxford Canal** linked the city up to the motorway system of its day. Previously coal had to be expensively shipped down from the East Coast through London and up the Thames. Now they could come straight from Midlands pits, making life cheaper, warmer and easier. The canal even had express passenger boats. But their profits would be short-lived both for passengers and for coal, thanks to the arrival of the railway age in the city in 1844, as you can still see from the long coal trains rumbling through Oxford on their way to Didcot power station.

1863: REFORM OF THE UNIVERSITY – LIBERAL REVOLUTION AND REACTION

The 19th century was a period of great upheaval for the gown if not the town. Until 1863, all Oxford dons had first to be Church of England clergy, and the students had to follow the Anglican Church too. By 1871, requirements of religious conformity were being dropped: strolling round the quads were the university's first Roman Catholics and Nonconformists. The centuries of hatred were falling away.

Meanwhile, the fossilised nature of academic thought was also being chipped away at – by the **discovery of fossils**, led by Oxford dons. If these showed that the world had not been created with every creature we know already in it, but that things had evolved, as Mr Darwin claimed, where did that leave the Bible, Creation, etc? The fuse was fizzing on the greatest intellectual and spiritual explosives since the Christians arrived on these shores.

What were these strange creatures which the palaeontologists were chipping out of the cliffs of Dorset and the Isle of Wight? **John Keble** (1792–1866), founder of the eponymous college, had no doubt. God put the fossils in the stones at the time of Creation for whatever purpose He deemed. Maybe to test our faith. And even today many people agree with Keble.

In the university museum, then a brand-new tribute to 19th-century engineering despite its traditional exterior, the key **Evolution versus Creation** debate took place in 1860. The conservative Bishop of Oxford, facing Professor Thomas Huxley, sneeringly asked whether it was on his mother's side or his father's that Huxley claimed descent from the apes.

Huxley crushingly replied that he would not be ashamed to have an ape as a remote ancestor, but he would be ashamed to be connected with a man 'who plunges into scientific questions of which he has no real acquaintance, only to obscure them by an aimless rhetoric'. The Bishop, his cheap jibe exposed, was humiliated.

Later – to lighten the tone a little – someone joked they gave an ape in a zoo a copy of Darwin's *The Origin of Species*. The ape looked at it, scratched his head and said: 'Is this true? Am I my keeper's brother?'

Another 19th-century revolution, the **Oxford Movement**, seemed to be going in the opposite direction. It was aimed at pushing the Anglican Church more towards High Church ritual, with incense, rich decoration and an almost Roman Catholic approach, but with a renewed, fervent devotion. In the end some of the key figures fulfilled the jibes of their enemies by actually becoming Catholics, but by that time, fewer people in the increasingly scientific and tolerant world could care.

Academic and religious upheaval notwithstanding, the town was surprisingly unaffected by the **Industrial Revolution** that surged through Britain from the late 18th century and increasingly during the 19th.

This had swept much of Olde Englande out of the way and replaced it with blast furnaces, mines, workshops and railways and their attendant pollution, but was largely disdained by Oxford in the 19th century.

It was suggested that the Great Western Railway's central workshops – a massive enterprise employing thousands of people – should come to Oxford but the powers that be were against it, fearing masses of working people would bring disease and irreparably damage the university nature of the town, giving town more influence than gown. The huge works were built in Swindon instead.

Although the ritualised grovelling of the town to the gown, which dated back to those medieval massacres was stopped in this century, the social nature of the city did not progress. The position of townspeople as rather conservative, deferential servants of the university – it was basically a company town from the Middle Ages until the 20th century – was confirmed by this turning away of great industrial employers. This was soon to change, however. In a change of heart, a different means of transport was to be welcomed into the city.

Talking of medieval massacres, far more Oxford men were soon to die in the slaughter of the World War I trenches: 2,700 were killed and several of those who returned said they found it hard to study surrounded by the ghosts of their friends. They couldn't accept that the stones and gargoyles of the colleges were still here as if that hell and upheaval had not happened. The eccentric warden of New College, William Spooner, even erected a memorial in the chapel for those who died fighting for the other side, for of course there were a few graduates from those countries who were killed in the conflict.

I N 1877, YOU COULD for the first time call the Oxford Fire Brigade by telephone. But only if you were in brigade engineer Neill's home. For there were only two phones.

Technical progress

WILLIAM MORRIS AND WILLIAM MORRIS

The late 19th century and early 20th saw Oxford influenced and revolutionised by **William Morris** (1834–96). To be precise, two William Morrises.

The first was the **Arts and Crafts Movement founder**, the socialist utopian who lived in Oxfordshire and proposed a whole new approach to design of everything from wallpaper to chairs. A return to elegant utility and a reaction to the gaudy trashiness that mass production and industrialisation had brought. A reaffirmation of the role of the designer-craftsman that is still influencing us today.

Morris lived beside the Thames at spacious Kelmscott Manor near Oxford and also at Kelmscott House in Hammersmith in London beside the same river, so the simple rural existence he seemed to want for others on next to no money wasn't quite his choice. At both places he could contemplate the superb sweep of the river, and if the thought occurs to you as it did to me, that it could be the same gallons of water at Hammersmith he'd seen at Oxford, then yes, it occurred to him too. When he wasn't busy running out utopian tracts on the Kelmscott Press, he went to the roadside to harangue passers-by about socialism. William Morris's wish to return to pre-industrial ways may or may not have been realistic, but his influence was far-reaching.

William Morris was involved with just about everyone artistic or intellectual of that age. The pre-Raphaelite group of mainly painters – that lot who swapped wives and mistresses, and took on beautiful models while assuring their parents everything would be chaste and then bonked them into next week, but nevertheless produced great works of art such as Millais's *Ophelia* (well, they had to do something while waiting for Raphael) – gravitated towards Morris and Oxford, becoming the pre-Raphaelite Brotherhood. They specialised in pale, ethereal beauties, whose great-great-grand-daughters seem to be still cycling through Oxford. And still Raphael hasn't bothered to turn up (maybe I have got that bit wrong. It's a bit like being post-modern: how can you be?).

Meanwhile, he gathered around him Left-leaning thinkers such as **George Bernard Shaw** (1856–1950) and **Sidney Webb** (1859–1947), a group of people without whom the British Labour movement and its 20th-century (and 21st-century) political expressions would never have happened.

To put it another way, the Lefties who inhabit Oxford Town Hall, flying the Red Flag or Campaign for Nuclear Disarmament flag, town-twinning the place with Um Bongo or somewhere right-on (as if it made a blind bit of difference), or flying the Rainbow Flag for social inclusiveness (ie: *excluding* the English and their flag which will be flown here on the day the Pope becomes Jewish), being Green with a capital 'G' and protesting

41

at acid rain from the giant Didcot power station (while expecting the lights to come on when they flick a switch, of course) wouldn't have existed without Morris.

Not that I'm anti-Left. I'm just anti-incompetence and woolly thinking of any sort. The Oxford City and County Councils in 2004, for example, somehow managed to spend £5million resurfacing Cornmarket and, having tried various surfaces, it ended up looking much like it did before they started. Absolutely amazing. If you're an old Oxonian, you'll remember when they resurfaced Cornmarket with rubber tiles to cut down the noise. A great success, except in the wet when buses slid 100 yards instead of stopping! Actually, for the ludicrous £5million Oxford could have rebuilt the picturesque medieval North Gate archway across the street – of which there are plenty of drawings – which was removed by idiot bureaucrats as a hindrance to traffic. Now traffic is being deliberately hindered as much as possible and is in fact banned from here. (Yes, put our lovely gate back!)

On the other, more positive, hand, Oxford's proud tradition of high-minded humanitarian socialism and

constructive charity – Oxfam was started here and so were many other charities – are the heirs to these pioneers who said, faced with the industrialisation of Britain, 'Hang on a minute, what about the quality of life? What about art and beauty? What about people?' Not everything is about money, they argued.

This arty William Morris loved Oxford deeply, but thought it then already damaged by progress:

Need I speak to you of the degradation that has so speedily befallen the city, still the most beautiful of them all, a city which with its surrounding world, if we had a grain of common sense, would have been treated like a perfect jewel, to be preserved at any cost.

Little did that William Morris know that just a few years later another **William Morris** (1877–1963) would be working in a bicycle repair shop in Longwall Street dreaming of one thing: building his own motor cars. This William Morris was to change Oxford more than any other single person, including his utopian namesake. His dream created the vast growth of **Cowley** and its factories to the east. The first William Morris would have been appalled.

Ironically, the **second William Morris** (later 1st Viscount Nuffield) created far more jobs and wealth for the working class, and drew in such numbers of Welshmen, Geordies and Cockneys to man his factories that socialist ideals – which had hardly interested the conservative lower orders of old Oxford despite the first William Morris's efforts – would really take hold. Trade unions, strikes, militancy.

It was a third Oxford that sneaked up on the old Town and Gown while they weren't looking or while wars were going on. It was an Oxford that the first William Morris would have disdained: the mindless work on assembly lines – attaching a flange grommet to the cringle gasket of thousands of cars, perhaps – and the bland terraces of cheap houses were just what he felt was so wrong with industrialisation. Ironically, it delivered to hungry coal miners fleeing the Great Depression in Wales and the North a standard of living they could only have dreamed of before. Electricity, a bath, hot water, an inside flushing toilet, enough food, which the utopian William Morris did not.

The second William Morris was a driven man (not just in his cars, that is). He had one brilliant idea, just as Henry Ford had thought of mass production (actually invented by Brunel to make pulleys in a Portsmouth dockyard, but Ford first applied it to cars). So Morris thought of assembling cars, not making them. He had assembled bicycles in this way at his Oxford workshop at the start of the 20th century – he would buy the best or cheapest brakes from one firm, the wheels from another, the tyres from another, saddles from elsewhere, lamps elsewhere. Why not apply that to cars?

The Bullnose Morris was the first mass-marketed model and eventually we saw Morris Cowleys and Morris Oxfords among the range. A sporty marque, MG, still exists – its name simply means Morris Garages. Morris Oxfords are still made in India, but the Morris brand was absorbed by British Leyland and then Rover as the industry lurched through crises in the late 20th century. Of course, during the war years Morris factories at Cowley turned to making and repairing aircraft and tanks.

At the time of writing, the old Morris car factory is no longer part of the Rover group but is owned by BMW and is producing the new Mini. Another little irony of history – the BMW roundel outside the factory, a shape that is a stylised turning aircraft propeller, less than a lifetime before adorned the engines of Luftwaffe bombers trying to destroy this factory and its workers. It's ironic, but by God it's progress.

TWENTIETH-CENTURY PRESSURES

Another irony is that mass ownership of the motor car, which created so much employment for working people and transformed Oxford, very nearly destroyed what was worthwhile about the city. The main streets became choked with traffic and fumes, the soft stones eroded even faster. The post-World War II solution proposed was the building of inner relief roads round the heart of the city, as was done elsewhere.

One was to go from the Magdalen Bridge direction right across Christ Church Meadow to relieve the High Street. It would have been monumental vandalism and the city council dithered. This was an era when old things were not much valued, when high-rise blocks, ugly dual-carriageway roads and concrete multi-storey car parks and shopping centres were seen as progress and old buildings as useless slums, so it very nearly came to pass.

In fact the continuation of this road was built: a road from St Aldate's and Folly Bridge west towards the station, connecting with roads up to the north to St Giles to make part of an inner ring road. A warren of medieval streets was bulldozed down at St Ebbe's and ghastly new shopping centres put up. Some of the people were shifted out to Blackbirds Leys beyond the ring road – a kind of Soweto to overstate things a little, a source of workers (and occasionally trouble) kept out of sight of the middle classes. These were huge errors, seen with the benefit of hindsight. Just about everything done in the 1960s and '70s would have been better not done and even now would be better blown up.

The one miraculously good thing is that the Christ Church Meadow road was never built, nor any inner ring road across the northeast, and the 'perfect jewel', the precious heart of old Oxford – the area east of St Aldate's and Cornmarket, that is the streets either side of the High Street as far north as St Giles and down to the Thames – was saved. It was a close-run thing.

Meanwhile, a revitalised Oxford had been making great strides in science. The first people saved by antibiotics, the discovery of various objects in distant space and within the atom, medical advances by the dozen.

One more irony about the two William Morrises. The car-maker made so much money he could make huge charitable donations and educational bequests and, as **Lord Nuffield**, started the influential Nuffield Foundation, Nuffield College and Nuffield Hospitals, and saved Pembroke College. He endowed medical professorships at the Radcliffe Infirmary, he financed the giant radio telescope at Jodrell Bank. This William Morris was almost the Getty of his day, his gifts worth billions in modern prices. A lot more use to working people than his utopian socialist namesake's arty wallpaper they couldn't afford, one might mischievously think…

Oddly, one more Morris played an important role in the eccentric history of Oxford, and of England, at around the time of the two William Morrises, but it wasn't a person. **Morris dancing** and the associated folk music, was about to become extinct when in 1895 Cecil Sharp, a teacher, came to stay with friends in Headington. He witnessed the

Headington Quarry morris dance and realised that this whole strange and ancient culture was on the brink of the abyss.

He determined to collect and record the dances and the music while they were still being performed and made it his life's work. It was because of his efforts that when the folk music and dance revival happened after World War II there was so much material left. True, if you come from rural England you may not think it eccentric to dance around with bells on your trousers waving hankies and whacking each other over the head with sticks or inflated pigs' bladders while onlookers inflate their bladders with beer but on a global scale it most certainly is.

None of this folklore would exist today but for those Oxford pioneers saving this little bit of eccentric, barmy Britain.

And morris men, who feature so strongly in Oxford's May Morning celebrations (pages 8–11) remind us of one more level of Oxford's life over the centuries. As poet John Betjeman put it in his book on Oxford – besides, first, the great architectural treasure house of a *University* and second, what he called *Motopolis*, the cosmopolitan East Oxford industrial sprawl caused by William Morris's success – there is still the third Oxford, the older county town, for which Betjeman borrows Hardy's name for Oxford, *Christminster*.

This latter county town is a busy small city of councillors, judges and local officialdom, where for centuries red-faced, if not red-necked, farmers have come with or without their beasts, to lunch on beef and beer in city pubs, where Cotswold and Otmoor villagers come to shop, to visit the market, get tipsy, appear in court, to hear music, to register births and deaths, see films and plays and see some city life. All three Oxfords have changed since Betjeman's time, but they all thrive, side by side. One of these three cities on its own would have something to offer, but all three superimposed make Oxford the fascinating, ancient and yet brand-new place it will always be.

ECCENTRIC LITERATURE

ALICE, THE PRINCE, THE NAZI AND MR TOAD

Alice Liddell was the delightful daughter of the Dean of Christ Church who famously became the inspiration – obsession even – that led to one **Charles Dodgson**'s unique and world-famous book *Alice's Adventures in Wonderland* (using the pen-name Lewis Carroll, of course).

Let's deal with one difficult thing first. There has been much seedy speculation about how much of a pervy paedo Dodgson was – speculation that was rather typical of the sex-obsessed and self-satisfied smug 1960s mockery of supposed Victorian prudery and hypocrisy. Knocking people off pedestals with a schoolboy snigger. While no sane person would defend for a moment any such perverted activity where it actually takes place, if Dodgson *was* so motivated, which I have yet to be convinced of, he kept his feelings concealed and the fact

is nothing at all happened. None of this even faintly dreams of excusing real paedophilia. But nor does it dent the brilliance of the Alice books themselves.

I am still happy, naively perhaps, to enjoy the image of Dodgson rowing Alice and her two sisters lazily up the river, the dripping oars passing over the glassy surface and dipping again with a quiet creak of the rowlocks... all under a cloudless blue sky, and the little girls saying: 'Just one more story from fairyland, please.' He could never refuse them, luckily for us.

Dodgson (1832–98) was a mathematics tutor. Queen Victoria was so impressed by *Alice's Adventures in Wonderland* that she had a lady-in-waiting write to Christ Church and say Her Majesty would be graciously pleased to accept the author's next book. So he loyally obeyed her command. It was *The Syllabus of Plane Algebraical Geometry*, which must have gone down like a lead balloon with she who was so difficult to amuse.

Oddly, if you are going to poke around in their stories you can dig up plenty of odd and eccentric connections, including Royals and Nazis.

Alice herself was unsentimental about the much older man's interest in her as a child, but it was hardly surprising given their age difference (compare it with Christopher Robin's annoyance at being a lifelong centre of the *Winnie-the-Pooh* stories about a century later). So although Dodgson had lovingly given Alice his manuscript in

1864, when she was a hard-up old lady of 76 in 1928 she sold it at auction for £15,000 (then enough to buy 15 decent houses).

But when young, her beauty clearly did do something for men in the college's cloistered environment. Queen Victoria's youngest son **Prince Leopold** fell headlong in love with her when an undergraduate at Christ Church, although he was barred from marrying a commoner.

It was commonplace in Victorian times that two from such different backgrounds could never be united, and that love was not the issue. The following century saw the problem repeated in the Royal Family, with it being decreed that Princess Margaret should not marry Peter Townsend, or that Sarah Ferguson was somehow better than Koo Stark. Compared to the British Royals, the Red Queen and the Mad Hatter begin to seem strangely sane, you may think.

Prince Leopold went on to marry some German Princess and they begat a boy, Charles Edward, Duke of Saxe-Coburg and Gotha in Germany and also in Britain a pukkah Prince, with the title HRH, and Duke of Albany, who became the only top Nazi who was born a British Duke (and who, ironically, played host to the only recent Royal who *did* marry for love against convention, Edward VIII, who had to give up the throne as a result).

After the end of World War I, in which he backed the Germans, he was deprived of all his British titles. Later he became an active Nazi and was seen in a storm-trooper obergruppenfuhrer uniform during the Hitler era – a bit rum for a British royal – and was punished for war crimes after World War II. He had earlier ended up marrying Victoria Adelaide, Princess of Schleswig-Holstein-Sonderburg-Glücksburg (snappy girl, snappy title!), and he died in 1954.

Marrying Alice would have been an awful lot simpler for Leopold, if she would have had him, and probably as Princess Alice wouldn't have produced a Nazi.

St Frideswide, Botley Road, has a door carved by Alice Liddell that portrays the saint in a boat, that is what she was in when Carroll told her the stories. Her favourite sweet shop across St Aldate's is still there selling the same kind of barley-twist sweets, and the lawns at the back of Christ Church (visible from the gates on Merton Grove, the path across the back of the college) are where the surreal game of croquet in the book was imagined. This gate can be seen on the first walk around the colleges described on page 129.

The Mad Hatter was said by many to be based on a milliner on the High, and 19th-century hatters really were mad because of the poisonous salts of mercury they used liberally in their hats.

So far, so fascinating, but that, of course, isn't enough for the literary detectives who love this sort of stuff. First, they showed that 'Mad as a Hatter' was used by previous authors such as Thackeray, so it was an existing phrase, which of course doesn't disprove the mercury theory or even that Carroll thought he'd invented the phrase. Then they claim that hatter was an old word for a snake or adder. 'Mad', they claim, was closer to the modern American usage, meaning angry. People at the University of Beaver Creek, or Vulture Gulch etc, make a living out of investigating this sort of stuff.

Then they say Carroll was in fact thinking of an eccentric Oxford furniture dealer Theophilus Carter who was known to be deeply strange and wore a top hat. They have even found his grave in **Holywell Cemetery**, behind St Cross, and yes, I've seen it. The fact that hatters in the 19th century were often deeply doolally (don't get me started on that word – look it up) was just a coincidence they claim, a misconception reinforced by the drawings used for the book. It is interesting, but aren't the academics the real crackpots here for spending a lifetime on 'facts' about a work of eccentric fantasy?

THE WIND IN THE WILLOWS AND REAL TRAGEDY ON THE RIVERBANK

Another Christ Church-connected children's book of true brilliance is Kenneth Grahame's *The Wind in the Willows*. It was written for Grahame's son Alastair who was an undergraduate here. In fact the stories were letters not intended for publication but to warn his son of the dangers of becoming like Toad, the overbearing character in the immortal book. Alastair, sadly, didn't grow old enough to express an opinion over being the focus of such a great book, as he died under a train at Port Meadow in 1920, two days before his 20th birthday. An ironic end – near another riverbank too – for one so thoroughly warned about the dangers of not railways but motoring by Toad of Toad Hall.

Actually it's a far sadder story than you might imagine. The boy was born with certain deficiencies but his father, who had wanted to go to Oxford when a schoolboy in the

city but was forced by impecunious relatives to become a banker instead, pushed and pushed the son academically until he reached Christ Church. It was thought Alastair couldn't face up to the expectations of his father or his tutors. His death was almost certainly suicide, and it wasn't the first or last of this type of tragedy in Oxford.

Of course, the parents may have been blameless and he may have been mentally ill but undiagnosed. Whatever the truth, they are reunited in the above-mentioned Holywell Cemetery (St Cross church), lying together not far from the gate.

The epitaph for Kenneth Grahame (1859–1932) says:

> *To the beautiful memory of Kenneth Grahame, husband of Elspeth and father of Alastair, who passed the River on 6th July 1932, leaving childhood and literature through him the more blest for all time.*

For the fascinating story of the treacle well mentioned in *Alice*, and where you can find the real thing, see Binsey, page 221.

OXFORD'S UNEQUALLED LITERARY PANTHEON

Oxford's rich contribution to the world's harvest of creative genius is unique. For a city of its size, it is surely second to none.

True, many are not that well known today. But who could need the name J R R Tolkien explaining in the early 21st century after the global impact of the films of his *Lord of the Rings*?

Here is a small selection of the genius that has flourished in the richly fertile patch of ground between the Thames and the Cherwell, either as students, dons or residents for some part of their most creative lives:

MATTHEW ARNOLD Balliol, 1841, Fellow, Oriel, 1845–47, poet, author of *Dover Beach* etc. Coined the most misquoted line about Oxford: 'That sweet City with her dreaming spires.' See page 224.

JOHN AUBREY Trinity College, 1642, The great diarist who demolished the famous with his waspish *Brief Lives* has a memorial in St Mary Magdalen, where he is buried.

MAX BEERBOHM Merton, 1891–94, friend of Oscar Wilde, author of the Oxford satire and romantic comedy *Zuleika Dobson*, which is set around 'Judas' College. More on page 161.

JOHN BUCHAN Brasenose, 1895–99, author of imperial heyday adventure thrillers such as *The Thirty-Nine Steps* lived at Elsfield, north of the city, where his ashes are interred. More on page 161.

LEWIS CARROLL 44 years at Christ Church, author of *Alice's Adventures in Wonderland* etc. Actually Charles Dodgson, and his model for the books was the Dean's daughter, Alice Liddell. See pages 49–55.

CECIL DAY-LEWIS A lefty undergraduate at Wadham, 1923–27, and later chum of W H Auden and Thomas Hardy, professor of poetry at Oxford from 1951, and poet laureate in 1968. Father of Daniel Day-Lewis, the actor. Died 1972.

COLIN DEXTER The creator of Oxford's most famous detective, the cerebral, irascible Inspector Morse, was in fact a Cambridge man, being a graduate of Christ's College (he read classics). But he moved to Oxford decades ago. He started writing – as many people have – when a holiday in North Wales ended up with his being trapped in a farmhouse by rain. That was the start of *Last Bus to Woodstock*, first of 13 books and, later, 33 very popular TV episodes, thanks partly to the grumpy portrayal of Morse by John Thaw. Not at all like Dexter, although their interests seems to coincide...

T S ELIOT Merton, 1914–15, poet, cerebral American creator of works ranging from the cryptic, not to say infuriatingly smart-alec poem, *The Waste Land* to *Old Possum's Book of Practical Cats*, origin of the musical *Cats*.

JOHN GALSWORTHY New College, 1885, author of novels such as *The Forsyte Saga*, serialised twice in recent decades on British television.

WILLIAM GOLDING Brasenose, 1930. Brilliant West Country author of *Lord of the Flies* (turned down by 21 publishers but sold a million, so there's hope for me and you) and other apparently pessimistic novels about the breakdown of human beings into depravity, obsession and madness under extreme pressures.

ROBERT GRAVES St John's, 1919, aptly named poet of World War I and many following decades. Graves took up his place in Oxford after fighting in the war. Ironically, he was treated with suspicion in both wars, having had a German mother and the middle name von Ranke.

THOMAS HARDY Poet and author of gloomily dramatic Wessex novels such as the *Mayor of Casterbridge*. Oxford becomes Christminster in *Jude the Obscure*, and many of the colleges are renamed, eg: Biblioll for Balliol.

HENRY JAMES Lived in Beaumont Street, 1894. American author of *Portrait of a Lady* etc.

JEROME K JEROME Author of *Three Men In A Boat*. A passage from this delightful comedy about the Thames is on page 226. He founded *The Idler* magazine, and having died in 1927 now idles in Ewelme churchyard, appropriately near the Thames, between Oxford and Reading. His middle name should have been something sensible, clearly. It was Klapka.

Interestingly, this is a rare case of someone naming themselves after their child, like Mercedes, who named the cars after his daughter and then himself after his cars by changing his surname. Equally, after Jerome K Jerome became so famous, his father Jerome Clapp renamed himself Jerome Clapp Jerome. Well, when in Jerome ...

T E LAWRENCE, Jesus, 1907–10, and All Souls. Heroic subject of the film *Lawrence of Arabia*, in which he seems to almost single-handedly free the Arabs from the Ottoman Empire, and troubled author of *Seven Pillars of Wisdom* etc. Met his Maker on a Brough Superior motorbike. His Dorset grave has the emblem of Oxford, the open book with *Dominus Illuminatio Mea* (God is my light) upon it.

C S LEWIS Author of *The Lion, the Witch and the Wardrobe* and one of the greatest exponents of Christianity. An unpopular tutor at Magdalen (before his conversion). Clive Staples Lewis converted from atheism, he said, on a

motorbike ride from Oxford to Whipsnade Zoo, getting on the bike godless and getting off it fervent. If it was a Brough Superior (see *Lawrence*, page 57), I'm not surprised. They do that to you. It's the high-speed handling. And why Whipsnade Zoo? In fact he said it was talking with Tolkien, fellow Inkling member, the previous night that did it. The ride just made him realise what it meant. Died 1963 – on the same day as President Kennedy and Aldous Huxley – and buried in **Holy Trinity**, Trinity Road, Headington. His grave is indicated by a sign on the wall.

GERARD MANLEY HOPKINS Balliol, 1863, poet and author of *The Windhover* etc. See page 197.

WILLIAM MORRIS Exeter, 1853–55, author, campaigner and chief instigator of the Arts and Crafts Movement. But didn't make cars. For more information, see page 40.

PHILIP PULLMAN The creator of the hugely popular *His Dark Materials* trilogy, which is not about soft furnishings as the name suggests, nor about luxury train building. It is in fact a much-loved love story set partly in the Botanic Gardens in Oxford.

As with Inspector Morse, there have been Will and Lyra walks and the Botanic Gardens are a favourite visiting place because of the bench where Lyra and Will have pledged to visit each other, at least in spirit, once a year. When I visited recently with a Pullman fan, we were hard pressed to spot THE BENCH. There were plenty of young people, even on a cold, damp day, wandering around wanting to be photographed on any bench.

Pullman was an impoverished schoolteacher here who went to work on a bicycle. My northern correspondent writes: 'Bicycle? Call that soooffering? By 'eck, it were loooxury. We had t' shoebox to live in and now't but clogs for breakfast.' Quite.

ROBERT ROBINSON His crime comedy *Landscape with Dead Dons* has a marvellous scene worthy of Beerbohm. The murderer is chased by the whole crowd of people at Parson's Pleasure, the place beside the Cherwell where naked male dons may sunbathe. The stream of naked angry men goes through Oxford causing various responses from astonished witnesses: cricketers are turned to stone; clergymen decide they must be Baptists; scientists decide it must be an optical phenomenon caused by the sun; it ends at the Martyrs' Memorial in a way that you'll have to read the book to discover. And yes, the author was the slightly smug radio quizmaster.

JOHN RUSKIN Fellow, Corpus Christi, 1871. Victorian philosopher-essayist with huge influence, leading to Ruskin College in Oxford.

EDWARD THOMAS Lincoln, 1898, much-loved poet of the Edwardian countryside and the horrors of World War I, in which he was killed. Absolutely classic Oxfordshire poem: *Adlestrop*. Go to that village in summer, if you love his poems, and wait not for the train to stop but a long gap in the road traffic and you will experience *exactly* what he says about the birds.

J R R TOLKIEN Fellow, Exeter, 1914, Fellow and professor, Pembroke, 1926–45, Fellow and professor, Merton, 1945–59. John Ronald Reuel, creator of *Lord of the Rings*, was born in South Africa and was persuaded to publish what he thought was the unprintable book *The Hobbit* by his chum C S Lewis. He died in 1973, rather annoyed at his increasing fame, and is buried in the Roman Catholic section of Wolvercote Cemetery in north Oxford, with his wife Edith. They are called Beren and Luthien respectively on the tombstone, a reference to the mortal man and immortal elf-maiden lovers whose story, which takes place 6,500 years before the events in *The Lord of the Rings*, is told in several of Tolkien's works, including *The Silmarillion*.

OSCAR WILDE Magdalen, 1874–78, author of *The Importance of Being Earnest*, etc, and self-declared genius, imprisoned after his (illegal) gay relationship with Lord Alfred Douglas, who was also at Magdalen. For more information, see page 150.

FURTHER READING

Oxford by Jan Morris, published by Oxford (1965 but revised since), £9.99, ISBN: 0192801368. Still the best in-depth book on Oxford, by this prolific, gifted and perceptive travel writer who, interestingly, like Christ Church's Old Tom, has changed sex – in this case not from a ding to a dong, but from being a doyen to a doyenne. Doesn't read as if long in the tooth, unlike Betjeman's book about Oxford, which is now very dated and ponderous.

The Surgeon of Crowthorne: A Tale of Murder, Madness and the Oxford English Dictionary by Simon Winchester, Penguin Books, £8.99, ISBN: 0140271287. About the dictionary, not the city, but a rumbustious, astounding and compelling yarn well told in a journalistic way. Best of his books.

Caught in the Web of Words: James Murray and the Oxford English Dictionary by his granddaughter, K M Elisabeth Murray: Yale University Press, £28. ISBN: 978-0300089196. An in-depth read but worth sticking to, an astonishing story of sterling service to our language. There is a blue plaque outside Murray's home in Banbury Road where the scriptorium used in this project was sited.

3:59.4: The Quest to Break the 4 Minute Mile by John Bryant, Hutchinson 2004, £14.99, ISBN: 0091800331. The well-researched full freshly played-out drama of the build-up to that wonderful day in Oxford in 1954 when Roger Bannister made athletics history.

Zuleika Dobson, an Oxford Love Story by Max Beerbohm. Since my complaint in the first edition of this book that it was out of print, now republished by three firms. Including Standard Publications, £8.45, ISBN: 978-1605977249. If you like P G Wodehouse, you'll love this.

Three Men in a Boat: To Say Nothing of the Dog by Jerome K Jerome (Penguin Popular Classics) ISBN: 0140621334, about £1.50. Jolly japes in this Victorian-Edwardian classic about silly adventures on the Thames.

Adventurers All by R Ricketts, Blackwell's 2002, £12.99, ISBN: 0946344353. A history of the Blackwells, this most eccentric Oxford family of publishers.

Oxford's Gargoyles And Grotesques by John Blackwood, Charon Press, £20, ISBN-13: 978-0951102800. Highly recommended, amusing, great pictures and a good souvenir. I have bought it a few times and lent it to visitors who don't return it. Don't you hate people who do that?

ECCENTRIC PEOPLE

AN ECCENTRIC OXFORD DON: RICHARD COBB

A typical eccentric Oxford don – and that is an oxymoron, because there can be no typical eccentric, but at any rate an excellent example – was the brilliant historian **Richard Cobb** (1917–96).

His period was revolutionary France, and his muse was lashings of French wine and reeking Gauloises cigarettes that dangled from his lip as he talked, as if stuck with glue. The booze caused problems from time to time. For example, when at a state dinner at Buckingham Palace, he started swaying disturbingly while talking to Princess Alice. That made him think of the Oxford Alice, as in Wonderland, so when he saw Prime Minister Harold Wilson wearing court dress (frock coat, tights and buckled shoes) he started saying: 'White Rabbit! He's going to bring his watch out now!' Sadly, he was taken away to sober up before he could confuse the real Queen with the Red Queen.

None of this should obscure his brilliance as a scholar of the French Revolution. He was revered on both sides of the Channel and fluent in both languages. Indeed, his books were written and published in French, and his English was sometimes infused with French. Bizarrely, his first books were translated by someone else into English, but he wrote many, many great works on his return to his mother country.

He was famed in Oxford for taking the parts of the principals of the Revolution and acting them out, even on the college balcony in Broad Street, I'm told, and even at night, which might have been a bit worrying for passers-by. Once he was fired up, he really *was* the characters, and this was his strength – it was no mere dead history, it was alive and thrilling for him, and therefore for his students, such as future Tory minister, later last Hong Kong Governor, European  Commissioner and probably BBC chief (blimey, how many top jobs can one bloke get after being rejected by the voters?) Chris Patten, who would never forget him.

He applied his historical perspectives to the politicians of his own day, thus dubbing Labour leader Michael Foot 'the Cornish Robespierre'. He also inspired a whole new generation of British historians, such as Simon Schama.

Cobb had gone to Shrewsbury School, which he left early under a cloud, and had no sooner arrived at Merton College than he became entangled in a strange libel case with the mother of a school friend, who wrote to every college in Oxford and Cambridge warning against him. The outcome was that he was offered a scholarship at Merton and she was murdered by her son, but not until Cobb had been to France to recover from the almighty row. This visit started his lifelong love affair with that country and its history.

At his viva (live examination) at Oxford, by the way, Cobb's strong views caused his examiner Sir George Clark to say: 'Good God, man, you're a bloody anarchist,' to which Cobb replied: 'Why, thank you, Sir.'

He went on to live in France after war service, and married two Frenchwomen while flirting with Communism. His favourite mode of transport was train, and it was lucky for the impoverished unpaid historian that one of his wives was an employee of SNCF, so he had free rail travel around France.

One town mayor reported later that the diligent Cobb probing his town's archives had been the first person to open the dusty revolutionary ledgers since they were written more than a century and a half before, which speaks volumes about Cobb, if not about French scholarship.

He returned to Britain to become an academic and marry an Englishwoman, coming to Balliol, where he caused no end of trouble (he was once sentenced to dig the gardens for his awful rendition of Irish songs outside the Master's house late at night), and then Worcester College.

Even in his later life his love of schoolboy pranks, good wine and France of two centuries before was undiminished.

THE DEEPLY ECCENTRIC ROBERT HAWKER

Pembroke College, overshadowed by the wealthy, aristocratic giant across the street that is Christ Church, was known for providing a home for less well-off grammar-school types. Dr Johnson famously ran out of money there, as did one of the most eccentric clergymen ever produced by the Church of England (a magnet for such eccentrics), **Robert Hawker** (1803–75).

Hawker came up to Pembroke in 1822 but after a year his father, a poor Cornish parson, told him that he could not afford to continue at Oxford. Hawker, then 20, jumped on his horse, without stopping to pick up his hat, to ride to his godmother, one Charlotte Eliza Rawleigh I'Ans, a wealthy spinster of 41. He proposed to her and rode back to Oxford with her on the back of his horse, allowing him to continue his studies.

He followed his father into the Church. As **Vicar of Morwenstow** in Cornwall, one night in July 1825 he decided to play a trick on the superstitious people of Bude, who were always going on about sea serpents and mythical creatures.

Under a full moon he rowed out to some rocks, plaited himself a wig from seaweed and wrapped his legs in more weed to resemble a tail. He sang and crooned to awestruck crowds, returning each following night as the 'mermaid' story spread through West Country villages like wildfire. Eventually Hawker became fed up, sang *God Save The King* in a male voice and plunged into the waves.

When entering church to take services, he was always accompanied by nine cats. He rode a mule bareback around the parish, followed by a pet black pig called Gyp.

Morwenstow Vicarage, which he built, is embellished by odd chimney stacks, which are miniatures of various church towers that took his fancy. There is a ship's figurehead as a memorial to victims of a wreck. He is also credited with inventing the **Harvest Festival service**.

But it turned out his strange marriage wasn't just for money. When his first wife and godmother Charlotte died – she was after all 20 years older – he was so bereft he decided to eat nothing but clotted cream, morning, noon and night. Mind you, he did wear a strange pink fez at her funeral but claimed the Orthodox Church allowed this. He later married a woman called Pauline Anne Kuczynski. A classic Oxford-reared eccentric.

THE LAST GREAT ECCENTRIC? BARON BERNERS

One of the great English eccentric figures of the 20th century – indeed some say the last of his type – was **Lord Berners**, a minor aristocrat/diplomat/homosexual/poet/artist/composer/translator/dilettante from Faringdon, a small town near Oxford.

Gerald Tyrwhitt-Wilson, 14th Baron Berners (1883–1950), is worth recalling not only because he was such fun but also because he left a splendid folly, a tower soaring above the tree tops that has never had any purpose whatsover.

The baron – a composer and a diplomat of a sort – had a funny thing about notices and he attached one to the top of this folly saying: 'People committing suicide from this tower do so at their own risk.'

If you don't find that surreal, he also ordered workmen to nail up notices every 40ft round the perimeter of his estate saying simply: 'People throwing stones at these notices will be prosecuted.'

But then he had some charming habits as well as bizarre ones. He dipped his doves in food dye – it's quite safe, try it at home – and they came out gorgeous pinks, mauves, yellows and blues.

The last time I went to **Faringdon**, they were still doing it. The doves, I mean.

These and many other of his foibles, such as dogs running around with jewelled necklaces, are recreated in the Lord Merlin character, based on Berners, in Nancy Mitford's 1954 novel *The Pursuit Of Love*. He would invite people on horses into his elegant drawing room and serve the horses tea and cream buns off bone china. There's a picture somewhere of Penelope Betjeman and her horse enjoying just such a tea.

One of his friends, a certain Salvador Dali, moved the grand piano into a shallow pond and put chocolate eclairs on the ebony keys. Berners was delighted and sat down to play a tune.

But then he had a piano in the back of his Rolls-Royce so he could pull up at the roadside if he had an inspiration and hammer it out. In fact, he requested to be, after his death, stuffed and installed at the top of his folly, endlessly playing an automatic piano. His heir funked it, saying he couldn't get the piano up the narrow stairs.

The gardens – not now open to the public, although the nearby folly is (for more about this odd building, page 216) – also hold diverse durable testaments to his ideas. There's what appears to be a castle but turns out to be Oxfordshire's only crenellated swimming pool. The changing room has a floor made of pennies set in cement and stained-glass windows; two fearsome wyverns sit at the shallow end. (Wyvern trivia: There was a Vauxhall Wyvern car in the 1950s and every Vauxhall car badge still includes one.)

Nearby, outside the Orangerie, sits a bizarre half-submerged statue of General Havelock. It suits the spot perfectly. He looks like he might be relieving himself, apt for the hero who relieved Lucknow during the Indian Mutiny.

While Evelyn Waugh tried to conjure up Oxford aristocrats who had nothing to do but enjoy life, get drunk, drive expensive cars and make love to people of various sexes, Berners was the real thing, and frankly much more interesting.

His slightly oddball approach to life was demonstrated at an early age when he was told if you threw a puppy in a river it would instinctively learn to swim. He took his mother's spaniel upstairs and threw it out of the window, reasoning that it would instinctively learn to fly. It didn't.

Two stories about Berners illustrate his attitude to pomposity and snobbery.

First, Edith Sitwell recalled: 'My brother Sacheverell, my sister-in-law and I were lunching with Lord Berners (Gerald to his friends), when his stately, gloomy, immense butler Marshall entered the room, bearing an immense placard. "The gentleman outside says would you be good enough to sign this, my Lord?" Gerald inspected the placard and wriggled nervously. "It wouldn't be any use, Marshall," he sighed. "He won't know who I am – probably never heard of me." It transpired that the placard was: "An appeal to God, that we may have Peace in Our Time.'"

The second one concerned some snobby friends who were telling Lord Berners that the head waiter at a posh restaurant had inexplicably failed to notice their importance.

'We had to tell him who we *were*!' the unbearable woman trilled.

'And who *were* you?' inquired Berners.

OXFORD'S MOST ECCENTRIC SCULPTURE

The Englishman's home is his castle, goes the cliché, but then it's all the more surprising how dull most of them are (the homes, that is).

Most people live in suburban conformity, reinforced by planning restrictions that are exactingly petty in the prettier places – all part of the price of living on an over-populated island with some of finest heritage going.

So it is in suburbs, not massive stately homes, that the occasional fantastic whims really stand out. And Oxford has the oddest of the lot: a massive **shark sculpture** plunging from the sky into the roof of a staid Oxford terrace house.

The slates are scattered as if the dramatically unbelievable had just happened and it has dropped from the sky. The 25ft glass-fibre shark is, in fact, supported against the gales by internal girders. Apart from its astonishing roof embellishment, the house is otherwise quite ordinary.

The man behind it is long-term Oxford eccentric and BBC Radio Oxford presenter **Bill Heine**, who first came to notice (being another American student who wouldn't go home) with his various cinema schemes, and needs little introduction to the locals.

He first leased a derelict cinema on Cowley Road in 1976, which he carefully restored and called the Penultimate Picture Palace. It was decorated, I recall, with a fine giant glass-fibre sculpture of Al Jolson's white-gloved hands: a portent of things to come.

He sold that off, after making a success of it as an alternative cinema, and it is today the Ultimate Picture Palace, which is not quite as alliterative and sadly has lost the splendid hands.

He then took over another old cinema in Headington in 1980, where a planning wrangle had been going on over the previous owner's desire to call it the Moulin Rouge and decorate it with a turning windmill, as in the Parisian one. The boring planners thought this misleading (as there were no cancan dancers) so Bill called his cinema Not the Moulin Rouge, to remove any ambiguities, but got his sculptor chum John Buckley to produce a pair of high-kicking legs, which caused another planning wrangle.

In the end the cinema was sold and demolished, but not before Bill had cocked the biggest snook in the history of Oxford (a city where snooks come pretty big) at the council by installing his now famous shark sculpture in 1986 in a house in the same road, New High Street, Headington. It still amazes me every time I go to have a look and draws visitors from around the world.

It was said to commemorate various events – such as the American bombing of Libya on the day Bill bought the house – and of course the council demanded its immediate removal. Meanwhile Bill argued that it was a work of art and the wrangle went on for years at various levels of government. One official suggested moving it to a swimming pool, which totally missed the point of its eccentric incongruity.

Despite much gnashing of teeth by the twitching-net-curtain brigade, the sculpture was eventually allowed to stay by junior planning minister Tony Baldry, who said, to his everlasting credit: 'I do not believe the purpose of planning control is to enforce a boring and mediocre conformity.'

Today Bill still presents his outspoken Radio Oxford show in his strange mid-Atlantic drawl and occasionally creates controversy despite his now silver hair. He gets a reaction, positive or not. Mind you, not long ago, the BBC Radio Oxford website was inviting listeners to 'shoot Bill Heine', which seemed a bit strong. It turned out to be a computer game.

Meanwhile, the astonishing shark remains. As one passer-by remarked: 'My God, that shark must have been going some speed when it left the water!'

POLITICAL ALSO-RANS AND POLY DOLLIES

Oxford, perhaps not surprisingly, has an awful lot of hanger-on colleges that aren't quite or aren't even vaguely in the university but somehow manage to bask in the glory of all that golden stone. And the students at these lesser institutions don't mind either.

And then there are those who come to Oxford for some brief purpose but give the impression they were at Oxford, if you know what I mean.

Former Tory Party vice-chairman, globally successful

novelist and disgraced jailbird **Jeffrey Archer** (b. 1940) was one who, ahem, could have been more open about his relationship with Oxford. He let the impression rest that he was educated at Wellington and Brasenose, Oxford. Except that it wasn't the famous Wellington public school in Berkshire but a lesser school in Somerset; and his time at Brasenose was just a one-year diploma of education, during which Archer somehow ran for the university. So on this occasion the alleged CV embroiderer was more or less telling the truth. While Archer was at Oxford he met Mary Weedon, a brilliant Nuffield College student who became the long-suffering and famously fragrant Lady Archer. She probably understood: the chap just likes to tell stories. Doing so in court, however, led to jail.

Many of the colleges make some serious boodle running summer schools for the offspring of rich Americans who possibly aren't bright enough to come to Oxford as proper students. They get to swan around historic quads and may also say: 'when I was at Oxford' although it's just a form of tourism or very posh summer camp.

Talking of politicos who almost went to Oxford, there's **Ruskin College** in Jericho, sometimes labelled 'the working-class Eton'. Technically not part of the university, this was set up to give flat-capped working-class oiks, as it were, a taste of cloistered life enjoyed by the top-hatted haughty toffs next door at Worcester. Ruskin's recent alumni have included built-like-a-brick-outhouse northern political bruiser **John Prescott** (b. 1938), whose path from young ship's steward to deputy prime minister was definitely opened up by this idealistic college set up in 1899. Precisely the type of chap Ruskin was supposed to help. Or as Mr Prescott has been quoted, it was the greatest thing that ever happened to him and 'taught me I had no need to feel inferior to anybody.'

Oh good, absolutely no chip on his shoulder then. Still, Prescott is variously known as 'Mr Grumpy' for pulling a face like a bulldog that's swallowed a bee, or 'Two Jags' for having two of the gas-guzzling cars that he used on the least pretext while lecturing everyone else about public transport, or 'Two Jabs' for taking a powerful swing at a political heckler who'd perhaps thrown eggs at him.

Ruskin was the 19th-century essayist after whom all kinds of institutions were named by a grateful nation. Would it happen today? The Boris Johnson College?

More of a bugbear for those who want to protect the elite university's name is the other university on the hill – **Oxford Brookes University**, up between Headington and a mental hospital, which used to be the Oxford Polytechnic until these institutions were moved up a category, and it had even been a mere technical college before that. (Giving rise to one Oxford resident's caustic comment, somewhat unfair, that: 'You can call a lump of coal a diamond if you like, but it's still coal.') It's particularly galling when the Poly (sorry, Brookes) beats the 'real' Oxford at its own sport, rowing, which they did not long ago. Rowlocks to you lot.

But what is Brookes like? Is it so much less academic?

A recent London newspaper article highlighted Oxford's 'Poly Dollies' and said they are not like normal students (in being poor and tatty, that is). 'They shop at Joseph, Jigsaw and Whistles, get their highlights done at Michaeljohn and won't step out of the house with less than perfect make-up.'

So they're smart-in at least one sense of the word, but possibly not in the other. The article pointed out various glamorous Brookes girls – Miss England 2002 **Danielle Luan** for example. There is also plenty of 'posh totty' at Brookes, the article argued, citing society figures such as **Laura Parker Bowles** (as in Camilla). This classier crumpet, apparently, study degrees carefully selected to make them unsuitable for real work, such as history of art.

Hmmm. Put like this, it reminds one a bit of finishing schools where debby but not particularly bright gels learned secretarial skills and deportment while waiting to snare a rich, titled boy who had a real job or, even better, real estate (and these are in bulk supply down the hill from Headington, as the article points out).

Meanwhile, one imagines the bluestockinged *real* Oxford women, fresh-facedly beautiful (or not) without an inch of make-up in that very English way, cycling down Catte Street not knowing who Dolce e Gabbana are (an opera?) or caring about anything so trivial as styling and just determined to be a professor of neuroscience, a great doctor, philosopher, engineer or explorer.

In fact the truth is, of course, less simple. Yes, there have been a few not very clever but stunningly pretty females at Brookes, but there are also many brilliant ones who are determined to succeed in their own career (and do very well), not merely measured by their potential husbands' incomes and status. And even dippy degrees like history of art have led to some high-flying careers. Honestly.

SEX AND THE VAR-SITY

Nor is Oxford University totally immune from glamour when it wants to be. Consider the amazing get-ups at the end-of-year balls, for example. But could female allure influence even high-minded Oxford?

A survey of Oxford University admissions policy in 2004 came up with the result that you were more likely to gain a place if you were female. One of the researchers thought paternalism or 'the male lust hypothesis' (that's an academic's way of saying 'Phwoar!') on the part of the ageing, mostly male, tutors could be a factor, and the tabloid newspapers leapt on this saucy titbit, as they do. Possibly, although many of Oxford's dons frankly look well past the stage even a bucket of Viagra and an armful of adrenalin could revive. Could the dons' fear of allegations of sex discrimination from a constantly nagging government, when not enough girls apply to balance the sex score, be another factor? In other words, positive discrimination for political correctness: get more girls in, pretty or not.

Naturally, Oxford women undergrads were outraged at the suggestion that their looks may have been a factor. 'It is the quality of the hemispheres in our skulls not under our shirts that matters,' sniffed one. Another was quoted as saying: 'It's pretty insulting to the general level of intelligence of applicants.' *Pretty* perhaps wasn't the best adjective to pick, Miss.

As a cynical working journalist, I fancy the whole brouhaha had more to do with the low level of intelligence of newspaper executives – or more precisely their low opinion of that of their readers – than that of Oxford students. I expect the papers had fun with headlines about 'university lecherers', and lines such as: 'You want to study science? It's all down to the chemistry!' (Which reminds me of a headline my former colleague Robin Popham waited a whole career in journalism to write and never had the chance: 'Geometry teacher in love triangle'. Now it's in print. Bet it was true once in Oxford.)

And of course the simple fact remains that you don't have to be plain to be clever. Even top Oxford academics such as **Susan Greenfield** (who collects tabloid headlines such as 'Britain's sexiest scientist' and 'baroness brainbox'; b. 1950) can put on the glitz and enjoy the spotlight. Why not? Who would dream of suggesting leather-miniskirted Professor Greenfield (once an undergrad at St Hilda's in Oxford) is a bimbo? Isn't expressing surprise that someone outwardly glitzy and attractive is not stupid a bit sexist? And do people, by the way, assume hunky himbos are stupid too? Do the many gay dons have a bias as well?

It all illustrates the old truth about judging by appearance. Being dowdy doesn't make you brilliant, being beautiful doesn't make you thick. The same applies to whether you are an extrovert, party animal or an introvert stay-at-home type. These factors, too, are not the same as being clever or dumb, despite our prejudices. Or as an Oxford man, Magdalen's great eccentric Sydney Smith, put it so much better:

Do not assume that because I am frivolous I am shallow;
I don't assume that because you are grave you are profound.

THE *WHAT* SPORTS CLUB?

The trouble with one of the most eccentric of Oxford student societies, the **Dangerous Sports Club**, is that its activities are, well, a bit dangerous. It was all very well when the Oxford-based club's activities included inventing bungee jumping, skiing down the slopes of St Moritz in full tailcoat seated at a grand piano, crossing the Channel in an inflatable kangaroo, having a black-tie dinner party at a properly laid silver-service table on the lip of an active

volcano, or steering
a blowup elephant
down an Alp.

Many of
these extreme,
eccentric or
downright silly
activities could have
ended in tragedy (and
indeed when bungee jumping
became a worldwide phenomenon, someone in
New Zealand did once forget to tie the other end on).

The worst thing that happened to the Oxford-based
Dangerous Sports Club founder, David 'Captain' Kirke,
was when he flew his microlite into a tree in Tatsfield,
Kent. He fell into the garden of an astonished old lady
in a heap of wreckage. Dazed and confused, he stood up
woozily and demanded directions for Paris.

Where the Dangerous Sports Club went tragically
wrong was with building a copy of a medieval siege
weapon, the trebuchet, a massive tripod-like object with
a swinging arm brought down by a huge weight. At the
other end, in the original, was a sling to throw a rock to
batter down walls, or prisoners' heads, or a plague-ridden
corpse. But not a live willing passenger. No-one would be
that stupid. Not until the Dangerous Sports Club thought
of flinging people several hundred yards into a net. In
November 2002, several people were successfully hurled
through the air to land in the net. Then it was the turn
of a 19-year-old Bulgarian student, a member of a group
called the Oxford Stunt Factory. He landed on the ground
with a sickening thud and died in hospital.

The glamour had gone out of the Dangerous Sports
Club. People realised it was, after all, what it said it was.

ECCENTRIC
COLLEGES

COLLEGES, THEIR ECCENTRIC
DONS AND OTHER ANIMALS...

There are around 39 Oxford colleges, depending on how you define them, all with their own eccentric ways. The colleges listed here are given a **foundation date**, and sometimes two as they may have started as private halls or other lesser institutions and than transmogrified into pukkah colleges – a process taking from a couple of years to about six centuries. The money figure is a recently reported **level of endowment** but shouldn't be taken too seriously; where it's missing it's probably because it's somebody's penny jar and a couple of out-of-date foreign notes (again not seriously). But it does give you some idea of the relative richness of the colleges, and the fact that collectively they own £2 billion worth of clobber. Annoyingly, not quite enough to tell the Government to get stuffed when it interferes. All of them take the word College after their names given except Christ Church (who will get the screaming heeby-jeeby ab-dabs if you do that), the ones end in Hall, and the ones already ending in College. That would be silly, but we could not bring ourselves to write just 'New' or 'University'. **Alumni** sometimes includes Fellows as well as plain grads, therefore people can appear twice, or even at a rival college-studied mouldering bog lost in the mists of eastern England.

There are about six things that seem like an Oxford college that aren't: they are private halls or religious establishments, and lesser creatures. One of these is Regent's Park College, which is neither in Regent Park nor a College, but a hall in Pusey Street. Equally, there is one college – St Edmund – called Hall, although it isn't one but is a college. Equally there are 54 colleges that really don't exist in any dimension except hypothetical or putative. These are the fictional colleges in novels, films, *Inspector Morse* TV episodes, etc. Some are about a subtle in a brick in a blancmange – I mean All Saints College is pretty thinly veiled for All Souls (Elizabeth Gaskell's *North and South*), or Brazenface College for Brasenose (Cuthbert Bede's *The Adventures of Mr Verdant Green*). Judas College (Max Beerbohm's *Zuleika Dobson*) is suitably funny, however.

ALL SOULS

(FOUNDED 1438, HIGH STREET, £230M)

An oddity in that it takes neither undergraduates nor even mere graduates. Only research Fellows may study here, so it's deadly serious, which is appropriate for a college that was founded as a war memorial. Not the last war, nor even the one before the one before the one before the one before. In 1438 the College of All Souls of the Faithfull Departed, to give its full title, was founded as a memorial to the dead of the Hundred Years War with France. Not that it stopped another 400 years of occasional belligerence between the Brits and the French. Whether it is truly a serious place is hard to say when you hear that an All Souls man stood up to eat his porridge every time it was served. Asked why, he said: 'Sir, no Scotsman sits down to eat porridge.' Breakfasts seem to have been an eccentricity here, with silver lids for Marmite jars among the oddities. Don't miss the cosmic **Wren sundial** (for which he charged £32) which you can see from the tower of St Mary's. By the way, that sundial could be in the wrong place. An eccentric old chap recently left a share in £888,000 to All Souls if it returned Wren's sundial to where it ought to be, by his reckoning. The college refused, although you must admit that moving sundials must be fraught with difficulties. The Bodleian Library, who received the cash instead, was far from miffed.

T E Lawrence (of Arabia) ended up here and devised a scheme for driving all Magdalen's deer into the grounds of All Souls (or some say it was Jesus, his undergraduate college – that's the trouble with these stories). It never happened, perhaps being more difficult than virtually single-handedly destroying the Ottoman Empire and creating the modern Middle East.

ECCENTRICITIES: Utterly bonkers ritual **Hunting the Mallard** every 100 years (see page 2). Fees are about £14,000 a year and sometimes a lot more – but *they* give them to *you*. Entry is by the hardest exam in the world. Recent question: Does the moral character of an orgy change when the participants wear Nazi uniforms? Plus long translations from classics. You can't enter unless you have a First from Oxford, and even then they require a vivat exam and a dinner before deciding to appoint one or two or none of the candidates each year. Duties and syllabus required or ordained from members: None.

Alumni

Lord Curzon (1859–1925), Viceroy of India; **Cosmo Lang** (1864–1945), Archbishop of Canterbury; and **John Redwood** (b. 1951), 'The Hon member for Vulcan'. More fun are the people who didn't get in, such as writers **John Buchan** (1875–1949) and **Hilaire Belloc** (1870–1953).

BALLIOL

(Founded 1263, Broad Street, £78m)

Doing penance was the medieval version of community service. You might be ordered to do something totally pointless but difficult (such as crawl to York) or you might be told to do something useful. When powerful baron **John de Balliol** (before 1208–68) insulted the Bishop of Durham, he was given a sound thrashing with birch twigs (something certain Tory MPs pay good money for nowadays) and ordered to found a place of learning for poor scholars. He took a house in Oxford in 1263-ish which eventually became known as Balliol College.

Balliol, which has indeed had a strong Scottish connection from the start, was known to be useless in the 18th century, with ruinous buildings (the President of neighbouring Trinity said he would sometimes lob a brick through a window to complete the picturesque ruin effect) and no effort at education (one of the aforementioned Scots, the great economist **Adam Smith** (1723–90), said there was no pretence of teaching anything). Things got a bit better in the 19th century with an eccentric Master, Dr Jenkyns. He was once riding down the Banbury Road when he was stopped at the toll gate. He had no money but considered his importance sufficient:

> Dr Jenkyns: *'Don't you know who I am? I am the Master of Balliol!'*
> Gatekeeper: *'I don't care who you are, you're not coming through here unless you're the master of tuppence!'*

Poor Jenkyns had to ride the long way round.

He liked to keep an eye on his undergraduates by peeping through their keyholes. Once a student, Sir William Hamilton no less, realised someone was looking through his keyhole, rushed out and held the poor screaming man dangling over the top of the stairs. After a while, Sir William realised it was the Master and brought him back with:

> *'I'm terribly sorry, Sir, I had no idea it could be you.'*

OTHER ECCENTRICITIES: Left-wing tortoises (well, named after Marxists) are cared for by an official known as Comrade Tortoise. The Nepotists' carol concert held last Friday of Michaelmas term includes a satirical song The Gordouli, about Trinity College, long-term enemies and target of occasional sabotage.

ALUMNI

Prime ministers **Herbert Asquith** (1852–1928), **Ted Heath** (1916–2005) and **Harold Macmillan** (1894–1986), writers **Graham Greene** (1904–91) and **Aldous Huxley** (1894–1963). The BBC's **Robert Peston** (b. 1960), **Stephanie Flanders** (b. 1968) and **Peter Snow** (b. 1938). Poets

Swinburne (1837–1909) and Southey (1777–1843). Politicians **'Woy' Jenkins** (1920–2003), **Yvette Cooper** (b. 1969) and to correct the Lefty lean, there's bumbling bouffant blond 'Bojo', **Boris Johnson** (b. 1964), Mayor of London at the time of writing. Boris has somehow got away with indiscretions that would have crippled lesser politicians, although he did have to grovel to Liverpool, Portsmouth and Papua New Guinea after allegedly insulting them (he was actually sent to Liverpool by Tory chiefs, and said he would strive to include PNG 'in my global itinerary of apology'). The bumbling bit, like TV 'tec Columbo, is an act – I think. Anyone who quotes Tacitus at the oiks from redtop newspapers and gets away with it is a good egg, surely. In one supposed scandal he said journalists were creating 'an inverted pyramid of piffle'. As a working journalist, I have to say such flowery denials are often followed by finding out much of it is true. Middle name: de Pfeffel. Things in London tend to become in headline terms Boris bikes, Borismaster buses, Boris island airport. Ethnic origin (according to him): 'One-man melting pot.'

Bodleian: not a college, but a library

The Bod has the most splendid building for a library in the entire world. It keeps a copy of every book published in English, and inhabits not only the original fantastic structure, festooned with marvellous gargoyles and grotesques (some of which turn out to be dons leaning out of a window on close inspection), plus inscriptions more beautifully Latin than Jennifer Lopez, but also the stunning Radcliffe Camera. Plus the New Bodleian across Broad Street, linked by tunnels carrying books back and forth.

BRASENOSE

(Founded 1509, Radcliffe Square, £98m)

Means simply a brass nose, or a particular brass door knocker to be precise. It is a particularly well-travelled knocker, as when the students fled turbulent Oxford in 1533 they took the brass nose with them to Stamford, Lincolnshire. They eventually moved back to Oxford and missed the brass nose terribly for the next six centuries, despite having made another one in the meantime. Eventually they bought the entire *house*, by then a girls' school, in 1890 just to get back the door knocker, now installed in pride of place above the Principal's table. The knocker on the front door is a mere upstart by comparison (and yes, a pair of knockers is better than one).

Talking about pairs, the Principal of Brasenose in the 18th century used to hire an extra horse to pull his coach for the last few miles into Oxford, as he put it: 'Lest it be said that the first Tutor of the first College and the first University of the world entered this city with a pair.'

Known for great boozing, Brasenose had an eccentric pair of brothers who helped found the **Phoenix Wine Club** in 1781. One of them, Reggie Heber, could famously hold vast amounts of booze, but returning sozzled to the college one day crashed into a don called Port and fell to the ground. He would recount later that it was the only time port got the better of him. He became Bishop of Calcutta and drowned in his bath. His brother Richard was an obsessive book collector and died owning 146,827 volumes. All different.

A later 19th-century club, the **Hell Fire Club** (named after the 18th-century aristocratic dilettantes), was disbanded after a don looked up at a window and saw a

Hell Fire Club member struggling with what looked like the Devil amidst flashes of blue fire. He rushed to the room and found the student dead and strange marks upon him. It was said he had summoned the Devil himself. Either that or he had invented high-voltage electricity…

OTHER ECCENTRICITIES: For five minutes a year, a connecting door to Lincoln College is unlocked. Any Brasenose members who get through must be served an antique ale flavoured with ivy, which sounds disgusting if not dangerous. It commemorates a dim and distant day when Lincoln let in their own members but shut out a Brasenose chap to be murdered by the mob: penance, if that was true. And the world's oldest boat club.

ALUMNI

Prime ministers **David Cameron** (b. 1966) and **Henry Addington** (1757–1844); Rugby inventor **William Webb Ellis** (1806–72); writers **William Golding** (1911–93), **John Buchan** (1875–1940), **John Mortimer** (1923–2009), and **Michael Palin** (b. 1943); and sixties sex and spy scandalee (and, it must be said, later saintly chap) **John Profumo** (1915–2006).

BROOKES

Definitely not a college, but another university that happens to be in Oxford. Well, a poshed-up polytechnic, which was a poshed-up technical college (see page 74).

CHRIST CHURCH

(FOUNDED 1546, ST ALDATES, £228M)

Some of this college's eccentrics, including 13 more or less batty British Prime Ministers, are listed on page 133. It's big, has the biggest quad, the poshest quad, the bossiest bulldogs. Does this make it sometimes arrogant or pompous? Well, is the Pope a Catholic? Do bears poo in woods?

The reply from a Christ Church Dean to the Dean of another college in 1840, to a perfectly civil question about examinations, ran: 'Alexander the Great presents his compliments to Alexander the coppersmith and informs him he knows nothing whatsoever about it.' It is not done to refer to Christ Church followed by that word beginning with 'c' (sssh! Colleges), which describes all these places; you just say Christ Church. Christ Church men call it 'the House' anyway, and they write it down Ch:Ch: A friend of mine, enquiring where Christ Church College might be, was snootily informed: 'I believe that is in New Zealand, Sir.' Ch:Ch: men also get the right to graze one cow on Christ Church Meadow. A top-hole Ch:Ch: eccentric was the 19th-century Professor of Geology **William Buckland** who would serve guests at his Tom Quad lodgings mice cooked in batter, or horseflesh cooked in wine, or crocodile steaks (where he got those from

I don't know). He shared his rooms with a bear and guinea-pig who may or may not have ended up in his cookpot. He tried mole but found them hard to eat. He could tell bat's urine by the taste. On a visit to nearby Nuneham Park stately home the chatelaine proudly opened a silver box and declared: 'What do you think of that, Professor Buckland?' He seized the lump of meat and scoffed it down before they could explain it was their treasured embalmed heart of Louis XIV. Buckland merely licked his lips and said: 'I've never eaten the heart of the French King before.'

Alumni

Alice in Wonderland creator **Charles Dodgson** (1832–98; pen name Lewis Carroll); broadcasters **David Dimbleby** (b. 1938) and **Ludovic Kennedy** (1919–2009); poet **WH Auden** (1907–73); Archbishop of Canterbury **Rowan Williams** (b. 1950); 18th-century Methodist founders **John and Charles Wesley**; nearly all the Governors-General or Viceroys of India (11); and the **seventh Earl of Cardigan** (1797–1868), who ordered the Light Brigade to charge at Balaclava (thus, with his companion Lord Raglan, cementing three bits of knitwear into one military disaster).

Scientists **Joseph Banks** (1743–1820), who took part in James Cook's first voyage, **Albert Einstein** (1879–1955) and **Robert Hooke** (1635–1703). An Egyptian Prince; two of the **Bhuttos** who led Pakistan; **William Penn** who founded Pennsylvania; **King Edward VII** who ruled the biggest empire the world has ever seen, and the **Winklevoss** twins (b. 1981) involved in creating Facebook, who also rowed for Oxford. Apart from that, and the 13 prime ministers, no one much.

CORPUS CHRISTI

(FOUNDED 1571, MERTON STREET, £58M)

A small college, with fewer than half the number of students as neighbouring Christ Church, it has a beautiful quadrangle with a totally bonkers pelican sundial. Never in the history of humankind has so much effort been wasted, some may think, as on Oxford's many elaborate and expensive sundials, as there is little sun to make them work from November to April. On the other hand, digital doobries wouldn't be the same. Dr Thomas Arnold, the founder of Rugby School and father of Oxford poet Matthew, used to hurl bottles at this sundial when angry. Asked why, he said it was the only thing round there which didn't hurl them back.

The college hosts the slowest sport in Oxford: the annual tortoise derby.

An eccentric Corpus Greek don was concerned whether the histories were right that in one battle the Greeks ran a full mile in full armour in full summer to attack. He built himself a suit of classical Greek armour, took himself down to the battlefield and waited for a really hot day, ran the full mile and, waving his sword around, declared himself ready to fight all-comers. A Greek farmer looked up briefly, and then ignored him, as if this happens every day round there.

The name of the college means the body of Christ. Not Corpus Christie, as one current guidebook has it, which would be something to do with a certain crime writer.

ALUMNI

Include Labour politico brothers **David** (b. 1965) and **Ed Miliband** (b. 1969); 'Banana Man' and 'Wallace' to some.

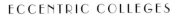

EXETER

(FOUNDED 1314, TURL STREET, £47M)

This college on Turl Street and Broad Street has the most perfect Gothic Revival chapel, whose ludicrously huge roof one sees so clearly from up the tower at St Mary's. This is well worth a visit if it is open, for it is by **Sir George Gilbert Scott** (1811–78), and has all the High Churchy almost Roman Catholic decorations, and indeed is based on Saint-Chapelle in Paris.

It's just potty – Victorian bad taste, some may think – and Christopher Wren would have hated it. By the way, the tapestry is by William Morris (the artist, not the mechanic, although it's hard to tell, see page 40). The whole chapel is totally out of scale with its setting, making it feel like a stage set for *Gormenghast*. How do they fill the place up? A Dean of Exeter was once delighted to find that the statutes of the college allowed him to compel a particularly irreligious don to attend chapel. The don looked at the statutes and agreed it was so – as long as the Dean wore the stated skull cap, yellow coat and yellow stockings. The matter was allowed to rest.

ALUMNI

Runner **Roger Bannister** (b. 1929); writers **Alan Bennett** (b. 1934), **Martin Amis** (b. 1949), **Philip Pullman** (b. 1946), **JRR Tolkien** (1892–1973), and **Will Self** (b. 1961); actors **Richard Burton** (1925–84) and **Imogen Stubbs** (b. 1961); politico **Tariq Ali** (b. 1943); textile designer **William Morris** (1834–96), and composer **Charles Parry** (1848–1918).

GREEN TEMPLETON

(Founded 2008, Woodstock Road)

All postgrad. Two newish colleges merged in 2008, making this the newest. The endowment figure is, in fact, not known to us. Scientific and medical hotbed but a bit serious.

HARRIS MANCHESTER

(Founded 1786, 1996, Mansfield Road, £8m)

Smallest college, origins nonconformist Christianity. Ditto.

HERTFORD

(Founded 1282, 1740, Castle Street, £52m)

The one joined by – sigh! – the alleged Bridge of Sighs across New College Lane. Hertford once came close to closing completely, getting down to just one member in 1814, after which the building fell down. But it survived and one famous graduate was **Evelyn Waugh** (1903–66), who did so much to immortalise a certain kind of foppish Oxford.

Alumni

Newsreaders **Fiona Bruce** (b. 1964) and **Natasha Kaplinsky** (b. 1972); writer **Evelyn Waugh** (1903–66) and poet **John Donne** (1572–1631).

JESUS COLLEGE

(FOUNDED 1571, TURL STREET, £119M)

Setting for one of those probably apocryphal stories about naive American tourists, this was where one supposedly was not impressed by the architecture.

> Tourist to porter: *I'm not sure I could tell the difference between Lincoln and Jesus.*
> Porter: *Sir, that's the trouble. Hardly any Americans can.*

Traditionally a Welsh college, which is why a leek is hoisted up the flagpole on St David's Day. Students used to wear the Welsh veg in their caps around town but received such disrespect and trashing that they desisted. It was said that if you shouted 'Jones!' in the quad 50 heads would pop out of windows.

A student drunkenly clambering in across the roofs (as one had to in the days of the curfew) mistakenly climbed into the Principal's bed. The Principal's wife woke up and was about to scream for help when the student put his hand over her mouth and said: 'Hush! *Really!* You'll wake up the Principal' and left through the window again.

ALUMNI

T E Lawrence 'of Arabia' (1888–1935) studied here, as did twice prime minister **Harold Wilson** (1916–95).

KEBLE

(FOUNDED 1870, PARKS ROAD, £47M)

Sometimes likened in its redbrick gloominess to a Victorian insane asylum. This is totally unfair. None of them was half as gloomy as Keble is on a rainy day.

Seriously though, Keble is famous for a great painting given by the widow of the OUP superintendent **Thomas Combe**. *The Light of the World* by Holman Hunt, which is displayed next to the suitably gloomy chapel, but even *The Light of the World* doesn't brighten up this place on a dull day. In fact Holman Hunt was so outraged that it was stuck here (or that they were charging people to see it) that he painted another copy and gave it to St Paul's Cathedral in London. Keble's architect was Butterfield, whose exteriors and interiors always seem to me like some display for brick and tile samples, using as many different ones as possible in a garish visual equivalent of a cacophony. In a style you could reasonably describe as Italian Zebra Renaissance or Early Horizontal Dolly Mixture, the college was famously avoided by Ruskin on his daily walk to avoid falling into a bad mood. I seem to remember that a society at one of the other colleges had as its entrance requirement a brick from Keble. Carry on chaps. Only another eight million to go…

John Betjeman, the mid-20th-century poet and architecture buff, said of Keble:

> It is unfortunate that William Butterfield … should have paid so little regard to the texture and colour of Oxford stone in this, his largest work in Oxford.

That's the nub of it: it would fit in fine in Birmingham, but not Oxford.

Betjeman isn't totally hostile and praises the work when seen in a dull light, objecting to it only in full daylight (just a slight drawback, then, Butterfield, old chum). In a caption Betjeman says of Keble: 'A monochrome photograph, such as this, shows up the originality of his detail and his excellent sense of proportion: it lessens the violence of his colour schemes and juxtaposition of textures.'

Simple. You just need a totally colour-blind friend to go with you holding a video camera while you hold and watch a connected small black-and-white telly, looking through toilet roll centres glued to sunglasses so you don't see the building itself. Try not to fall over.

Of course I'm simply having fun along with those who have teased Keble. I have friends who have gone to this college and love the place, rightly so. If its brickwork were at, say, St Pancras station, it would probably have been praised to the girders. Daring to be different wasn't really the end of the world. Imagine if a really wild and brutally ugly modern building were erected in Oxford ... ARGH!! Around the corner on the Banbury Road, here it is. Oxford's ugliest building, the **Physics Department**.

Keble is named after **John Keble** (1792–1866), the 19th-century Fellow of Oriel who started the Oxford Movement, pushing for Roman Catholic-style rituals and ornament in the Church of England. Keble thought the students should lead lives of almost monastic poverty and asceticism (not that current students seem to do so, having got all sporty in the meantime). And the whole place was aimed at High Church incense-swinging religion. A Keble wit who once posted a letter mockingly to 'Worcester College, near Oxford' (because it is nearly in Jericho) received a reply to 'Keble College, near Rome'. Good thing Latimer, Cranmer & Ridley (rather a good name for a firm of solicitors) aren't still around.

Alumni

Sally Bercow (b. 1969), leggy wife of the titchy Speaker of the Commons (though she dropped out after two years); Labour politicians **Ed Balls** (b. 1967) and **Andrew Adonis** (b. 1963); Pakistani cricketer/politician **Imran Khan** (b. 1952); US President **Ronald Reagan** (1911–2004; honorary fellow), and picky food writer **Giles Coren** (b. 1969).

KELLOGG

(Founded 1990, 1994, Linton Road)

Alumnus

Author **Umberto Eco** (b. 1932; honorary fellow).

LADY MARGARET HALL

(Founded 1878, Norham Gardens, £34m)

Founded for women, now co-educational. And what formidable women!

Alumnae

Pakistani PM **Benazir Bhutto** (1953–2007); celeb chef **Nigella Lawson** (b. 1960); journalist **Dame Ann Leslie** (b. 1941); author **Lady Antonia Fraser** (b. 1932); actress **Diana Quick** (b. 1946), and politician **Ann Widdecombe** (b. 1947).

LINACRE

(FOUNDED 1962, PARKS ROAD, £13M)

ALUMNI

Dr David Kelly (1944–2003), ill-fated bio weapons expert; and journalist **Yasmin Alibhai-Brown** (b. 1949).

LINCOLN

(FOUNDED 1427, TURL STREET, £69M)

The **Bishop of Lincoln** founded it as 'a little college of true students of theology who would defend the mysteries of Scripture against those ignorant laymen who profaned with swinish snouts its most holy pearls'. Well said, old bean.

One Rector of Lincoln, the **Reverend Tatham**, used to give interminably boring sermons lasting up to three hours at the church of St Mary the Virgin. Students and dons alike would sneak out after a while, and once, only one member of the congregation remained, strangely immobile. It was found he had died during the sermon. Another Lincoln preacher was founder of Methodism **John Wesley** (1703–91), who preached 40,000 sermons in the early 18th

century, many at the same church until he was banned from there. When he met Beau Nash, the elegant dandy of Jesus College, on a narrow pavement, Nash said arrogantly: 'I never give way for a fool.' Wesley, being a Christian, stepped into the muddy street, saying: 'I always do.'

Alumni

Children's writer **'Dr Seuss' Theodore Geisel** (1904–91); author **John le Carre** (David Cornwall b. 1931); **18th Duke of Norfolk** (b. 1956); actress **Emily Mortimer** (b. 1971); and 'Adlestrop' poet **Edward Thomas** (1878–1917).

MAGDALEN

(Founded 1458, High Street, £153m)

Academically, top dog. More than half of its 2010 finalists received first class honours. Five members in the Cabinet at time of writing. More Nobel prizes than most entire countries. For the best grounds, the most eccentric ceremonies, the most fabulous gargoyles, grotesques and statues, fascinating architecture, the stories of wild Wilde and C S Lewis, see page 150.

Alumni

Oscar Wilde (1854–1900); **King Edward VIII** (1894–1972); **T E Lawrence 'of Arabia'** (1888–1935); **Andrew Lloyd Webber** (b. 1948); **Sir John Betjeman** (1906–84); **C S Lewis** (1898–1962); politicians **William Hague** (b. 1961), **Chris Huhne** (b. 1954), **George Osborne**

(b. 1971), **Jeremy Hunt** (b. 1966); and **Dominic Grieve** (b. 1956). **J Paul Getty** (1892–1976); **Ian Hislop** (b. 1960), **Martha Lane Fox** (b. 1973); **Louis Theroux** (b. 1970), and the **Ninth Earl Spencer** (b. 1964). Do you know what? If you're British you didn't need labels explaining that lot.

MANSFIELD

(Founded 1886, 1995, Mansfield Road, £12m)

Small, non-comformist originally. One of the porters, Hugh Flint, was a drummer for John Mayall's Bluesbreakers.

MERTON

(Founded 1264, Merton Street, £142m)

Likes to say it is the oldest college, which absolutely infuriates University College, which thinks it is, but isn't. It *is* the oldest college. It has long been known for eccentrics, such as the undergraduate who, when stopped by a bulldog for being drunk, lay down in the street and flayed his arms about, shouting: 'Save the women and children! I'm all right, I can swim.' Or the Merton chef in World War I who was handed a white feather in the High Street by a woman who said: 'How dare you just stand there while everyone is fighting to save civilisation?' The chef looked the women in the eye and said: 'Madam, *I* am the civilisation they are fighting to protect', gave the white feather back and stalked off. This somewhat unenthusiastic attitude to warfare was not entirely gone from Merton in World War II, when an American officer leading a huge convoy over Magdalen Bridge hailed a Merton student and said: 'Hey, you boy, can you direct me the way to Buy-ses-ter?' The student, peeved at being so addressed, helpfully explained that Bicester is pronounced to rhyme with sister, and directed the trucks down the increasingly narrow Merton Street. By chance he met another lost convoy further up the High Street, which he directed down King Edward Street, converging with the other lot on Oriel Square. It took a day to sort out the mayhem. (For more on Merton's buildings, see page 138.)

OTHER ECCENTRICITIES: People here will tell you the Mob Quad is the oldest such courtyard in Oxford. It isn't, It isn't even the oldest in Merton – Front Quad is older. Some of the buildings have no chimneys because they had not been invented yet; another has a steeply pitched roof because it was made of stone to make it fire proof; it's where they kept the money.

ALUMNI

Authors **JRR Tolkien** (1892–1973) and **Max Beerbohm** (1872–1956); runner **Sir Roger Bannister** (b. 1929); poet **TS Eliot** (1888–1965); alliterative musician **Kris Kristofferson** (b. 1936), and war hero/philanthropist **Leonard Cheshire** (1917–92).

NEW COLLEGE

(FOUNDED 1379, NEW ROAD, £143M)

New in the sense that the New Forest once was; this college is many centuries old. Has a memorial to three

New College men who died for their country in World War I. They were all fighting for the other side, being German, but I imagine it took some courage to put this up in 1919. Mr Chips would have understood. Great modern 'gargoyles'.

An early aviator, Mr Pring of New College, didn't do well in the 1921 Oxford and Cambridge air race, when six biplanes, three with tails in Cambridge blue and three in Oxford's darker colour, raced round a 120-mile course. Pring failed to complete the course, coming down midway and tangling with some railings. The headline should have been 'Pring prong prang.' For the great eccentricities of New College's Dr Spooner, see page 152.

ECCENTRICITY: The Lord Mayor of Oxford and his corporation must process along the city wall which is part of New College once every three years, to check on a 14th century deal that it would be repaired. Even though the rest of the walls have largely fallen down and no one remembers what they were for. Beautiful chapel and cloisters. Possesses two 'unicorn horns'.

ALUMNI

Actors **Hugh Grant** (b. 1960) and **Kate Beckinsale** (b. 1973); politicos **Tony Benn** (b. 1925) and **Hugh Gaitskill** (1906–73); and authors **John Galsworthy** (1867–1933) and **Geoffrey Wheatcroft** (b. 1945).

NUFFIELD

(FOUNDED 1937, NEW ROAD, £146M)

Small, all graduate, good spire. Paid for by Morris Oxfords and similar cars (see page 43).

ORIEL

(FOUNDED 1326, ORIEL SQUARE, £77M)

Properly called 'The House of Blessed Mary the Virgin in Oxford', it is not surprisingly now better known by the name taken from Oriole House which stood here. This had an oriel window (an upstairs-only bay window).

ALUMNI

Explorers **Sir Walter Raleigh** (1554–1618) and **Cecil Rhodes** (1853–1902); historian **AJP Taylor** (1906–90); and dandy **Beau Brummell** (1778–1840).

PEMBROKE

(FOUNDED 1624, ST ALDGATES, £40M)

Much associated with the great contradictor, **Dr Johnson** (see page 36), who famously didn't graduate, being too poor to finish. After being punished for not going to a lecture, Johnson remarked: 'Sir, you have fined me tuppence for missing a lecture that was not worth a penny.' Oddly, a continuation of Pembroke Street is Penny Farthing Place, which sounds like a reasonable compromise for the worth of the lecture. Anyway, the remark is very Dr Johnson in that it sounds witty and wise, but how did he know what the lecture was worth if he didn't hear it, the smart alec?

Pembroke (founded in 1624, and somewhat over-shadowed by the richer and grander Christ Church across the way) was also home to Robert Hawker (see page 66), surely one of the most eccentric clergymen the Church of England has ever produced. He, like many a Pembroke undergraduate, was also too poor to continue but found a remarkable solution.

Pembroke is also said to have the most beautiful small college chapel. The college's hall, built in 1848, nearly made Pembroke broke because it was, in fact, much larger than necessary. The college owes its survival to William Morris (the car-maker, not the utopian of the same name) who rescued it from penury.

I visited Pembroke once with my Boswellian companion, and we sadly noted at the porter's lodge that it was closed to visitors (afternoons are best for most colleges). A porter spotted his Pembroke tie. 'You're a Pembroke man, aren't you, Sir?'

'Yes, that's right, I came up in 1963.'

'Well you're welcome anytime, Sir. Do come in and look round.'

We looked round and as predicted it is on a much cosier scale than mighty Christ Church. On our way out, the porter popped his head out. 'Do come back and see us again, Sir.'

I can't really define the young man's attitude to the old man. It certainly wasn't fawning, or fake deference, or patronising. Family, almost.

Oxford Union

Not a college but a strange combination of gentleman's club and debating society, with guests ranging from Kermit the Frog to former Presidents of various countries. Few can resist the invitation. Elections to the Presidency are close-fought and close-fraught.

The Oxford Union Society outraged public opinion – and would it be doing its job if it didn't occasionally? – in 1933 when it was proposed that 'This House will in no circumstances fight for its King and Country.'

Set against the careless slaughter of Oxford men of World War I, and given the youth of the students, it was perhaps not totally surprising that the motion was carried by 275 votes to 153. But it caused outrage in the wider country. Many people naturally saw it as an insult to their fallen heroes. Fleet Street newspapers had a field day laying into Oxford. The *Daily Express* called the students 'communists, practical jokers and sexually indeterminate' (no change there, then, you may mischievously think). Another letter to a magazine attacked the students as 'aliens and perverts'. On a grammatical point, as we don't know the moral standpoint of aliens, should that have been aliens or perverts? In the event, confronted with the unimaginable evil of Hitler's Nazi Germany less than ten years later, Oxford graduates, including many of those who voted for the controversial motion, did their duty.

ALUMNI

Wine buff **Oz Clarke**; *Foyle's War* actress **Honeysuckle Weeks** (b. 1979); **King Abdullah II** of Jordan (b. 1962) and lexicographer **Samuel Johnson** (1709–84).

QUEEN'S

(FOUNDED 1341, HIGH STREET £131M)

Properly The Queen's College. Perfectly proportioned classical buildings. Founded on behalf of England's first black Queen, according to a list of 100 black Britons published in 2004, which might surprise many people. Edward II decided his son should marry Philippa, the bewitchingly beautiful daughter of a nobleman in what was going to be Belgium. They wed in 1328 and he became Edward III, tough dude, hammer of the Scots, etc. Was she really black? After all, her portrait suggests not. Ah, says the theory, the few black people in Europe at the time were painted white in pictures. And then there's her son ... the Black Prince. Perhaps that tag didn't refer to his armour. After all, he had the nickname as a child and the armour may have been made to match his complexion. Whatever, does it matter? Queen Philippa was a good queen and her chaplain **Robert of Eglesfield** (1295–1349) founded this college in 1341 'for honest, chaste, peaceful, humble poor persons from the North'. Chuffing 'eck, 14th-century cynics may have asked, who would they be then? In one of Oxford's typically arcane and eccentric rituals, dinner guests at Queen's are given a needle and thread. It is a French pun, *aiguille fils* (needle thread) supposing to make us recall Eglesfield. Daft? Well, we're remembering him nearly 700 years on, aren't we? Best dinner of the year: The Boar's Head Feast in December which recalls the day when a Queen's student out walking at Shotover was attacked by a massive wild boar. He managed to kill it by ramming his only weapon, a copy of Aristotle's works, into the pig's mouth, choking it. But then it is always dangerous to ram philosophy down anyone's throat.

ALUMNI

Comic **Rowan Atkinson** (b. 1955); philosopher **Jeremy Bentham** (1748–1832); internet inventor **Sir Tim Berners-Lee** (b. 1955); astronomers **Edmond Halley** (1656–1742) and **Edwin Hubble** (1889–1953); and hero of Agincourt **King Henry V** (1386–1422).

RUSKIN COLLEGE

(FOUNDED 1899, WALTON STREET AND HEADINGTON)

As said elsewhere, not part of the university but dubbed the 'working class Eton' for what used to be the 'deserving poor'. George Bernard Shaw was against the idea and said sniffily: 'A workman ought to have a vulgar prejudice against Oxford.' He was wrong, as usual, but wonderful though it is for people to say they are the first of their family to reach higher education, they still have to be good enough. Logically, though, if you devise stuff like this for the deserving poor, it stands to reason that there is an *undeserving* poor out there too. Here's a controversial essay topic for Ruskin students: Does the Labour Party's utopian determination to get half the so-called working class into university ignore the fact that some poor people are poor because they are lazy, thick, or both? If so, can this aim be achieved only by making universities increasingly worthless? So far in this process Oxford has stood firm against this political pressure as an unabashed standard-bearer of an elite, not nowadays by birth or money, but by effort and ability, and has not, yet, replaced its former upper-class twits with modern working-class twits.

Alumni

Labour politicos Jack later **Lord Ashley** (much respected; b 1922), **Dennis 'the Beast of Bolsover' Skinner** (much feared in debate; b 1932), and John **Lord Prescott** (er… well, John's John, as Tony Blair said after some debacle. But he did make it to Deputy Pie Minister. Sorry, Deputy *Prime* Minister; b 1938; see page 73).

ST ANNE'S

(Founded 1878, 1952, Woodstock Road, £40m)

The first women's college, so they have Alumnae not Alumni. Now has some men. Amongst its most famous alumnae are politician and John Major's canoodler Edwina Currie and broadcaster Libby Purves. Hmm. Must do better, girls… A student complained recently at being chucked out of the college accommodation for covering the walls with nail varnish and prints made from a female bottom smeared with ice cream, decrying it as unreasonably harsh. I'd say it depends on the flavour.

Alumnae

MP **Edwina Currie** (b. 1946); *Bridget Jones* writer **Helen**

Fielding (b. 1958); radio presenters **Libby Purves** (b. 1950) and **Martha Kearney** (b. 1957); columnists **Melanie Phillips** (b. 1951) and **Polly Toynbee** (b. 1946); and wealthy English deb and once active IRA member **Rose Dugdale** (b. 1941).

ST ANTONY'S

(FOUNDED 1950, 1963, WOODSTOCK ROAD, £30M)

All graduate. Social life includes a Halloqueen Night.

ST CATHERINE'S

(FOUNDED 1963, MANOR ROAD, £53M)

Unusual in that it was designed as an artistic whole right down to the cutlery used in hall by one great Dane, Arne Jacobsen, in the mid-20th century. He even designed the door knobs, light switches and specified which fish would swim in the pond. It'll all look suitably mellow after the usual ten centuries…

ALUMNI

Labour **Lord ('of the Dark Arts') Mandelson** (b. 1953); president of Pakistan **Farooq Leghari** (1940–2010); and Olympic rower **Sir Matthew Pinsent** (b. 1970). The aforesaid 'Dark Arts' were a popular reference to Mandelson's spin-doctoring days, and not entirely fair to a great public servant. But funny. Still, he and Michael Howard ought to be in a Dracula film one day, or something Harry Potterish.

ST CROSS

(Founded 1965, St Giles)

Small but perfectly formed, all graduate.

ST EDMUND HALL

(Founded 1226, 1957, Queen's Lane, £39m)

Always called Teddy Hall by Oxonians. Although it has been for many years a proper college, the name is a survivor of the dozens of halls that once provided homes for Oxford students in less than college-level surroundings, often with a rather dubious academic nature and rotten food, if any.

Alumni

Broadcaster **Sir Robin Day** (1923–2000); Monty Python **Terry Jones** (b. 1942); comedian 'the pub landlord' **Al Murray** (b. 1968); and mohawk physician **Oronhyatekha**, second aboriginal doctor in Canada and great scholar (1841–1907).

ST HILDA'S

(Founded 1893, Cowley Place, £39m)

Originally for women, known as Hildabeasts.

ALUMNAE

Her Royal Highness Princess Haya of Jordan (b. 1974);
Tory peeress **Lady (Gillian) Shephard** (b. 1940); and
brainbox **Baroness (Susan) Greenfield** (b. 1950).

ST HUGH'S

(FOUNDED 1886, ST MARGARET'S ROAD, £27M)

Originally for women and founded by Elizabeth
Wordsworth (1840–1932) great-niece of the poet.

ALUMNAE

Politicians **Barbara Castle** (1910–2002) and **Theresa May**
(b. 1956); and Burmese rightful leader and Nobel prize
winner **Aung San Suu Kyi** (b. 1945).

ST JOHN'S

(FOUNDED 1886, ST MARGARET'S ROAD, £27M)

Amazingly rich college. It was once said that you could
walk from St John's Oxford to St John's Cambridge
without leaving St John's land. Today you'd get squashed
on the M1. Founded in 1555 by **Sir Thomas White**
(1492–1567), an English cloth merchant who was told in a
dream to build a college at a place where three elm trees
grew out of one root. He wandered around the next day till
he found exactly one such triple trunk here. Luckily Dutch
elm disease hadn't arrived yet, and the thing survived until

a bossy bursar arrived in the 17th century and cut the thing down. Vandal! It should have been made into his gallows.

Scene of yet another tourist story. The gardener was offered £5 for the secret of the so-perfect lawn. Money changed hands and the chap said:

> *'Well, it's very simple, Sir. You just roll it and roll it, and then roll it some more, and carry on like that. Then 400 years later, it looks like this.'*

The college, which by the way has about the best gardens you could imagine, was hit by Parliamentary cannonballs in the Civil War and one is still to be seen in the tower over the gateway. Rather Tory, Right-wing, High Church traditionally.

THREE ECCENTRIC EVENTS FROM ST JOHN'S HISTORY: One President (not Laud who got his head chopped off for being too High Church and had prohibited football or anyone greeting him in college or street) used to arrive on a silver horse. Students (who knew their Bible) would quip: 'Behold the head of St John upon a silver charger.'

When the Dutch **Admiral Van Tromp** decided in 1675

he could drink St John's men under the table, he was taken back to his lodgings in a wheelbarrow, unconscious. (By the way, if you're a Turner fan – painter J M W – not Tina or Anthea – you'll know his seascape titled *Van Tromp Going About to Please His Masters* – it's a nautical term. This Van Tromp should have been painted in his wheelbarrow and titled *Van Tromp Going About to Displease His Masters.*)

Many years later when Dr James was President, an undergraduate entered the President's room to find two men on their knees and totally engrossed in sticking stamps in an enormous album. One was Dr James, the other a face familiar from most of the stamps: King George V. But then Royals have always been rather susceptible to philately.

Alumni

Jethro Tull (the original 18th-century land reformer, not the 20th century musician, 1674–1741); US Secretary of State **Dean Rusk** (1909–94); Dragons' Den presenter **Evan Davis**, (b. 1962); aptly named war poet **Robert Graves** (1895–1985); **His Imperial Highness Prince Akishino of Japan** (b. 1965); poet **AE Housman** (1859–1936) and recent Singapore police chief **Tan Sri Khoo Boon Hui** (b. 1954). Labour Prime Minister **Tony Blair** (b. 1953); novelist **Kingsley Amis** (1922–95); Prime Minister of Canada and Nobel Peace Prize-winner **Lester Pearson** (1897–1972), and the second-longest serving United States Secretary of State **Dean Rusk** (1909–94). Whether they stuck to founder Sir Thomas's dictum 'Every scholar within these walls should cherish brotherly love' is open to question. Tony Blair wasn't particularly active in politics but played in a student band called Ugly Rumours, rehearsing his cheesy grin and appearing an all-round decent straightforward kind of guy.

ST PETER'S

(FOUNDED 1928, 1961, NEW INN HALL, £34M)

Not the most architecturally inspiring college. Its first Master, **Christopher Chavasse** (1884–1962), lost a leg in an accident, ran 400 yards in the 1908 Olympics, became the peace-loving Bishop of Rochester and fought like a demon in World War I, winning the Military Cross. Not in that order, obviously, but not a dull life nevertheless...

ALUMNI

TV chef **Hugh Fearnley-Whittingstall** (b. 1965); BBC Washington correspondent **Matt Frei** (b. 1963); film director **Ken Loach** (b. 1936); President of Ghana **Edward Akufo-Addo** (1906–79); and Governor of the Falkland Islands at the time of the 1982 invasion **Sir Rex Hunt** (b. 1926). Luckily, help was on hand from the next college...

SOMERVILLE

(FOUNDED 1879, WOODSTOCK ROAD, £45M)

A late 19th-century foundation aimed at women; has produced the novelist **Dorothy L Sayers** (1893–1957) who set her book *Gaudy Night* there, plus **Iris Murdoch** (1919–99), a very eccentric French don **Enid Starkie** (1897–1970) and a certain **Margaret Thatcher** (b. 1925; she was told she'd 'make a reasonable second-rate chemist', which was damning with faint praise for the future 'Iron

Lady' who became Britain's first woman Prime Minister, smashed the nationalised industries, defeated the trade unions and the Argentines, and with her chum Ronald Reagan won the Cold War too).

ALUMNAE

Writers **Iris Murdoch** (1919–99), **Dorothy L Sayers** (1893–1957), **A S Byatt** (b. 1936), and **Vera Brittain** (1893–1970); politicians **Shirley Williams** (b. 1930), **Margaret Jay** (b. 1939) and **Indira Gandhi** (1917–84); and Nobel prize winner scientist **Dorothy Hodgkin** (1910–94). Admits males now – but none is eminent enough yet.

TRINITY

(FOUNDED 1554, BROAD STREET, £67M)

Properly 'the President, Fellows and Scholars of the College of the Holy and Undivided Trinity in the University of Oxford of the Foundation of Thomas Pope, Knight'. Or just Trinners. A smaller college but none the worse for that. Located right in the middle of the city.

ALUMNI

John Aubrey 17th-century writer of *Brief Lives* (1626–97); prime ministers **Pitt the Elder** (1708–78) and **Lord North** (1732–92), who respectively temporarily saved and lost the American colonies; comic writer/musician **Miles Kington** (1941–2008); and playwright **Terence Rattigan** (1911–77).

UNIVERSITY COLLEGE

(Founded 1249, High Street, £91m)

Has a naked reclining white man on display. Not as old as Merton, whatever they tell you. Alumni include poet laureate **Andrew Motion**.

Eccentricity: The grace said before formal meals at nearly all Oxford colleges is long and Latin. The one at Univ, however, requires responses from the diners and it is preferred, though not required, that all will learn it by heart:

Scholar — *Benedictus sit Deus in donis suis.*
Response — *Et sanctus in omnibus operibus suis.*
Scholar — *Adiutorium nostrum in Nomine Domini.*
Response — *Qui fecit coelum et terras.*
Scholar — *Sit Nomen Domini benedictum.*
Response — *Ab hoc tempore usque in saecula.*
Scholar — *Domine Deus, Resurrectio et Vita credentium, Qui semper es laudandus tam in viventibus quam in defunctis, gratias Tibi agimus pro omnibus Fundatoribus caeterisque Benefactoribus nostris, quorum beneficiis hic ad pietatem et ad studia literarum alimur: Te rogantes ut nos, hisce Tuis donis ad Tuam gloriam recte utentes, una cum iis ad vitam immortalem perducamur. Per Jesum Christum Dominum nostrum. Amen.*
Scholar — *Deus det vivis gratiam, defunctis requiem: Ecclesiae, Reginae, Regnoque nostro, pacem et concordiam: et nobis peccatoribus vitam aeternam. Amen.*

No wonder the bods are starving at the end of all that. I'm not suggesting it, but you could get a sneaky Scotch egg down in the scholar's last bit.

114

Alumni

Poet **Percy Shelley** (1792–1822), expelled, drowned and then in statue form having his bits painted blue; Russian **Prince Felix Felixovich Yusupov** (1887–1967) who killed Rasputin (and that was a harder job than you'd think); US President **Bill Clinton** (b. 1946); British PMs **Clement Atlee** (1883–1967) and **Harold Wilson** (1916–95); Australian PM **Bob Hawke** (b. 1929); writers **C S Lewis** (1898–1963), **Richard Ingrams** (b. 1937) and **Paul Gambaccini** (b. 1949); actors **Warren Mitchell** (b. 1926) and **Michael York** (b. 1942); and physician **John Radcliffe** (1652–1714) after whom about a trillion things in Oxford are named.

WADHAM

(Founded 1610, Parks Road, £66m)

One Wadham man, the Earl of Rochester, took advantage of King Charles I being in Oxford during the Civil War to chalk up on his door:

> *Here lies a great and mighty King,*
> *Whose promise none relied on.*
> *He never said a foolish thing,*
> *Nor ever did a wise one.*

Amazingly, the King took no offence because he thought it more a slur on his ministers who didn't do the wise things rather than himself who didn't say foolish things. Which just goes to show how foolish he really was.

A pupil of Wadham who did very well under his son,

Charles II (reigned 1660–85), was architect **Christopher Wren**, designer of Oxford's Tom Tower and the Sheldonian Theatre. Wren made his name just in time for the Great Fire of London in 1666 to give him the dream commission: to build the new St Paul's and dozens of beautiful and different city churches such as St Bride's in Fleet Street. His tomb is in St Paul's, marked *Si Monumentum Requiris, Circumspice* (if you require a monument, look around you). Eccentrically, he wasn't a trained architect but an astronomer.

The great eccentric early 20th-century conductor, **Sir Thomas Beecham** (1879–1961), was also a member of Wadham. An heir to the Beechams powders fortune (an amount not to be sneezed at), Sir Thomas was wonderfully outspoken. For example, in the 1930s he met a woman he vaguely recognised in Fortnum & Mason's. After exchanging greetings rather awkwardly (we've all done this, haven't we?), he asked: 'What's your husband doing nowadays?' The answer was: 'Oh, he's still King.'

But he could be more forthright as a conductor. To a cellist he once thundered: 'Madam, you have between your legs that which could give pleasure to thousands. All you do is sit there and scratch it.' Another time, asked if he had conducted any Schoenberg, he said: 'No, but I stepped in some.'

Once he described the sound of the harpsichord as: 'Two skeletons copulating on a tin roof' and he said on another occasion that the bagpipes were a fine instrument in the right place – about a mile away.

Wadham student japes have included buying rotten fish in the market and then posting them in every post box in Oxford, and perhaps less odorous but as odious, summoning 1,000 students by official-looking letters to outside the Sheldonian one morning in 1928, then calling the police and the proctors to report a riot at the same spot, then calling the fire brigade and saying there was a huge fire needing at least ten engines, then sitting back and watching the mayhem that ensued. It took half a day to sort out.

Wadham College's greatest don of the 20th century was **Maurice Bowra** (1898–1971), Warden from 1938 to 1970 (surely an interesting period). Bowra, much respected and loved, was a generous host and described himself as:

A man more dined against than dining.

Asked once why he was interested in a rather unpretty woman (and this in a widely homosexual college), he said instantly:

B*ggers can't be choosers.

He was sitting in his study once when he heard a half-drunk student, attempting to beat the curfew, clamber in the window and then hide behind the curtain trying not

to make a noise. Bowra read on for three hours until he finished the book, slammed it shut and said loudly: 'Well I don't know about you, but I'm going to bed.' On another occasion he was sunbathing naked at the male nude-bathing spot called Parson's Pleasure on the Cherwell. A punt containing females came into view and the assembled dons hurriedly put towels round their waists. Bowra left his bare, wrapping a towel round his head instead. 'It's my face they know. Not my genitals,' he explained. His face, by the way, is preserved in a quite extraordinary sculpture of him in the college garden, half-chair and half-man.

The homosexual links go back a long way and were, of course, once scandalous rather than de rigueur. An 18th-century limerick went:

There once was a Warden of Wadham
Who approved of the folkways of Sodom,
For a man might, he said,
Have a very poor head
But be a fine Fellow at bottom.

The Master concerned fled the country. The sex and sexual orientation of members, as it were, is now unrestrained, thankfully, but there was a time when even women servants were banned, except for laundresses who were of 'such age, condition, and reputation as to be above suspicion'. I think they mean old bags who would not attract, nor stand for, any hanky-panky.

Alumni

Writers **Monica Ali** (b. 1967) and **Alan Coren** (1938–2007); admiral **Robert Blake** (1598–1657) who made the Mediterranean 'The English Sea' for three centuries,

NZ PM **William Fox** (1812–93); a **King of Malaysia**; actress **Rosamund Pike** (b. 1979); and TV know-all **Melvyn Bragg** (b. 1939).

WOLFSON

(FOUNDED 1966, 1981, LINTON ROAD, £33M)

The Wolfson Colleges in Oxford and Cambridge, which are aimed at graduates and mature students, are just one small part of yet another almost incredible rags-to-riches story. Isaac Wolfson was born in the roughest part of Glasgow in 1897, son of a Jewish cabinet maker, Solomon Wolfson, who had fled from a part of the 'Empire of Russia' (as the naturalisation papers said) which later became Poland. He founded a mail order, clothing and furniture company, Great Universal Stores, in the 1920s, and it was so successful that the family set up their philanthropic foundation in 1955. In its first half century, this has given away a billion pounds in real terms to good causes around the world, mostly in health and education, without using up the capital. Two thoughts to add: All this would have been cruelly lost had the family stayed put in time for the Holocaust. And that's a lot of achievement to start from a few decent dovetail joints in the Gorbals.

WORCESTER

(FOUNDED 1714, WALTON STREET, £32M)

A hundred years ago the favourite Worcester sport was to release of a cage full of rats in the quad and then try to beat them to death with hockey sticks. A more recent deeply eccentric Worcester don was Richard Cobb (page 63). Like Starbucks, has extensive grounds. And a lake.

ALUMNI

Authors **Richard Adams** (b. 1920), who wrote *Watership Down*, and **Thomas** 'opium eater' **De Quincey** (1785–1859); fashion-writer and novelist **Plum Sykes** (real first name Victoria, geddit?; b. 1969); *Dr Who* producer **Russell T Davies** (b. 1963); Aussie-American multi-media mega-mogul **Rupert Murdoch** (b. 1931), famously the victim of a custard pie in the House of Commons (or was it humble pie on the menu that day?) and Academy Award Winning composer **Rachel Portman** (b. 1960). Remember her when a chauvinist old git asks you to name a great women composer. She is best known for film music and has composed around 70 movie scores, including classics such as *Chocolat*, *The Cider House Rules* and the remake of *The Manchurian Candidate*. She won her Oscar for *Emma* (the Gwyneth Paltrow one).

ECCENTRIC CHURCHES

NAME THAT SAINT

Oxford has some pretty eccentric saints remembered in its church dedications. Where else can you find churches of, for example, St Alban, St Aldate (who doesn't exist), St Aloysius, St Barnabas, St Bartholomew, St Clement, St Cross (again, no such saint), St Ebbe, St Edmund *and* St Frideswide and (separately) St Frideswide, St Giles, St Peter le Bailey and St Peter in the East, not forgetting St Thomas A Becket?

The older ones also get a street named after them, such as St Ebbe's, off Queen Street in the city centre. She was an otherwise forgotten 7th-century abbess in Northumberland (Christianity having arrived in Britain from the top).

ST FRIDESWIDE isn't much known outside Oxford, but she performed a miracle here and is patron saint of Oxford, so she gets one-and-a-half churches, in Botley Road and Iffley Road. (For her story, see page 25.)

St Cross is one of those almost meaningless church names – what Saint Cross? – that pop up from time to time around England, like St Sepulchre. Usually they started life as something like 'The Church of St Edmund, the Holy Sepulchre, the Blessed Virgin and the Holy Cross', which locals, not unnaturally, shortened to something easier to handle, if nonsensical.

St Giles also gives its name to the great broad street south of it where a fair is held each autumn (see page 19). Set as it is amidst the hurrying traffic on the nose of land separating Banbury and Woodstock roads, one might expect St Giles to be patron saint of road-crash victims, and indeed he is patron saint of cripples. It is the most oddly laid-out building in that few of the walls and angles are right. All are slightly too long, short, or wonky.

In fact, if it's *the* St Giles, he was also patron saint of lepers, a common and incurable disfiguring disease in medieval England. Edinburgh's grand Princes Street was going to be called St Giles's Street until someone remembered this – and the fact that St Giles's slum in London was then the notorious haunt of thieves, murderers, loose women and pickpockets.

People feared lepers because of contagion and their terrible deformities, so some medieval English churches have a 'leper's squint', a spyhole tunnelled through the wall at an angle so the unfortunate sufferers – treated like lepers, literally – could see the service from outside. At Oxford they were cared for out of sight beyond the edge of town, but at least they had their own chapel (see page 177).

ST MARY THE VIRGIN, HIGH STREET

It is probably hard for those who have not studied history to comprehend that 16th- and 17th-century Oxford seemed to consist largely of one lot of Christians burning, beheading and hanging another lot for what may seem small theological differences, but then these things were clearly life and death to them. Whether statues were allowed in church, for example. The Catholics and High Church Anglicans loved them, but the puritan Protestants were so convinced an image in a church was a sin they were prepared to kill or be killed (which seems to be putting aside the sixth commandment in favour of the second). The Roundheads, you will recall, smashed any stained-glasswindows they could find and beheaded many a statue. They didn't like saints, they loved witch-hunts, and they despised statuary in churches.

A case in point is the **elaborate porch** in the beautiful St Mary the Virgin church, surely Oxford's finest (which would spend half its time, if it could speak, saying 'No, actually I'm *not* the cathedral').

The ornate south porch was linked to Charles I – the king who was besieged here in Oxford and then lost the Civil War and his head to Parliament – and to his High Church **Archbishop Laud**, who was Chancellor of Oxford University at thetime.TheArchbishop's chaplain donated it and it was sculpted by Charles I's master mason, the aptly named Nicholas Stone. It features helical columns supporting a curly pediment with a shell niche containing a statue of the Virgin and Child. Big mistake when humourless, Roundheads were about to ban everything like this, plus theatre, Christmas, maypoles and just about any kind of fun or art; the ayatollahs of their day.

In Laud's 1641 trial, this 'scandalous statue', which caused someone entering to bow or pray at it, rather as Roman Catholics might (so claimed the prosecution witnesses), was a vital part in getting Laud executed. Just what the Roundheads thought is indicated by the bullet holes in the statue which were made after the King was driven from Oxford in the Civil War. In fact, they were decapitated for a while.

(For much more on this church and its great viewpoint tower on the north of the High Street walk, see page 144.)

The church is where much university teaching and the degree ceremonies took place before the university's own buildings arrived, such as the Sheldonian in 1669. Historic events in this church include the **hearings** into the supposed heresy of Latimer, Ridley and Cranmer (Protestant bishops burned in Oxford) in 1554–56; **John Wesley's last sermon** before setting up Methodism (in which he attacked the sloth of university officials); and the **birth of the Oxford Movement** to reform Anglicanism in 1833 (which thought statues in churches an excellent thing after all).

ECCENTRIC DETAIL: a roof boss in the north corner of the West Gallery depicts an unexpected thin Indian gentleman sitting cross-legged and wearing a simple loincloth. It is, you soon realise, Mahatma Gandhi.

CHRIST CHURCH CATHEDRAL

You could be forgiven for missing this, Oxford's cathedral, for it is so tucked into Christ Church the college that it looks like a mere college chapel (which it also is).

Actually it is an ancient church site, going right back to the 8th century when Oxford's patron saint, St Frideswide, founded it. It was burned down twice in the next 400 years, once deliberately in 1002 when a group of Danes had taken refuge in it. The Danes, it should be explained, were not tourists bringing nutty pastries but were the raping and pillaging sort that came up rivers in their longboats to create mayhem. Still, an expensive way to massacre people, burning down your main church. Whatever happened to sanctuary? Perhaps it didn't count if you were heathens. The Danes are still trying to get their revenge, judging by the little wooden spikes you get hidden in roll-mops from that country.

In 1829 there was some discussion of demolishing the 'despised and desecrated church' and perhaps they should have done. Instead it was restored and altered for about the 100th time. Unsatisfactory, architecturally, you may think, and almost invisible from the outside, buried as it is in academia's dreaming spires.

ST THOMAS OF CANTERBURY, ELSFIELD

Reached by a lane of less than a mile from Marston, having crossed the A40 ring road, a fine walk if you have the time, or a great bike ride (see page 218). A simple Early English-style church (much restored in Victorian times), the graveyard not only offers the best view of Oxford but includes at its best viewpoint a monument to **John Buchan** (1875–1940), author of the turn of World War I thriller *The Thirty-Nine Steps*. The monument, which covers his ashes – he was killed in a World War II plane crash in Canada – is of a strange circular design with a Greek inscription. For such a truly great spinner of yarns, it is perhaps appropriate that his title was Lord Tweedsmuir.

ST GILES, HORSPATH

Has a very odd stone figure playing the bagpipes and a matching one looking amazed, as one often is. Particularly if it's spin doctor Alastair Campbell doing the piping.

ST BARNABAS, HORTON-CUM-STUDLEY

Wacky name, wacky church. By the brick-banding busybody Butterfield who created Keble College (see page 93). A little more successful here, you may think.

WALKS: CENTRAL OXFORD

THE ARCHITECTURAL CROWN JEWELS

The best bits of Oxford lie in a surprisingly small area, just 300 yards north and south of the High Street, yet are so condensed and layered that those who have lived in the city a lifetime still find the odd surprise and hidden quirk. But then, architecturally, this city centre is one of mankind's greatest gems.

Of course, being Oxford, it is not as other high streets in Britain. There are no chain stores, thank God, with their bland glass and plastic frontages that could be in Milwaukee or Manchester or Melbourne, to defile the face of this 'the noblest prospect in all Europe' as it was once called. It has a Gwyneth Paltrow-style curve to it (gracefully gentle but not too much), so you cannot see both Carfax Tower at one end and Magdalen Tower at the other.

It is, all in all, surprisingly unspoiled (unlike some other parts of Oxford, it must be said) and intact; perhaps there is some truth in the notion that Hitler wanted Oxford for his capital and so it wasn't bombed flat, as were other city centres. If you have no time for the outlying areas, the villages, the pubs and the museums of Oxford, you *must* explore this one patch. Otherwise you have not seen what more than a millennium of many-layered culture can offer.

Let's look at the south and the north of the High Street in two walks that you can enjoy by walking literally, or read in an armchair to select the bits you really want to see. Our starting and finishing point can be Carfax, the crossroads at the centre of Oxford. This means four ways, but there is no road called Carfax, as all four streets have proper names. Like Oxford University, it exists as a concept, a focus, not a place.

From the old **Carfax Tower** on one corner, a church tower that has long lost its church, one may enjoy superb views of central Oxford, and it is from up here that the Mayor must proclaim a new King or Queen. On the face of the tower stand the quarterboys who ring the bells every quarter-hour and remind us with their Latin inscription that Strength is Truth, or probably more clearly Truth is Strength, which sounds a bit less fascist. It was from on this tower, first mentioned in 1032 so around 1,000 years old, that the outraged townspeople in 1355 rang bells to call the citizenry to battle the university in a three-day massacre that killed 63 (page 29). Leaving aside that bloody blip in Town-and-Gown relations, it is still an excellent view. What you can't see from up here is the fascinating labyrinth of lanes and paths either side of the High Street. Time to explore...

Walk: South of the High Street

A superb stroll that can be done in less than two hours, or easily take twice as long, or more, with stops to look at things, taking in most things of interest south of the High Street. It's a good walk in midwinter, if you are proofed against the weather, and on a fine day in spring, summer or autumn, it is just cosmic.

Set off down the road south marked St Aldate's ('What St Aldate?': another Oxford eccentricity, there isn't one, it probably means old gate) on the far side from Carfax tower, so you are going past the **Town Hall**.

At the far end, a monument mentions the city's Jews who lived in this area (till expelled from the county in 1290) and, tucked into a corner, is the **Museum of Oxford**. This is inexpensive but not brilliant: it contains

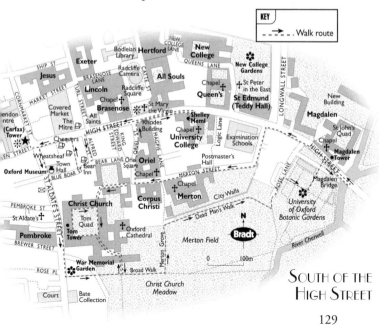

SOUTH OF THE
HIGH STREET

129

a few interesting objects from history, maps and photos, and some reconstructions of things, arranged in a linear walk-through pattern, but unless you have time to kill on a rainy day it's frankly better to see the real thing. The video presentation I sat through in the small theatre couldn't have been more boring. (It reminded me of a Oxford newspaper editor called Eddie Duller, whose presentation I once attended. It was called, jokingly, something like 'how to make a Duller newspaper'. It certainly wasn't. This certainly was.)

Next to it is inviting Blue Boar Street which we cross, keeping on down St Aldate's, with its smattering of pubs. Down Pembroke Street on the right is the **Museum of Modern Art**, and tucked away on the left of that street **Pembroke College** (home of several great eccentrics such as Robert Hawker and Dr Johnson – see pages 66 and 36), very much the poor relation compared to the most splendid of Oxford colleges, **Christ Church**, which is on our left facing down St Aldate's. In fact, it is sometimes called the coal scuttle, to denote its inferior wealth and social status to the overmighty place across the road. This has been conspicuous all the way down the street because of the **Tom Tower**, the beautiful construction Sir Christopher Wren added in 1682 to house Great Tom, the bell once in the great Osney Abbey down by where the station now stands, destroyed by the Reformation in the previous century.

Oddly, the bell was female when it lived at the abbey, being Great Mary, but with the Protestant suppression of the cult of Mary, its change in gender en route to Tom Tower, via a time at the cathedral and recasting, was perhaps explicable. It definitely has a deeper dong now.

This sonorous bell still tolls a curfew at 9pm each evening, with 101 tolls for the 101 students of 1682.

Eccentrically and rather typically, that is 9pm Oxford time, so it is 9.05pm Greenwich time. Each town in Britain once had its own time, as before the railways and telegraphs came, there was no need for one exact time across the country, depending on how far west it was. Bristol was 12 minutes behind London, Oxford just five minutes. Only here is there a remnant of the old system.

Looking through the gate that somehow hasn't fallen down despite holding up Tom Tower and its seven-ton bell, one can see the classic Oxford quadrangle of perfect lawn and smooth-worn honeyed stone, yet the visitor's way is firmly barred by bowler-hatted porters (unless you are in a wheelchair). It is not that Christ Church won't let you in at all, it just won't let you in by the front door, nor the next gate, but the third, through some railings on the left almost halfway to Folly Bridge.

Notice at this gate set in the ground a brass sword pointing the way, and a war memorial quotation from John Bunyan. Don't omit to read the regulations allowing you into the **Christ Church Meadow**, which urge the Meadow Keepers ('What do you do for a living? Oh, I keep meadows') to 'prevent nuisance and indecent, rude or disorderly conduct of every description', which would seem to cover a wide scope, and also prohibits kite flying, bowling of hoops, throwing balls, shooting arrows or firing guns and pistols. I couldn't help wondering if I could get away with doing as many of them as possible at the same time. I also began to understand the Town's centuries-old resentment of the humiliating controls the Gown forced on every aspect of their lives for so many years since that St Scholastica's Day Massacre (see page 29) started up in Carfax.

On the other hand, the college has done you a favour by forcing you round to this side to see the **Broad Walk** before us, across a little stream. I have read one respected authority say this is all that remains of Trill Mill Stream, a once filthy medieval open sewer that ran through the St Ebbe's slum area (and still runs forgotten underground), and that adventurous students have tried exploring it underground by punt. In 1920, he said, a Victorian punt was found down there with two rat-gnawed skeletons in it. I just hope they weren't paying by the hour.

This Broad Walk goes straight ahead right down to the **River Cherwell** about 600 yards ahead. To the right, across the meadow can be seen the line of the River Thames (or Isis as it is known by Latin-loving pedants with which Oxford is infested), and a lovely walk may be had in summer beside the rivers, watching punters slowly bothering the dozy ducks. The view from the riverside walk or a punt upon the Cherwell back towards the city of dreaming spires could not be bettered, and we thank God again for those in the 1960s who stopped an insane scheme to drive a huge road across this meadow.

Assuming we leave the riverside pleasure for another day, on the left we are finally allowed entrance to **Christ Church**, which they may charge you for (it's a bit vague – I merely said I was a graduate of another place and not over 60, and was allowed in free. Maybe it was because I wanted to see the cathedral). If you ignore the cathedral for a moment, walk through to **Tom Quad**, the around 260ft square of architectural perfection we saw looking through from St Aldate's. In the centre is a statue of Mercury which, one day when the pond was frozen thickly, the students dressed as a doctor of divinity. When the authorities wanted to remove the garments the next day, however, the ice proved less robust…

This one college has supplied Britain with 13 prime ministers, so might you expect some gravity from such characters? Not a bit of it. The **Earl of Derby** (1799–1869), one of the 13, knocked Mercury off his pedestal in 1817. **Sir Robert Peel** (1788–1850), another one who more or less invented policemen (hence Peelers and Bobbies are two nicknames for the boys in blue) played a particularly nasty prank on a freshman on his second day at Christ Church. He sent a message that the Dean was coming to test him on Greek, and turned up in disguise with an accomplice dressed as a bulldog (the university police, that is, not the canine creature). He denounced the quaking freshman, who fled the university and never returned.

Tom Quad is not only a visual delight but opens into another more splendid quad, the 18th-century **Peckwater Quad**, at the far side, then another, **Canterbury Quad**, leading to the grand arch of **Canterbury Gate**, whence we should retrace our steps, getting another look at the superb architecture on our return.

The doors around the quads lead to the men's rooms at this, perhaps the most prestigious of Oxford colleges;

their names painted up have often included Lord so and so, the Honourable so and so. Eton College, which stands further down the Thames near Windsor, funnelled boys in here with hardly any academic hurdles, and degrees were awarded with some studied carelessness.

Many a young aristocrat left without bothering to sit the laughable examinations, as their time at Oxford was seen a social and mind-broadening experience. Things may have changed, although in the 1960s tiny Pembroke across the road was still known as 'the little place for grammar-school boys', that is a place where a boy of humble background could gain entry through mere brilliance, not connections.

Mention of the doors recalls another Christ Church eccentric, one **Marquess of Waterford**, who was annoyed at the authorities objecting to his hunting in pink (it's red, but it's one of those daft upper-class things like white horses being called grey). He painted the Dean's door red, or pink as he might have called it, in revenge. (In fact the Marquess's family were deeply eccentric. One had a hunt tattooed down his back with the fox going to earth at the appropriate aperture, another paid a railway company to crash two engines head-on just for fun, another placed a donkey in the bed of a traveller at a wayside inn, another set his bloodhounds to hunt the terrified village parson, the hooves of whose horse he had painted with aniseed to drive the dogs crazy.)

In fact Christ Church was named and founded twice. Once by **Cardinal Wolsey** (1473–1530), Henry VIII's right-hand man, who started it off in 1523 and called it Cardinal's College. He crushed 22 monasteries and sold their treasures and lands to do this; but as a churchman at the cathedral told me, he might have been serving the Church rather well by doing this. The monasteries were corrupt big businesses, the nunneries – including one at Sandford near here – dens of vice and prostitution. As Wolsey said: 'Neither God was served in them, nor religion kept.' But Wolsey fell from power over Henry's attempts to break with the church of Rome, and it was left to Henry to restart the college as Christ Church, at the same time making what would have become the college chapel (a church which was here for around 350 years before Wolsey started his college) the cathedral of the new diocese of Oxford. Henry could afford to do this by copying Wolsey's trick: suppressing the vast abbeys and convents that owned so much of medieval England.

Oxford Cathedral, therefore, which you can easily look in on your way back to the entrance of Christ Church (the entrance is on the left as you leave Tom Quad), is very small and the congregation sit facing each other, as in a college chapel. There is no choir screen, so what you see is what you get. The somewhat piecemeal construction is hemmed in by Christ Church buildings and offers no imposing vistas, and nothing more inspiring than most other college chapels.

There is, however, the reassembled remains of the **shrine of St Frideswide** (see page 25) – only its base, the Protestants having attacked anything reeking of saint worship, including knocking off the heads of several sculptures nearby – and a watching loft from which pilgrims would keep their vigil all night.

Back outside on the **Broad Walk** and turning left to continue the way we were going, turn left by some railings instead of continuing to the end. This path is Merton Grove and the field to the right **Merton Field**. Don't miss the bowling green-flat lawn seen through the gateway in the wall to the left, not just for the splendid view over Christ Church and the Cathedral, but for the fact that this lawn was the one where Charles Dodgson watched a game of croquet and imagined this surreal scene:

> *'Get to your places!' shouted the Queen in a voice of thunder, and people began running about in all directions, tumbling up against each other; however, they got settled down in a minute or two, and the game began. Alice thought she had never seen such a curious croquet-ground in her life; it was all ridges and furrows; the balls were live hedgehogs, the mallets live flamingoes, and the soldiers had to double themselves up and to stand on their hands and feet, to make the arches.*

Alice's Adventures in Wonderland

The college ahead down the path and to the right is **Merton**; the one to the left is **Corpus Christi**. However, turn right along the long side of Merton Field, along its long back wall. We are now on **Dead Man's Walk**, so called because the Jews (mentioned on the plaque back at the Town Hall) were not permitted to be buried within the city, so the dead were taken down here to a Jewish cemetery, which was where the **Botanic Garden** is ahead of us. You might wonder if the brilliance of its flowers might be in part owed to their bones. But the Jews had been forced out of the country in 1290, long before this garden was properly established in 1631. Later that same century the Jews were finally allowed back into England. The upstairs bay window of Merton College that overlooks the wall with a great view across the meadows is, by the way, where *Lord of the Rings* creator J R R Tolkien worked for many years.

Further down Dead Man's Walk look out for the plaque on the wall marking where **James Sadler** (1753–1828) made the first English hot-air balloon ascent in 1784, landing near Woodeaton about six miles to the north. This ascent in a 170ft-circumference 'fire balloon' must have utterly astonished the population which had never seen a man fly – and he went to 3,500ft – in the way that walking on the Moon did for people in 1969. Imagine his view as he drifted directly over Oxford's spires, the first time anyone (apart from angels) had seen such a perspective. You can also see his grave at **St Peter in the East** (now part of St Edmund Hall), where you will also find the grave, eccentrically, of someone who died on 31 February.

Have a look at this very early **botanic garden** with its samples from around the world by popping through the gate in the wall. Depending on the time of year, it can be quite wonderful. The London Plane tree, which I had always assumed to be a natural form and which is probably more loved by shade-seekers and more loathed by leaf-sweepers than any tree in the world, was in fact created here as a hybrid. At the far side is the River Cherwell.

On a fine day this is a great place to take a rest, but then continue to the left and out of the front gate to regain the **High Street**. Here we are eventually going left, but if you are new to Oxford first take a short stroll to the right to **Magdalen Bridge**, **College** and **Tower**. This college is festooned with gargoyles and grotesques of a most detailed nature and well worth examining. Notice the bishop on the corner blessing those who cross the bridge, for example. The river pool by the bridge is one of the places to pick up a punt, and much craziness happens around here on the morning of 1 May (see page 7).

Returning past the Botanic Garden, it's worth noting the **memorial** in the hedge near the entrance put up by the Americans to the eight Oxford doctors who pioneered the practical use of penicillin, and thus antibiotics. I doubt if anyone else has saved so many lives in the history of the world. (I recall when I was younger, one of these named, a genial old gent called Norman Heatley, coming round to my mother's house for a drink in North Oxford from time to time. If only I had fully understood then what they had achieved. They should have all been knighted, not just Fleming – an apt name for a curer of chest infections. They gave away their breakthrough to American manufacturers rather than make money from them, figuring that in the constraints of wartime that was the best way to help the most people, and they were right.)

Take the next left road heading away from Magdalen, Merton Street, and go down past the rather stately **Examination Schools** on the right. The Schools are not as old as they pretend to be architecturally, but curiously once had a chute for the dead. No, not a punishment for plagiarism. That's been an increasing problem at Oxford, we were told recently, particularly among foreign PhD students. All right, I admit it, I copied that from a newspaper. So why the chute for the dead? More sadly, this building served as a hospital for badly wounded soldiers in World War I.

Further down **Merton Street**, round the corner, there are few cars, few tourists but a cobbled street that is so unspoilt it could go straight in a Jane Austen film. Further down we reach **Merton College** on our left (notice the massive and superb, almost comical gargoyles which look like they're badly hungover and about to vomit over the lawn; can you see some of them have two heads?) and behind us as you look at them is the ancient postmaster's hall. Somewhere on here is a plaque to an MP and gentleman commoner of University College (between us and the High Street now) which notes he was a 'Republican and Wit' as if sharing the two things were then thought unlikely. Would we now put up 'Feminist and Wit' or 'Vegetarian and Wit'? Discuss. A good question for the Examination Schools round the corner.

Merton, if it is open for visiting, has various treasures: the oldest quad in Oxford is the 14th-century Mob Quad (the third and smallest from the road), a library with medieval chained books, and a Max Beerbohm room full of the caricatures of the early 20th-century satirist who wrote the hugely funny *Zuleika Dobson* about Oxford life. There is also a very strange carving of St John the Baptist in the Wilderness on the gatehouse by the street – just look at the detail. Some wilderness! For more Merton eccentricities see page 98.

At the end of Merton Street, passing between **Oriel College** on our right and little **Corpus Christi** on our left, we come out into an agreeable open space, **Oriel Square** (if this shape is a square then geometry teaching wasn't very good, was it?). The great arch is the suitably pompous **Canterbury Gate** of Christ Church we may have seen from inside that college. Plunge into the right fork at the top of the square, which is narrow Oriel Street, with its houses painted in strangely gay seaside colours.

At the top turn right to catch some vistas and eccentricities we missed on the High Street. First is a good view of **St Mary the Virgin** opposite (much more like a cathedral than the cathedral, more on page 122), and on the end of Oriel College on this side of the road is the **Rhodes Building**, featuring Cecil Rhodes himself at the top. He who looked to Africa and diamonds for a fortune, founded Rhodesia (thus sharing that rare quality with Simon Bolivar of having a whole country named after himself), started the Cape to Cairo railway and invented Rhodes scholars at Oxford is here stuck looking, totally inappropriately, north.

Further down, still looking across to the other side, after Catte Street (down which you can glimpse the round Radcliffe Camera) is **All Souls** (see page 80), while sticking to this side we come to **University College**. This is worth a quick visit for just one thing: the **Shelley Monument**. If it is open for visits (and even if it isn't, if you ask at the Porter's Lodge sweetly for this one thing you may be lucky) you may enter the quad and go immediately to the nearest right-hand corner. Off the staircase at the corner ground floor is a quite extraordinary white marble monument in a very strange hall to the eponymous poet, Percy Bysshe Shelley (1792–1822), portrayed freshly drowned, as he was in 1822. It was considered too erotic for its first-intended location so ended up here at his old college. As the chap said:

> *A lovely youth – no mourning maiden decked With weeping flowers, or votive cypress wreath, The lone couch of his everlasting sleep.*

To bring things down to earth a bit, every so often the rugby team break in to the enclosure and paint Percy's percy blue. While they're at it, they could put a bolt through his neck in memory of his wife Mary Shelley's creation, Frankenstein. Enough Bysshe bosh.

Back on the High Street, go a few yards further east (to your right coming out of University College) simply to glimpse the glorious street name on the right, **Logic Lane** which, logically enough, went past a philosophy department. Yet again we reverse (Logic Lane isn't as interesting as it sounds and only dumps us back in Merton Street) and return towards Carfax, past Oriel Street and parallel King Edward Street which both lead back to Oriel Square. Now we are in sight of our journey's end, but with one more diversion, which involves a number of splendid pubs you may well be in need of.

Go left down Alfred Street to have a look at the ancient **Bear Inn** at the end (for how truly ancient and how much the Bear Inn, see page 248), and turn right on to Blue Boar Street after stopping (or not) for a drink. Instead of going up to the Town Hall, take the narrow passage very soon on the right, **Wheatsheaf Yard**. Up this narrow passage is another surprisingly large pub on the left and on the right has, until recently, a legendarily old-fashioned hardware store called **Gill's**. One of those places that smells of paraffin (kerosene to Americans) and string and candle wax, where old dons come in and order four No 8 screws and take them away in a paper bag without having to buy an unopenable blister pack of 20. Splendid: dons and loose screws go together. Up the passage to the High Street, turn left and Carfax tower, our start and finish point, is just ahead. Do notice the holey sign of the Chequers and have a look down that intriguing passage too for another splendid old pub if you fancy a self-congratulatory bevvy or three…

WALK: NORTH OF THE HIGH STREET

This walk encompasses some of the finest colleges in the history of mankind, the most exquisite architecture, the most ancient books you have probably ever seen, a gaggle of eccentric dons and loony students, a fantastic viewpoint, a truly wonderful gem of a pub as perfect as you'll get this side of paradise, and a bloody good fried breakfast if you need one. The walk starts and finishes at **Carfax tower**. This took me two-and-a-half hours but would have been an hour less if I hadn't stopped in churches, pubs, coffee shops, etc. I didn't stop in the colleges on this occasion, so it could very reasonably take all day. As with the other walks, you can, of course, follow it to the letter, or just read it to help establish what you'd like to see. Again, most colleges are open only in the afternoon in term time, so if you wanted to go into any of them, you won't be able to in the mornings.

Setting off east from Carfax down the High Street, you almost immediately come to entrances to the **Covered Market**. This is a fascinating place, but if you need a good

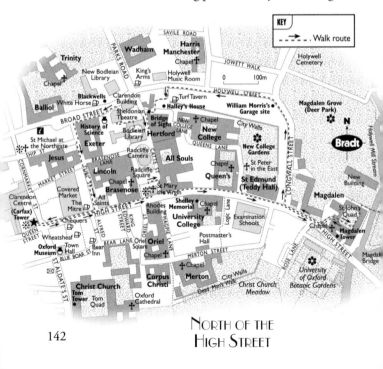

NORTH OF THE
HIGH STREET

breakfast to set you up then you could do worse than pop in here and find Brown's, where a full English costs less than a fiver at the time of writing.

But staying on the High, as it is known, note the **Mitre** pub, a truly ancient establishment first recorded in 1227 and probably considerably older. Under here are great stone crypts, now mostly bricked up, which were used as wine vaults and extended right under the High and Turl Street. In fact, rumour has it that because Henry VIII's soldiers bricked up some of these monks in the tunnel that once crossed the High Street, they are now haunted and the cries of the persecuted monks can be heard in the dead of night. Someone once said that because of the Town-and-Gown riots, there is not a spot of ground between the Mitre and Carfax that has not been soaked with blood. It was true that in the 1825 riot, a particularly good one from the point of view of spectators who watched these things from upstairs windows, the landlord of the Mitre was asked to supply broom handles, chair legs and rolling pins … for the Gown side to use as weapons. He gladly agreed, as the Town had torn down his pub sign and lamp. Many heads were broken that night.

'Why is this road we are crossing, **Turl Street**, like the Church of England?' demanded my Boswellian companion, and offered the answer: 'Because it goes from Broad to High, taking in a bit of Jesus on the way.' If that doesn't yet make much sense, it will later.

We are passing a brilliantly bespired redundant church, **All Saints**, now a college library. This is followed by **Brasenose College** on the left (it means brass nose, see page 85) and then the rather extraordinary **University Church of St Mary the Virgin**, set alongside Radcliffe Square behind. Note the barley-twist porch and the rather Roman Catholic Virgin and Child above – Archbishop Laud paid for this embellishment and then paid with his life (see page 123).

Let's leave the High for a moment, assuming the church is open, and go through the entrance and across the church diagonally, noting the plaque on the pillar that tells of the three bishops who were tried here for being Protestants and then burned in Broad Street. Don't forget to look back at the glorious west window. Head for the gift-shoppy area in the north porch. Here a real treat awaits, unless you are greatly afraid of heights, an unfit old codger, or extremely corpulent (I nearly ticked 'all of the above', but went anyway).

You pay a small fee and you ascend the tower through the door behind the cash till. There are 127 steps but it's broken up in stages, as you pass the library (actually the first university library in 1337, when students had to vow not to wear wet clothes or kindle fire), the bell-ringing loft and finally a narrow spiral staircase. In high summer it may be wise to shout 'coming up' and 'coming down' to decrease the chances of meeting people, but there are places such as arrow slits where you can squeeze past.

At the top, you are out among the gargoyles (and far be it from me to suggest that is where you belong!).

In fact you can see for once the stone channel down their backs, which makes them gargoyles (that vomit or

THIS IS A GUIDE to what you're looking at, starting with the first side (north) and left to right in each view:

Views from St Mary the Virgin

North

The grey very steep and rather French roof with one slender spire, **Exeter College Chapel**; the nearest quadrangle between you and it, **Brasenose College**; the small green and white dome to the left of the huge one, the top of the **Sheldonian Theatre**; the vast dome right before you, the beautiful honey-stone round **Radcliffe Camera** (camera meaning chamber, as in camera obscura or darkened room, the one you hold in your hand being a later miniature version), being part of the university library that has outgrown that room downstairs somewhat; a white block in the far distance to its right, the **Science Area**; the elegant quad surrounded by many small spires and featuring the first of many sundials, **All Souls College**; and behind that, **New College bell tower**.

East

The last two again to the left; on the horizon a great white thing like a distant ocean liner, the **John Radcliffe Hospital** (Radcliffe again, there is a monument to him downstairs, he did a lot for Oxford); the tower with a small green dome, **The Queen's College**; the wooded hill behind, **Headington Hill**; the High Street curving towards **Magdalen Tower**; if you imagine this curve continuing and it is, unluckily, a clear day, you can see the ghastly sprawl that is **East Oxford** leading to the ugly distant **Cowley** car works and unattractive estates beyond (architectural judgments only, of course).

(CONTINUED OVERLEAF)

Views from St Mary the Virgin

(CONTINUED)

South

The last two again to the left; a quad with many small triangular gables, **University College**; the pinnacled tower and long grey roof to its left, **Merton College Chapel**; the green sward immediately behind it, **Christ Church Meadow**; the line of trees at the end of that, the **River Thames**; the green-roofed buildings much nearer with more Dutch gables and pompous sculptures facing the High Street, **Oriel College**; the inelegant stubby spire, **Christ Church Cathedral**; the open space between us and it, **Oriel Square** and the lane leading back to the High Street, **Oriel Street**; the more elegant large domed tower that looks as if Nasa might light the fuse, **Tom Tower** in Christ Church; the smaller spire to the right, **St Aldate's Church**; the hill behind it, **Boar's Hill**.

West

The last three again; the spire surrounded by a ring of columns, **All Saints** (which we just passed on foot, the spire being an attractive but illogical compromise between Gothic and classical architecture); the red-roofed college in front of it, **Brasenose College**; behind it and right a little, **Lincoln College**; a distant green spire, **Nuffield College**, and to its right a distant stone spire, the **Wesley Methodist Church**; and so back to **Exeter College Chapel**.

gargle, hence gargoyle, water), unlike the other statues without such spouts looking down from roofs all over Oxford that are really grotesques. The tower was built before the spire (yes, of course it would be, but 40 years before, so they must have had second thoughts) in 1280. The views from the top are just tremendous and the best way to orient yourself in the city. Do take time to gaze at them.

There are few places where you can see so much of Oxford and also how (if you pretend East Oxford's semi-industrial sprawl isn't there) compact it is and surrounded by green hills.

Leaving the church by the entrance (north) in the bookshop, I fell headlong over the step. Boswell pointed out that it was helpfully inscribed, if my Grade 3 Latin is up to it: 'May the Lord look after your entrances and exits.' I must have done something to offend Him that day…

Don't succumb to the attractions of going on north, beyond admiring the totally glorious **Radcliffe Camera** (the round building so much the colour of Crunchie bars that I almost fancied a bite. You haven't tried Crunchie bars? You haven't *lived*).

By the way, a sottish Brasenose don once got so blind drunk that he couldn't see properly and clinging to the Radcliffe Camera railings felt his way round five times before dawn came up when he was spotted and helped to bed by a Fellow. Or so they tell you. When you think that dons have drunk themselves to death in this famously alcoholic city, it could well be true.

Turn right (as you come out of the church) alongside the church up Catte Street (site of medieval book scribes and binders) to return to the High and turn left, passing **All Souls College** (which has no undergraduates, page 80).

147

Opposite is **University College** and looking ahead on our (north) side of the street, don't freak out that students are about to commit suicide by jumping from the roof. They are merely sculptures, which Oxford grows as readily as mushrooms, adorning **The Queen's College** (page 104), rapidly followed after Queen's Lane by **St Edmund Hall** (Teddy Hall).

One eccentric Queen's College man who made a name for himself in 20th-century politics was **Sir John Stokes**, a Conservative MP who thought Mrs Thatcher was not Right-wing enough. He was dubbed 'The MP for the 17th century' in his reactionary views. He urged Mrs Thatcher, for example, to return to using the upper classes to find government ministers: 'To remind the public of the glorious part the nobility has played in the history of England. There is no better qualification for a minister than to have been to Eton and served in the Guards.' He called for more hereditary dukes to be created to save the country. His recipe for dealing with strikes then paralysing the motor industry in factories such as Cowley was straightforward: 'Shooting a few strike ringleaders, Pétain-style, would end trouble at British Leyland.' And he thought no-one should serve on a jury who didn't wear a collar and tie. That would cut out a few women, as well as most of the working classes, clearly. He died in 2003 aged 85, about 200 years too late.

Crossing Longwall Street, we reach **Magdalen College** on the left, a wonderful building well endowed with fabulous and fantastic (using those words properly for once) gargoyles and grotesques all along this frontage, and with a few real eccentrics and oddities inside over the centuries (page 97). Christ Church may think itself the most magnificent of colleges, but Magdalen, open most afternoons for a small fee, is more magical. You also get a leaflet to guide you, so I'll just touch on highlights here to help you decide.

What's great about it is its diversity of tone. Going into **St John's Quad**, it feels medieval. There is an open-air pulpit high on the left from which a strange annual service is conducted (see page 16).

The oldest part, **Chaplain's Quad**, is through the arch under this, with a strange modern sculpture and a view of the tower. From this on May morning Latin hymns are sung in a deeply eccentric ceremony (see page 7). Less welcoming were the sharp stones stored up there to be hurled at Cromwell's troops as they crossed the river in the Civil War. But although the tower was used to keep watch through the siege of Oxford, no attack ever came by this route.

Don't miss the **chapel** itself (access from St John's Quad), or rather the extraordinary massive ante-chapel filled with huge works of art. Plus the wonderfully carved medieval misericords (choir's bum rests) and the elaborate screen of saints' statues at the far end of the chapel itself, one of whom is Oxford's own fair Frideswide.

And outside there are two sets of memorials to the Magdalen men who fell in the two world wars, both, to their credit, with the Germans included. Have a look.

If you go through to the **Cloisters Quad**, the atmosphere changes and we are at the end of the Middle Ages. Look through the cloister arches at the wonderful and deeply strange carved animals sitting on the buttresses. Can you imagine C S Lewis, creator of *The Lion, the Witch and the Wardrobe*, sitting here watching the snow gathering on their backs, imagining Aslan breathing life back into them?

This quad also allows access to the **Hall** (refectory) which is typical, and offers the unlikely prospect of Lord

Denning (the former Master of the Rolls) eyeing up Oscar Wilde as their busts face each other.

Leaving the cloisters by narrow passages at the far end, you are faced with the hugely different **New Building**, a typically 18th-century massive construction that was intended to form the far edge of a huge quad. This would have meant demolishing the building we have just left.

Do make time to go through the blue gates on your right, across a branch of the Cherwell and into **Addison's Walk**. If you are lucky enough to come in early spring, this is the spot where the otherwise rare purple-and-white snake's head fritillaries grow in a sea of colour. You can see the deer park to the left – there are enough to give the denizens the benison of venison fairly regularly – and you can make a pleasant circular walk in riverside woodland, forgetting you are in the heart of a busy city.

Among the many, many eccentric types at Magdalen over the years, **Oscar Wilde** (who arrived in 1874) was famous for such bizarre behaviour as taking a live lobster for a walk on a piece of string. More likely on Magdalen Bridge today is meeting a 'crocodile' – that is a group of choristers crossing from their school to the college for evensong.

Wilde wasn't popular with the other students (which is not surprising, somehow) and they trashed his room and boiled his pet lobster. Another time they trussed him up and took him up a hill, lectured him about what a smug prig he was, ungagged him and asked him angrily what he had to say for himself. He said: 'What an exquisite view.' This is clearly the man who was to arrive at customs off a liner one day and say: 'I have nothing to declare but my genius' or on his deathbed: 'Either that wallpaper goes, or I do.' He also said at that time: 'I am dying beyond my means.' Actually, he had a point about French wallpaper. It's ghastly and they put it on the ceilings too.

Other eccentric Magdalen types have included poet **John Betjeman** (1906–84; thrown out), *The Lion, the Witch and the Wardrobe* author **C S Lewis** (see page 55), and cuddly **Dudley Moore** (1935–2002), late comic star of the films *Arthur* and *10*.

Retreating to **Longwall Street**, where there is likely to be queuing traffic, cross it and turn right and walk up it.

HOW GOOD ARE OXFORD colleges? Christ Church may have produced 13 British prime ministers but no fewer than seven Magdalen fellows have been awarded Nobel prizes. Many entire universities would be glad of just one or two.

Did you know?

The original city wall was built on the left here – hence the street name – and a short plod of about 230 metres is necessary to reach the next point of interest, although you may note a splendid modern sundial on the buildings to the right. On the corner ahead, there is the **garage** where William Morris built the first bull-nosed Morris Oxford in 1912, starting a revolution in British transport.

And beyond that, the pretty cottages of **Holywell Street** are on an invitingly human scale. This, like Merton Street to the south of the High, is a taste of the real old Oxford. Going down here, **New College** is now on the left and we have turned round an outside corner of the old city walls, which continue between the street and the college.

New College was home to a famous Warden (head) whose mangled speech rapidly gave us a new word for linguistic mayhem: Spoonerisms. **William Spooner** was Warden from 1903 to 1924, but had spent more than 60 years at the college in all. A typical Spoonerism would be to *intend* to call for: 'Three cheers for the dear old queen' but in fact say: 'Three cheers for the queer old dean.'

One famous angry tirade at a student supposedly went: 'You have tasted a whole worm, you have hissed my mystery lectures and you were found fighting a liar in the quad. You will leave by the town drain.'

He came off the worse with Oscar Wilde (of course) whom he ordered to copy out a chapter of the Bible because of some Wildean cheek. Wilde copied until Spooner thought he had done enough, and was then told to stop. Spooner was perturbed to find Wilde copying out more and more and not leaving the room. He demanded to know why Wilde had not stopped. Oscar said he had been so excited to find out what happened in this book, and that when he got to the end he wanted to come and tell Spooner (thus neatly exposing the pointlessness of the exercise).

THE ARCHITECTURAL CROWN JEWELS

Wilde, by the way, once perturbed his fellow students by asking for extra paper only a third of the way through an exam, then walking out two-thirds of the way through. He still won the highest marks.

A fellow of New College a century before was the eccentric clergyman **Reverend Sydney Smith** (1771–1845), whose waggish wit was notorious. He would sometimes wear a sort of suit of armour filled with hot water to keep him warm. Among his better known sayings are:

Marriage resembles a pair of shears, so joined that they cannot be separated; often moving in opposite directions, yet always punishing anyone who comes between them.

I never read a book before reviewing it – it prejudices a man so.

And less-often quoted:

Among the smaller duties of life I hardly know any one more important than that of not praising where praise is not due.

Mansfield Road on the right leads to **Mansfield** and **Harris Manchester colleges**, and then on the right is the **Holywell Music Room**, said to be the oldest still in use in the world. Ignore it and plunge down **Bath Place** opposite. The Bath that it referred to, by the way, isn't here because it blew up shortly after its opening. Most inconvenient if one didn't have a towel handy.

Here are more homely cottages – mentioned in Hardy's *Jude the Obscure* – once lodgings of the great writer **Dorothy L Sayers** (1893–1957), and now, although you'd hardly notice, the rather eccentric Bath Place Hotel (see page 256).

153

Take the passage to the left near the end to find Oxford's worst-kept secret, the **Turf Tavern**, one of those places that has no road to it, doesn't advertise yet is often busy. The low-beamed pub itself is small, but the yards (I recommend the further one, because you can sit beneath the medieval wall built to repel the Danes and in the cooler months they light a coal brazier here) are spacious and cool in the summer. The beer is usually excellent (14 real ales or pints of bitter as we call them) and so is the food. If you come

Goings-on in the Turf Tavern

IN 1963, AUSTRALIAN FUTURE PM **Bob Hawke** downed a yard of ale (two-and-a-half pints) here in a record-breaking 11 seconds, and future American president **Bill Clinton** also visited here, but if he smoked wacky backy he didn't inhale. But then he was to do very, very strange things with cigars later.

Less rude games that have been played here in what should be properly called the Spotted Cow (no one has for at least a century because so much illegal betting went on here) include 'bumble puppy' and 'shovel groat' (and if you know what the former was, I'm dying to find out). Hardy's Jude in the book courts Arabella the barmaid here, and if she was anything like the present lot, you can see why.

from some poor benighted country where the beer is always chilled and sterile, this could be the scene of your C S Lewis-style conversion. It is an acquired taste, but believe me, after just three pints, bitter is better.

Sober or not, leave by the other path (left in the yard, and properly known as Hell Passage) to emerge in **New College Lane** and enjoy one of the great unexpected views – under the **Bridge of Sighs**. At this point I am nearly killed by a large mad cyclist who was more Dawn French than Arabella from the Turf – 'Bridge of Size 22,' quips my Boswellian companion. Seriously, being silent, bikes are a real danger to look out for and it did not surprise me to hear someone was killed in a bike crash close to here.

Although the bridge is thus known, the Bridge of Sighs in Venice is not like this at all. It's a mistake. This is a copy of the Rialto Bridge, but then that wouldn't sound so right for a bridge linking two halves of **Hertford College**, would it?

The view looks invitingly towards a splendid and unique set of buildings. But hesitate for a second.

If you like gargoyles and rude jokes as well as the finer points of architecture (and if you don't skip to the line mentioning Clarendon Building in bold below), take a fascinating and amusing short diversion to the left out of Hell Passage (that is away from the Bridge of Sighs). The house on the left before the corner with the odd structure on the roof was home, by the way, to **Edmond Halley**

(1656–1742) as in comet, the astronomer, the structure being where his observatory was.

In line with the buildings is an old tower, part of **New College**, which has a gargoyle (or grotesque) covering his face to avoid seeing what goes on in the Turf Tavern below (second on the left) and others featuring, appropriately, the **Seven Deadly Sins**. Follow this strange, canyon-like lane under an arch and around yet another sharp corner (watch out for bikes) and notice the **line of grotesques** on the long side of New College on our left. Each face features hidden (well not very hidden sometimes) male and female genitalia. If you like this sort of satirical cartoon in stone, go round the next corner and there is another tower (formerly a church). This blows away the idea that all these carvings are medieval (they would have long-since eroded and are replaced every century or so) by featuring the college bursar (the grotesque holding two moneybags) and another don with a squash racket. Some of them are wearing glasses; not very medieval. Retrace your steps to the Bridge of Sighs.

Go under the mock-Venetian bridge, which connects two bits of Hertford College, to the corner to enjoy the wonderful prospect. We are now amidst the most splendid architecture that the 17th and 18th centuries could muster. This is the heart of the university and surely one of mankind's greatest gems. Let's get our bearings.

The building across the road right in front of us is the **Clarendon Building**, originally the base for the Oxford University Press. Hence the ancient muses done in lead on the roof. Actually the middle pair aren't lead but merely lead-coloured fibreglass copies filling in what was for many years a gap. What students thought of this is shown by the muse for music (facing the Bodleian) who has lost her flute. Do not be surprised if she is playing a parsnip, or something sillier.

Left of this, along this road (Catte Street) is the Bodleian Library, then the Radcliffe Camera which we saw from St Mary's which is further behind that. Looking between the Bodleian and the Clarendon Building we can see the **Sheldonian Theatre**.

To our right is a crossroads, with another good pub, the **King's Arms**, on the further corner of Holywell Street, if the Turf was too busy. On the other (left) far corner is the New Bodleian Library, a more modern extension. The road that goes left at the crossroads is Broad Street.

Go left up Catte Street a few yards and into the front arch of the **Bodleian Library**. Go through the front arch and savour the splendid stone quadrangle. Above the doors are the various original schools in Latin – *Schola Moralis Philosophae*, etc. Turn around and see the quite astounding gate tower, which was designed to show off all the classical orders of architecture – note how the style of the pillars and capitals changes as you soar upwards.

King James I (and VI of Scotland) – dubbed the wisest fool in Christendom because of his obsession with witches – is featured with his greatest legacy, the wonderful *Authorised Version of the English Bible*. He set scholars to produce this, surely the most influential book of the millions stored in this vast library with its seven underground storeys linking across Broad Street to the New Bodleian, and he is shown taking the good book from an angel and handing it over to academia, represented by alma mater.

Even amidst this pomposity, I'm glad to note, the grotesques at parapet level around the quad mock and make satirical or rude gestures. TB, by the way, carved here and there, is not Tony Blair but **Thomas Bodley** (1545–1613), the founder of this extraordinary library to which a copy of every book published in English (yes, even this one!) must be sent free of charge.

Its collection goes back to the quite fantastic illuminations of hand-scribed medieval texts, and there are still chained books in the famous **Duke Humfrey's library** within this building. Readers have to stand and read aloud this declaration:

> *I hereby undertake not to remove from the Library, or to mark, deface, or injure in any way, any volume, document, or other object belonging to it or in its custody; not to bring into the Library or kindle therein any fire or flame, and not to smoke in the Library: and I promise to obey all rules of the Library.*

Well, you don't get that in Neasden Central Library, but then the books there aren't worth, in some cases, many millions of pounds each. As for not kindling flame, this – as you might have seen at St Mary's Church where this all started – goes back centuries before tobacco arrived from the New World. So what were students likely to do? Flick a lighter and say: 'Hey, dude, cool, I wonder what this could be for one day?'

You can enter the buildings by the door opposite the gate tower and they usually have on display some of the wonderful medieval texts. Don't miss the magnificent fan-vaulted ceiling in the cloister-like **Divinity School**, where heavy stone roof bosses seem to hang by magic (and notice how they all feature people reading books) and the largely glass walls allow in floods of light. The perpendicular style (a trademark of which is the window mullions running straight up) is the ultimate triumph of Gothic architecture, which started with little pointed windows and thick walls of clumsily built rubble with crude decorations before finally reaching this mason's miracle, like King's College Cambridge, where an amazingly intricate stone roof is seemingly supported by walls of mostly glass (the buttresses doing that job instead). It also marked the end of the road for Gothic (until the Victorian revival). Outside, the classical style which took over for the next 200 years dominates the buildings, such as the Radcliffe Camera and the Sheldonian, built as if the Gothic era had never happened.

Here in the library, in the **two pulpits** ahead of us the clerics would present thesis and antithesis and debate some fine point of doctrine for hour after hour. Through the black door at the end was the tiny university court, another example of the Gown having privileges over the Town. Scholars could insist on being tried here, but if their crime was severe they could be hanged on the **university gallows** near the Turf Tavern. On the right-hand wall of this library, note the elegant ogee door that looks as if it has been inserted in the wall at a later date. It has, as we shall see in a minute.

There are also details of guided tours of the rest of the building, and a souvenir shop.

Leave the Bodleian by the entrance now to your left (the north) and you come out by the **Sheldonian Theatre**, the building that made young Christopher Wren's name as an architect in 1663. It is open to visitors in late mornings and early afternoons (not Sundays). If you go in, paying a small charge, consider the 80ft ceiling span, which was amazing for the era, given the lack of long enough trees. Wren managed it – to give a clear view without any columns – by constructing ingenious braces of shorter timbers. This allowed the magnificent painting on it of the triumph of Religion, Science (the two were not yet rivals) and Arts over Envy, Hatred and Malice. It was painted by **Robert Streater** (1621–79) in London in 32 pieces and shipped to Oxford by river. If so, did he ever see

it as an entirety until it was put up, rather like that Italian chap who painted a ceiling lying on his back?

Talking of whom, the poet **Robert Whitehall** (1625–85), when he saw the new building, wrote in his poem 'Urania':

> *That future ages must confess they owe*
> *To Streater more that Michael Angelo*

As the future age in question, you judge if Whitehall was right.

If the attic and cupola are open, you get to walk over the other side of this gravity-defying ceiling. Sadly Wren's ingenious contraption for keeping it up was replaced in the 19th century, but if you find it dark up here, Wren wouldn't have had it so. His design had 11 elegant oval dormer windows on three sides, flooding this area with natural light, but by the 19th century these needed replacing. They should be restored now we can afford it. In fact the downstairs shows an aspect of his brilliance that was to be repeated in dozens of London churches: use ingenuity to give people an unobstructed view flooded by light. He didn't do churchy gloom.

If you are still outside the Bodleian, pause a moment before going round to the Broad Street side and go left instead between the buildings. The Sheldonian is, some have suggested, built the wrong way round. Everyone assumes that the Broad Street side is the front, and is attracted there by the monstrous heads on the railings. It isn't, it's the back. So thousands of visitors miss the imposing frontage, which faces south, towards the Bodleian's Divinity School. The Sheldonian is the ceremonial hub of the university, and thus it faces in towards the Bodleian, Radcliffe Square and St Mary's.

By the way, the door facing the Sheldonian was said to have been inserted in the Bodleian by Wren, and with its elegant ogee arch – the reverse curve that looks rather oriental – one can believe it. It has the initials for Christopher Wren Architect on it, but was decried at the time as mutilating a fine building.

As with many beautiful buildings in central Oxford, you have to stand back in a cramped space to get a view – they are too close together in some ways, people have complained. Wouldn't the Radcliffe Camera look better on a grassy hill in the middle of nowhere? Well, no. It would be out of context. You could see the Empire State Building better if the rest of New York was moved 50 miles away, but it wouldn't be the right place for it.

Going round to the Broad Street side (as I say, thought to be the front by many a tourist), the railing here was in fact the back, at the outer edge of the university's heart, but being by Wren, this side was magnificent too.

Note the rather imposing **Emperors** facing Broad Street in a curve that matches the building's end. According to one local legend, on Christmas Eve and May Day they jump down from their pedestals and make their way to the pub. I think I'd have another double whisky if these rather terrifying characters walked in one night.

Max Beerbohm, in his comic novel *Zuleika Dobson* – the still hugely funny story of a female undergraduate *femme fatale* who sends half of Oxford crazy with her beauty – has the Emperors' brows run with beads of sweat as the gorgeous Miss Dobson walks by.

If these look in surprisingly good nick for carvings over 300 years old, it's because they are the third set. If they wear out before you do, you may be able to buy one for your back garden (as various Oxford people have) when they are replaced. And no, despite the theories, they don't represent anyone in particular. If you have a small child handy, suggest finding a bird hiding in one Emperor's hair and the sculptor Michael Black's initials on another's shoulder.

We are now in close proximity to millions of books. The rather plain building on the corner of Broad Street to the right, across Parks Road from the King's Arms, is the **New Bodleian**. As mentioned, like a nuclear bunker, this has far more storeys (and stories) below ground than above, and is connected with the old library by tunnel. Opposite us, across Broad Street, is the quintessential Oxford bookshop, **Blackwell's**. It, too, has a vast underground section, the Norrington Room, which extends under Trinity Quad (in the college to the left). Notice how a cheeky pub, the White Horse, interrupts Blackwell's, and indeed seems to interrupt its customers and staff in a pleasant kind of way. Very Oxford.

Although Broad Street fair smokes with history (more in the next walk, which you can jump to on page 180 for a seamless join), Boswell and I have had quite enough at this point, the beer from the Turf doing its stuff, and take a left turn up Turl Street. This quickly takes us back to the High Street with **Jesus** to our right (which in recent years had an eccentric don who kept a vicious-looking live eagle owl on a perch and would appal students during tutorials by fishing a cute cheeping yellow chick out of his pocket and tossing it to the owl, who would rip it to shreds and devour it) and on our left **Exeter** (alma mater of not only **R D Blackmore** (1825–1900) who wrote *Lorna Doone* but also at another time of *J R R Tolkien*) and then **Lincoln**,

All Saints spire being a great landmark at the end. There we turn right and are back in Carfax. Phew!

The Blackwells

THE BLACKWELLS OF THE Oxford book-publishing empire were hard-working and eccentric, creating a huge business from a start in one 12ft-square room in 1879. They were mavericks, rebels almost, at any rate paid-up members of the awkward squad.

Joshua Blackwell, grandfather of Benjamin Henry, a tailor in London's East End, turned teetotal simply to deprive the government of the tax. It's like leaving your car at home not to cure pollution but because the government is ripping you off on fuel tax.

His son, Benjamin Harris, took a different tack, organising lectures to demonstrate the evil effect of drink on the liver, and his son, Benjamin Henry, cocked a snook at the doyens of the University as an outspoken Liberal Councillor. The third B H Blackwell, the almost-legendary Sir Basil, resented modern traffic rules and liked to walk down the white lines in the middle of the road. I wouldn't try it on the Oxford ring road today.

Much more recently, Miles Blackwell, the great-grandson of the founder of 'Blackwell's of the Broad', who took his turn as chairman of the business, left a large sum of money – many millions, some say – to some sheep. Some Manx Loghtan sheep, his favourites, to be precise, which have extremely strange unicorn-style horns, and

(CONTINUED OVERLEAF)

The Blackwells

(CONTINUED)

a few other frankly weird animals such as Scots Dumpy chickens. So he alternated from rare breeds to good reads. Perhaps as a typical snub to the Establishment, Blackwell's took to publishing works by 'young poets unknown to fame'. Many writers, some very odd, some mainstream and some who are now household names, made their debuts at Blackwell's. Among the early Blackwell adventurers were **Beeching** in 1879, followed shortly by **A E Housman**, the **Huxleys**, the **Sitwells**, and **Dorothy L Sayers**. Spurred on by his father, and turning a blind eye to small financial losses, Basil launched *Oxford Poetry*; a series that has withstood the test of time despite the original scorn of the critics. During his time a contribution had come his way from one of the most famous of B H Blackwell's alumni: **Ronald Tolkien**. Years later, writing from his study in Merton, momentarily relinquishing his lands of myths and hobbits, he reminded Basil Blackwell of this fact. His first published poem Goblin Feet had seen the light of day in a 1915 issue of *Oxford Poetry*: 'So you (Blackwell's) were my first publisher', he wrote decades later. Following in his footsteps came more famous names: **Auden, MacNeice, Graham Greene, C Day-Lewis** and **Stephen Spender**. And you know what? Somewhere in the slim volumes in this quirky Oxford bookshop-publishers lurks one of the greats of tomorrow.

WALKS:
EAST OXFORD

ENTER THE FREAKY
COSMIC TRIANGLE

It's like the Bermuda Triangle, only not so wet. The area between Cowley and Iffley Roads, the ying and yang of East Oxford, close to where they diverge at the Plain beyond Magdalen Bridge, is suffused with mystic powers. No-one who lives there is ever quite the same afterwards. Or so some people say.

Certainly it's deeply alternative, with a ley line of cosmic forces seemingly lined up along Magdalen Road, which forms the short side of the perhaps half-mile-long isosceles triangle between these two East Oxford thoroughfares, the apex being at the Magdalen Bridge end. Along this apparently ordinary street are gathered the most extraordinary collection of eccentric oddities, an alignment that goes beyond any reasonable coincidence. If you like crop circles, pyramid power, UFOs or ancient spiritual sites, you'll like **Magdalen Road**. And if you want a decent

coffee, a delicious cake or a tap washer you're in the right place too. This whole area's well worth an exploration because it's so different to the pompous architecture and stately buildings just over Magdalen Bridge. This is low-rise, low-brow, low-rent and lo and behold. (Well, it *used* to be low-rent.)

Cowley Road itself is a ribbon of straggle-taggle shops, eating houses, places of worship that are so diverse and surprising that they put the 'eck in eclectic. Posh it ain't. If you want a Polish restaurant or Indian spices or Asian jewellery or Chinese traders or Russian groceries or English tattoos, Cowley Road will have it.

'If you sit here in the Manzil Way Gardens,' I was told by Boswell, a denizen, 'every nationality and look of people on the planet walks past. Every colour, creed, age, race, sex – and a few in-between, frankly. The thing about Cowley Road is that it's never boring, there are people arguing in Urdu, students in love, a fierce man dressed in highland plaid, hippies, batty old dons, care-in-the-community oddballs, and we get some good murders from time to time. You can hear Old Tom at Christ Church at night, but you hear the police helicopter sometimes too. Having said that, we all rub along pretty well, I think.'

Cowley Road's development was driven by Victorian land division and then by the working-class boom of the 20th century caused by the motor-car works at the far end, still churning out Minis today, but once a huge employer.

Iffley Road, on the other hand, is a bit staider, more genteel, and more residential. It's not that long ago in Oxford terms since you could encounter old people who could recall coming down Rose Hill, the gentle rise a mile or so up Iffley Road, towards Oxford and seeing nothing much between them and Magdalen Tower but countryside. Little of East Oxford is very old.

But if you fancy a stroll into another dimension, a trip to an alternative world with not a dreaming spire in sight, take a look at the Cosmic Triangle.

A STROLL ROUND THE COSMIC TRIANGLE, GENTLY TAKING THE MICHAEL

If you were to take a stroll round this Cosmic Triangle, the obvious place to start would be the Plain, the convergence of roads on the far side of **Magdalen Bridge** from the city

THE COSMIC TRIANGLE

167

centre. Straight away the mystic intensity of the place – you have to take all this with a wheelbarrow of salt – is apparent. For here was not only a well with miraculous powers but also a symbol of peace.

When I say that there was nothing much this side of Oxford until the last 150 years, that's ignoring the area tight up to the River Cherwell known at **St Clement's**. Here there was a medieval huddle of houses around St Clement's church, flattened (and rebuilt in Marston Road, around the corner) to make the Plain and take its traffic when the main roads arrived thanks to the bridge.

The drinking fountain in the middle of the road, although dating from only 1899, replaced an earlier well of supposedly miraculous properties. Today it would be a miracle if the fountain worked and if you could get to it without being squashed by traffic. The fountain stands where a tollhouse once regulated traffic over the turnpike road.

The green space in the middle is all that remains of St Clement's churchyard, so presumably there are a few bones rattled by the buses under there. On one of the lampposts a monument to peace was put up. 'Peace was proclaimed in the city of Oxford 27 June, 1814.' I rather like the idea of peace breaking out. You could declare peace against another country.

Actually this is the one peace that shouldn't have been marked by anyone. It seemed to mark the end of the Napoleonic Wars between France and Britain, with old Bonaparte carted off to Elba. As you may remember, Boney escaped and rallied France before being thrashed (just) at Waterloo in 1815, so the peace was pretty short-lived.

Peace and miraculous wells proving elusive, we could strike up **Iffley Road**, or if you're not up to walking a couple of miles altogether, get any bus No 4 (that is 4a,

4b etc) and ask for Magdalen Road. These buses come from Carfax at the other end of the High Street if you're starting from there.

The pub between Iffley Road and Cowley Road was once called Cape of Good Hope because it is on a peninsula like the end of Africa.

Here, unlike the unvarnished cheapness of Cowley Road which we'll soon see, we are soon on the left-hand side strolling past 19th-century houses that proclaim their middle-class credentials. Pleasant ornamental details such as fancy finials, arched windows, first-floor plaques which might have carried presumptuous names, patterns in the brickwork with red and grey bricks, oriel windows (upstairs bay windows). As if to emphasise the middle-class virtues of this stretch, along here the **Cricketers' Arms** pub has a plaque with a man holding a very straight bat.

The roads on the left here, which start very short in this sharp end of the Cosmic Triangle (the first, Circus Street, recalls the last use of the land before development in 1861) are actually part of political gerrymandering. It was almost as blatant as a certain Tory council leader in the 1980s who flogged off council flats cheap to anyone who would vote Conservative, more or less.

Here a Liberal-supporting society was selling off plots of land so that ordinary people could build homes that were freehold – and vote Liberal too. They parcelled up the first four streets and set the low-rise and architecturally varied tone for the southeastward march of Oxford. The fifth street, James Street, has at No 16 a **plaque** stating **William Morris** (1877–1963), later Lord Nuffield, lived here from 1896 to 1903. It was here in the garden sheds he assembled bicycles, the start of one of the world's biggest car-making companies that was to transform the fortunes of working people in Oxford.

The houses on Iffley Road become increasingly elaborate, not to say pretentious, with the terrace at 85–94 particularly ornamental with gaudy brick banding that makes Keble College almost seem restrained. Actually, here I quite like it. Further elaborate decoration, in the form of ironwork, is visible at Nos 133 and 137.

But I'm basically suggesting you fair sprint or bus up the half-mile from the Plain to Magdalen Road, despite the architectural detail (for this is the unexciting genteel street that the cosmopolitan craziness of Cowley Road will provide the contrast to). In fact a man who could have done this distance in under two minutes was **Roger Bannister** (b. 1929), who is commemorated by a street name, Bannister Close, off Jackdaw Lane on the right. For it was behind the boring close-boarded fence on the right- hand side of Iffley Road that athletics history was made on 6 May 1954, when he ran the first under four-minute mile at the athletics ground (see opposite). He later became Master of Pembroke and it was said that he had an unusually slow heartbeat which helped him achieve the goal men had dreamed of for so long.

The church on the right, by the way, is – I could reasonably assert – the only church in the world dedicated to **St Edmund and St Frideswide**, the patron saint of Oxford, with a plaque of the Virgin and Child indicating that it is Roman Catholic (page 24).

Iffley Road and the four-minute mile

IT WAS AN ASTONISHING achievement that went round the world. It was one of the great British moments of the 1950s, like the Coronation and conquest of Everest the previous year. The running of the world's first under four-minute mile.

When **Roger Bannister** (b. 1929) a few years earlier had arrived as a rather lanky undergraduate at Exeter College, he found another would-be athlete and they took themselves off to a track for a practice. A groundsman watched and told them afterwards: 'You've got the making of a fine runner, Sir, but' – turning to Bannister – 'I'm afraid you'll never do'. Happily, Bannister took no notice.

The 1954 event nearly didn't come off at all. Bannister had come down by train from the hospital where he by then worked, St Mary's, Paddington, and paced up and down while the wind and rain went on. Medicine to him was far more important than the running which brought him fame.

He, and his pacemakers **Chris Brasher** (later a founder of the London marathon) and **Chris Chataway**, looked anxiously at the flag on the squat church tower across Iffley Road. It streamed out in the steady wind. Then in the early evening, as it often does, the wind dropped. The flag drooped for the first time that day. The race was on!

A false start only added to the tension. The gun went again and Bannister said later that his legs seemed to flow effortlessly. He thought the first two laps passed too slowly and urged his pacemakers to go faster, but they were on the target time for the half-mile mark. On the last lap Bannister was on his own and sprinted for the tape.

(CONTINUED OVERLEAF)

Iffley Road and the four-minute mile

(CONTINUED)

Had he really done it, he must have wondered as he flew through.

Norris McWhirter, one of the twins who later set up the *Guinness Book of Records,* helped run it. When he announced the time of three minutes, 59 seconds, four-tenths of a second, he recalled just before the 50th anniversary (Norris died less than a month before it): 'Nobody heard the seconds and tenths of a second as the roar went up after I said three minutes.'

What he actually said, the record shows, was a rather cleverly teasing build-up: 'Ladies and gentlemen, here is the result of event number nine, the one mile. First, number 41, Roger Bannister of the AAA and formerly of Exeter and Merton Colleges, with a time which is a new meeting and track record, and subject to ratification, will be the new English native, British national and British all-comers', European, British Empire and world record. The time is three...' and the rest was lost in a deafening roar of joy from the crowd.

Another odd fact about that rainy 6 May at the Iffley Road track in 1954 was that a certain timekeeper was **Harold Abrahams** (1899–1978). He was one of the heroes who triumphed against the odds at the Paris Olympics of 1924, as depicted in the film *Chariots of Fire.* His reaction summed up the importance of the four-minute mile: 'When I heard the words "three minutes", it was as if an atom bomb had gone off.'

Insisting on a similar ornament at St Mary's in the city ensured Archbishop Laud's execution.

By the time we reach 217 or 233 Iffley Road there are really substantial properties and around here the Conservative Land Society were trying to sell off land in the 1860s to combat the efforts of the Liberals. Unfortunately, perhaps, for them, the one Conservative occupying the huge plots of land they envisaged had one vote where the Liberals would have squeezed in ten (the Tories might have preferred the arrangement before 1832 when only the bigger home owners had the vote). More to the point, the big villa-owning bourgeoisie could not be persuaded that increasingly proletarian East Oxford was the place to settle.

It was too near the spreading working-class estates on the Cowley Road, and they would within a few decades be voting for their own new party, Labour. One wants the proletariat close enough to be one's servants, as it were, but not so close as to cause a nuisance, and the Tory scheme to gentrify this patch fizzled out. This snob versus yob battle was typified by a court case involving boys being prosecuted for playing cricket in the street on a Sunday in Stanley Road using a metal box for stumps. You can imagine the noses turned up and the curtains twitching. A servant was sent for the police who said the boys were from the Cowley Road area and 'of a sort that could not speak without using profanities'. Their descendants are clearly still around. (If you think I'm exaggerating these British social attitudes, there was an estate in North Oxford, part-private part-public, where a Berlin Wall-style barrier was built and stood for many years in the 20th century, just to keep the riff-raff away from posh people's homes.)

Turning down **Magdalen Road**, the base of the Cosmic Triangle, the mystic forces start intensifying, particularly if you have had a swift bevvy or three in the **Magdalen** (excellent pub, good lunches, nice crew and totally recommended) at this end. Grab a copy of the *Guardian* if you want to fit in with the locals and hide your *Daily Mail*, if you have one, inside it. If you've got a beard, even if female, wear it.

On the right is the **Pegasus Theatre**, a stage for youth that, no doubt, utilises the creative juices of the strange street. Soon on the left there is **Thrangu House Buddhist Centre** and **Magic Café** and the **Inner Bookshop** on the right.

This is the spiritual centre of alternative Oxford, man. If you want to know anything about flying saucers, crop circles or the dangers of getting your dogma run over by a karma, this is where it's at. Here people buy books about ley lines and by deeply strange purple-wearing former sports reporter David Icke. Fruitcake? Available in the Magic Café, where they have good live music on Saturdays as well as much munchable. The Inner Bookshop couple were hoping to sell up and retire as I write this, so best of luck to them and the shop. I love independent bookstores with their own character.

As if to emphasise the space-time warp happening around here there is a shop called **Retrozone** which seems to offer reincarnation for all your previous furniture. The oriental theme continues with the gorgeously coloured **Chudry Jewellers**, there's a cycle workshop and then the ultimate space-time leap, Silvester's hardware store. If you could do with a light bulb or a springlebracket grommet for the thingummyoojamaflip, boldly go in here. You will notice that by crossing the threshold you have gone back several decades and that the weird labyrinth inside is clearly much bigger, like Doctor Who's Tardis in the TV series, than the outside but a lot more useful. I'm not saying

the charming old chap who served me was a Time Lord, in fact he seemed perfectly normal, but be polite just in case. I did notice however that the passageways between the piles of stuff in this strange store are just the right shape for Dr Who's deadly enemy, the spooky Daleks...

Outside, notice the anti-Dalek humps in the street, more angular than normal speed bumps. If that's not the work of Time Lords, what is? The road also offers a Holistic Animal Centre, whatever that is, a wired and weird internet place which clearly benefits from the energy lines running deep here, some kind of goldfish aquarium thingy (I didn't go in just in case I went round and round inside for ever) and in case your number is up, a funeral directors and a bingo hall at the far end. In fact there are pubs at both ends and halfway down just in case it's all too much, man, plus three Christian sites along this street to add to its strange religious power.

Emerging safely (if indeed you do) on to Cowley Road and turning left back towards the Plain, I defy you to say the Magdalen Road experience has not changed your inner self. Forget the dark rides of cheap theme parks, Magdalen Road is the street of destiny, a tramway of time, a splinter of the fourth dimension, a meaningless comma in the sentence of the cosmos, a dialling tone in the phone booth of memory. And another thing, doesn't the order of all those strange shops change every time you go down there? Are you in fact *sure* they are still there now? Wo, freaky man!

Cowley Road, on the other hand, is more cosmopolitan than cosmic. As said before, you can meet every possible variation of humanity here (OK, and the odd borderline case too). There are so many faiths here that every day is somebody's Sabbath, so you can always have a day off.

One Sunday in June the Cowley Road carnival brings the whole melting pot to the boil. Music booms out to assault the ears, belly dancing and exotic coloured costumes bombard the eyes, ethnic food and incense enrich your tastebuds and nostrils and I can't think of anything to do with touch, but you get the idea. Sensory overload. There's a procession, floats, dressing up, music, and everyone has a great time.

But on any day along here there are wonderful foods from around the globe in various restaurants and takeaways. There are plentiful spices and more dhals than Roald's grandchildren in the Asian grocers along this street – and at a fraction of the price of most supermarkets – plus the unexpected glimpse of a full-blown mosque to the right.

What **Edward Thomas** (1878–1917), the Edwardian poet who lived at No 113, would have made of it all I don't know. His addle would have been stropped, probably.

But before I leave you to stroll back to the Plain along this street of many colours, let me mention another religious oddity less obvious than the mosque. If you went straight across Cowley Road from Magdalen Road, you could find a forgotten place very few Oxford people know about where people were treated like, well, lepers.

Up the path beside the vicarage (from where you should ask for the key) is **St Bartholomew's Chapel**, the only remaining part of a large medieval leper hospital run by Oriel College and once staffed by nuns and monks. It was damaged in the Civil War, when soldiers grabbed the lead from the roof to make bullets and pulled down some of the old hospital, but here it remains all these centuries later. Once deliberately set well away from the town, now the city laps around it. A strange survivor indeed. Returning west up Cowley Road, you might notice **Bartlemas Road**, an outward reminder of that forgotten medieval gem. And yes, since you ask, the chapel is lined up with the supposed spiritual forces of Magdalen Road. Spooky, man.

NOTE: My apologies to the good shopkeepers of Magdalen Road for gently taking the mickey. Like all genuine eccentrics, they will think themselves not unusual, but I assure them, they are a unique street, not a freak street. And I hope I haven't annoyed any Buddhists. It's so hard to tell because they are so easy-going. No chance of the fatwah from that lot. Or even a thinwah.

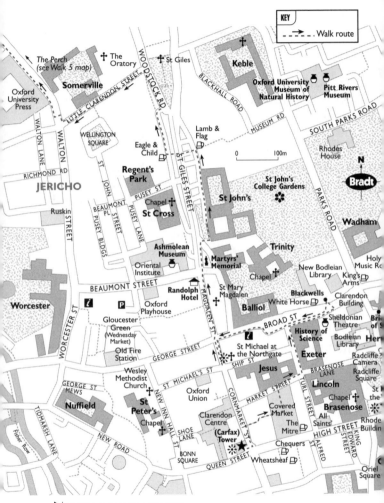

NORTH OF THE CENTRE

WALKS: NORTH OF THE CENTRE

FROM BROAD STREET TO THE BIRD AND BASTARD

From Carfax tower, cross Cornmarket and dive into the entrance to the **Covered Market**. If you haven't had breakfast, this is the place to get a hearty full-English one, and if you have, there are butchers and game shops galore, wonderful delis and everything a gourmet could desire: wonderful cheeses and fresh-roasted coffee. As they say, you don't necessarily live longer without eating stuff like this, but it'll feel a lot longer.

Leave the market by the far entrance into narrow **Market Street** (and if you have come out of the labyrinth into the High by accident, just plunge back in). Turning right you are immediately in **Turl Street**, but notice narrow **Brasenose Lane** running opposite. It has the remains of the medieval gutter or kennel in the middle down which all sorts of vileness used to flow, and Samuel Johnson is recorded standing astride this. Doing what, I don't want to know.

179

Go left instead down Turl Street, between **Exeter College** on the right and **Jesus** on the left. For a glimpse of their many eccentricities, see pages 90–2.

You emerge in Broad Street and I suggest turning right briefly, to see the **Museum of the History of Science** just before the emperor's heads of the Sheldonian (see page 159). This museum is not only a fascinating place in its own right – far more so than its name suggests – but is also the key to the highly eccentric roots of one of Oxford's and Britain's greatest institutions, the Ashmolean Museum (see page 184), which we will encounter later.

This original is a fine building but is less appreciated than it should be because it is surrounded by gems such as the Sheldonian, the Bodleian and the Radcliffe Camera. Also, like the Sheldonian, its Broad Street side isn't its front. Both buildings – like the TV personality Jordan – have rather improbable frontages, but they are less-often noticed than hers is. In the case of the MotHoS, the ceremonial front faces in towards the university heart, that is towards the Sheldonian (east). Another quality it shares with that building is that neither building was designed by a trained architect, this one being by a local mason, T Wood. That doesn't say a lot for trained architects, you may think!

The museum of the History of Science is great for anyone of any age interested in gadgets, technology, history, inventions, explosions or science (see page 211).

Assuming you don't stop at the museum all day, go left from here down Broad Street. The story that dominates the west end of this aptly named road is the burning of the Protestant bishops Latimer, Ridley and Cranmer by the 16th-century Roman Catholic Queen, 'Bloody' Mary. On the north side of the street is a **memorial** to them (see page 183), and in the centre of the road a cross set into the surface, where they actually died.

Going up to the end of Broad Street, if you look left (south) down Cornmarket, you can see on the left the Saxon church of **St Michael at the Northgate**, the oldest building in the city. You have to imagine that the city wall continued across the street from the church tower here, and that above the arch was the tiny Bocardo prison, where the bishops were held. This place was already old, for in the 13th century it was recorded that a second floor was added to allow women to be segregated. The number of 'loose' women detained there became so many at this time that they were moved to a tower called the Maiden's Tower because it was filled with prostitutes. The jailer made so much money from the bribes and fees he charged the prisoners for meals and privileges that instead of being paid by the city for his job, he had to pay the city.

This is where Thomas Cranmer, who under pressure or torture had recanted his Protestant beliefs, had to watch the other two bishops burn. The narrow arch and the Bocardo prison above it were such a hindrance to traffic down Northgate (now Cornmarket) that they were demolished in 1771. As the city council now spend a lot of their money trying to hinder traffic, why not rebuild the ancient gate to make Cornmarket far more interesting?

You can climb **St Michael's Tower** for a small fee. The views are excellent, although not quite as wonderful as at St Mary's, and the interior of the tower has much to show you.

There's the door to the cell in the now-vanished prison where the three bishops were held. There's also the **Bocardo Box**, with a slot for coins, which the prisoners used to lower for charity from passers-by. The original Saxon stonework is fascinating, being 1,000 years old, and includes a door, as you can see from the outside, that would open into mid-air halfway up the tower.

Do have a look at the view from the top, but don't lean as far out as did one Robert of Honiton on the Eve of the Circumcision of the Lord in 1301. He took a few days to die.

Turning away from Cornmarket, north up one side or other of St Mary Magdalen church in the middle of the road, we reach another wide thoroughfare, St Giles.

St Giles is a totally fascinating place. It is a wide street, even better deserving the title Broad Street than the one that is so called. Its shape is that of two wide roads converging at a shallow angle and then diverging again, like two straight railway lines crossing.

There is a pleasing symmetry. At either end it has a massive church to define its length as clearly as a Latin sentence, and a monument on the thinnest part of the peninsula between the converging roads; there are five more churches or chapels down just the west side (including the Oratory on Woodstock Road), and at least a couple more in the colleges to the east. Which perhaps gives the lie to the idea that Oxford students are a bunch of irreligious drunks, as there are only two pubs of note.

Yet once a year this wide street is home to the most unholy racket of the **St Giles Fair** (see page 19) which fills the street with noise, gaudy rides, bright-eyed children, trashy food, yobs and all that stuff. It is big and loud.

Having seen how Broad Street and St Michael at the Northgate are at the very centre of once literally burning hatred between Catholics and Protestants, thankfully forgotten in this country, there is more here. The first church between the diverging roads at the south end of St Giles is **St Mary Magdalen**, very High Church Anglican, and a base for the Oxford Movement reassertion of 19th-century religious fervour to an almost Roman Catholic degree. Just to the north of that is the recently restored

Martyrs' Memorial to Cranmer, Latimer and Ridley. It is known as St Giles Cathedral sometimes, for it looks like nothing as much as the spire of a cathedral that has sunk beneath the ground. In fact, a tourist was once persuaded that it was Oxford's subsided underground cathedral and the steps down were over there – pointing to the public toilets. Allegedly.

The memorial is by Sir George Gilbert Scott and was built in 1841–43 as the Gothic Revival styles swept out the classical. Twenty years before and it would have been some round Roman temple thing made of columns. Here it looks like some Hammer Horror space rocket. Students have often climbed the thing at great peril just to place a chamber pot or traffic cone on the top, which requires the fire brigade to remove it.

On the north side it warns of the 'Errors of the Church of Rome'. Which is understandable, except that a massive Roman Catholic institution is just on the left up St Giles (Black Friars) and in the distance may be seen the roof of the equally Roman Oratory. Fat lot of notice they took. But as Jan Morris points out so pertinently in her brilliant book on Oxford, this was not really aimed at Roman Catholics, given the church politics of the time, but at the lot who inhabited the church we have just passed, St Mary Magdalen, the Anglicans who were going semi-Catholic.

Level with the Martyrs' Memorial is Oxford's poshest hotel, the **Randolph** (see page 255), and across Beaumont Street the imposing frontage of the **Ashmolean Museum**,

The Ashmolean

THE FASCINATING FAR-FROM-RESPECTABLE origins of the now great and respectable Ashmolean Museum – which was after all Britain's first public museum – involve a raucous pub, an eccentric collector, a bit of a rogue, two widows, a legal battle, an attempted murder and a suspicious death. In the early 17th century an inveterate collector, **John Tradescant**, had put together an extraordinary collection of objects from round the world, known as the Ark, in Lambeth, London. The basic impulse was not so very different from pubs today, which might display a hundred kinds of hot water bottle or toilet seats from stately homes or some such daft idea, but far more eclectic and surprising. Then such collections were rare indeed, and without photography, television or any public museums, few people ever saw things from foreign lands. And, it must be said, the public was more credulous.

Tradescant had got together the most amazing collection of oddities: a vest from Babylon, a dodo from Mauritius, a Turkish toothbrush, a dragon's egg from Turkey, a bracelet made from the thighs of thousands of flies in India, blood that fell from the heavens on the Isle of Wight. Wonders indeed (and even odder things were to be added over the centuries). From the 17th-century catalogue of the collection:

4. Man's Skull with 5 Horns on it.

And later:

16. Calf that had been 3 years in the Cow's Belly, as hard as stone.

ꓴucous beginnings

And more famously:

26. Dadar-Birds, one of which watches whilst the other stoops down to drink.

These latter, of course, being as dead as a Dodo. Some of their legacy is still very much alive, however: if you are a gardener you will know the tradescantia plants that were first gathered by Tradescant and his son.

The son, also called John, formed a friendship with **Elias Ashmole** (1617–92), a graduate of Brasenose who had wanted, ever since being at Oxford, to be an antiquarian – that is a collector of just such old and curious things. He had just lacked the money, which remedy he fixed by marrying a rich widow (not the first or last Oxford man to do so), and in the process being threatened with murder by one of her family. After falling in with Tradescant the younger, Ashmole was promised the Ark's amazing collection for Oxford upon the childless man's death. Unfortunately upon this event in 1662, his widow Hester went to court to dispute it, and an enormously long (more than a decade) and expensive legal wrangle ensued.

(CONTINUED OVERLEAF)

185

The Ashmolean's raucous beginnings

(CONTINUED)

The obsessed Ashmole meanwhile moved into the house next door to the Ark to ensure she didn't disperse the treasures, and although initially she won in court, and there were threats to send the collection to Cambridge (arghhhh!), it somehow went to Ashmole after all. Being found dead in a pond probably didn't help her cause. In fact that 'accidental' fall changed Oxford and started Britain's great public museums, of which this was to be the first.

So the whole amazing shebang ended up here in Oxford in 1677. Little of the collection is in this building today, because the huge new Ashmolean (which we will see shortly) was built in Beaumont Street in the 18th century, and some of the Tradescants' original oddities may be found there.

successor to the original building in Broad Street. This stolid building seems to be from the apex of classical revival (but in fact was built in 1845).

It is worth a lot of time for its own sake and I doubt if many (if any) provincial museums in the world can equal its breadth and quality of exhibits. And certainly not the oddities, thanks to Ashmole.

The right-hand side of St Giles is mostly formed of two huge colleges: first **Balliol** (see page 82), which goes right down to Broad Street; then **St John's** (see page 108), which presents a fairly blank face to the outside world.

More welcoming and on a much-needed human scale are the two pubs set either side of St Giles. On the right is the sign of the **Lamb and Flag**, one of the impossibly odd connections that you see repeatedly around the country such as The Bear and Ragged Staff, but of course they all have origins. This one is the symbol of St John the Baptist, used on the crusades: it was also used on pilgrims' badges and on certain Tarot cards. Arabella of Hardy's novel about Oxford, *Jude the Obscure*, once worked here. **Graham Greene** (Balliol), possibly the leading British novelist of the 20th century, was transfixed by another real barmaid here. He wrote:

The young barmaid of the Lamb and Flag in St Giles whom we all agreed resembled in her strange beauty the Egyptian Queen Nefertiti. What quantities of beer we drank in order to speak a few words with her. We were too young and scared to proceed further.

Actually, one of Greene's chums did proceed further, in a punt, but as far as Greene was concerned, she was more *Nefer* than *Titi*. Much more important was Britain's greatest novelist of the era's right to use 'whom' in the above quotation? Discuss.

This pub belongs to **St John's**, as does most of St Giles and immense tracts of land in Britain and overseas, for this is one of the world's wealthiest colleges.

The college has, since its inception in 1555, been rather High Churchy and Tory, which makes it all the more odd that one of its alumni was Tony Blair, the recent Labour Prime Minister.

The pub on the other side of the road, the **Eagle and Child**, is a tiny place with, like the first pub, a surreal image on its sign. This concept is said to have originated in the arms of the Earls of Derby, or is read by pagans or homosexuals to have some special significance for them. Equally, fans of the fantasy books connected with this pub have found all kinds of deep meanings in it. It is a case, as another Oxford fantasy book put it, of a word meaning just what you want it to mean. However, to Oxford students it will always be the Bird and Baby or, more likely, the Bird and Bastard.

This pub has generated global interest out of all proportion to its size because of the giants of genius, the mega-masters of creative fantasy that once gathered here.

This little building – once a Civil War army pay office – was the unlikely crucible in which the concepts behind the *The Lion, the Witch and the Wardrobe* and *Lord of the Rings* were perfected. Here, in an informal group of writers and academics known as the **Inklings**, these books' great authors met with several others for convivial boozing and conversation on which it would have been fascinating to eavesdrop. The proof? In the back bar above the fireplace is a note to the landlord signed in their cups by these characters. It starts in inky scrawl, in mock-legal style: 'The undersigned, having just partaken of your ham, have drunk your health.'

I expect it was more the beer than the ham doing the talking, but Clive Staples Lewis sticks, as usual, to his initials and signs:

C.S. Lewis, Fellow of Magdalen sometime scholar of University College, late 13 Light Infantry.

Further down is:

John Ronald Reuel Tolkien MA Merton Professor of English language and literature, late professor of Anglo-Saxon (Pembroke College) and exhibitioner of Exeter College, and of the Lancashire Fusiliers (1914–18) and father of the above-mentioned C.R.T.

His son is listed above as an undergraduate of Trinity. An exhibitioner is someone who passed the entrance exams at such a high standard that the college paid him to be there. 'It wasn't much in my case,' said my Boswellian companion. 'About £40 a year and my name painted up in gold in the school chapel.'

The listing of which war was significant: at this tempestuous time in British history you were either old enough to be in the first German war or the second, or if extremely unlucky, both. How very lucky *we* are, then.

The food is as good as the Inklings found it, and as rumbustiously English. My Boswellian companion had one of those beef pies whose crust resembles an inflatable mattress (but thankfully doesn't taste like one). We chatted to an Oxford man who cheerfully admitted to having been an alcoholic and a schizophrenic, but seemed to have conquered both of them.

A strange little character with a whiny voice lurched past with two friends, going through to the conservatory.

'Gollum!' said Boswell, a little too loud for my liking.

'Boswell,' I said, 'I have to confess in this of all places that I didn't like *The Hobbit*. I think the world is divided into people who love Tolkien, and people who don't.'

'No,' said Boswell. 'The world is divided into two groups: those who divide it into two groups of people, and those who don't.'

FROM ST GILES TO JERICHO AND BEYOND

This great stroll takes you past Jericho to a forgotten word and a great rural pub. It will take about an hour-and-a-half plus stops.

Turn left off St Giles at the far end, near the church of the same name (and we are near Anglicans, Christian Scientists, Jews and Catholics here, so most options are covered), down Little Clarendon Street, we are already alerted by this name to the area's biggest employer. The Clarendon Building back in Broad Street was the first Oxford University Press. We are heading for the present establishment and it is even

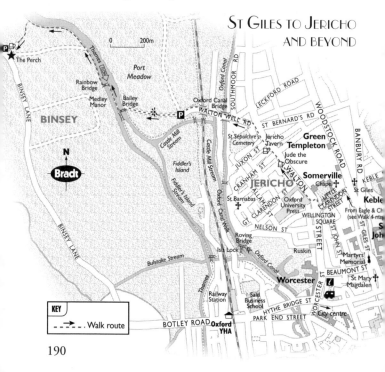

St Giles to Jericho and Beyond

grander than the original.

Little Clarendon Street offers a pleasing mishmash of shops and cafés. If you like stately architecture you could take a turn round **Wellington Square** halfway down on the left and enjoy the fine perspective south (on the far side) down **St John Street**. In one corner a sign mentions the little-known **Kellogg College**. If you listen at the keyhole can you can hear professors Snap, Crackle and Pop, those old favourites of British breakfast time.

Back in Little Clarendon Street, if you don't like stately architecture there's a pleasing juxtaposition of a shop selling '60s-revival plastic furniture (probably ghastly if you remember it first-time round, cool if you don't) almost opposite some modernist part of **Somerville College** on the other side. Or it may be a misplaced wing of Legoland. Or a stack of shipping containers with windows in.

Turning right into **Walton Street** (shopping guide, page 258), note, on the right, how well protected the backside of Somerville is, with high walls and barbed wire to keep the Somerville girls safe (or keep them in. Possibly).

Walton Street is great for browsing and shopping if you like boho chic, independent delis, coffee shops, cool bars, bookshops, great places to eat (in short the antidote to shopping malls and chain stores).

It is on the edge of **Jericho**, an appealing district, somewhat eccentrically named. I've seen the suggestion that it was jerry-built – which, in turn, raises the question of why we call anything thrown up badly jerry-built – but I prefer the second suggestion: that it was jokingly remote from Oxford. It's like someone saying: 'Oh, he lives in Timbuktu.' It doesn't mean he literally lives in said, no doubt worthy, African town but it's rather remote. There is even a link between the two – the suggestion that something jerry-built would fall down like the walls of Jericho when the trains blow their trumpets, as they do here. Lastly, isn't it possible that a wall of the ancient gardens here once fell down and the monks jokingly called it Jericho Gardens thereafter? You may not be convinced by any of these theories.

What is convincing is the low-rise friendliness, architecturally, of unpretentious Jericho, after the grandeur of central Oxford. It was once a workers' suburb for the men who manned (or women who wimmined) the **Oxford University Press** and the ironworks by the canal and, therefore, built cheaply with less pompous ornamentation than the rest of North Oxford. Like Brian Rix's trousers, the place has been up and down a few times.

Working-class and cheaply built it may have been, but with the growing fashion for intellectuals to appear more 'of the people', the area became bohemian, Lefty and intellectually middle-class by the later 20th century, and property prices motored ahead.

By 2011, a really simple and plain two-up, two-down terrace house with a front door straight onto the street and straight into the front room of the house (chilly in winter, muddy carpets) was going for an eye-watering £500,000. Ouch! It seems crackers when such a house would have gone for £5,000 when I was a child. Nice if you bought six of them then, of course. An example of the Jericho eccentric intellectual would be the aforementioned writer James Morris who not only became **Jan Morris** but wrote a great book about Oxford herself and many other good books. In short, the *Guardian* newspaper sells heaps here.

THE MOST EXPENSIVE AND amazing book yet produced at Oxford was unveiled in late 2004. It is the *Oxford Dictionary of National Biography*, containing 60 million words and weighing 280lb. Its 60 volumes, with 54,922 essays on famous and infamous Brits, take up 11ft of (very strong) shelf space. Yours for around £7,500 per copy.

Did you know?

It does, however, retain a diversity. Jericho has never been homogenous: it defies definition. And the flood of new money has certainly been a good thing. The threat to the shabby Jericho of the 1950s – the area's demolition and replacement by then- fashionable tower blocks and housing estates which would now be vile slums falling apart punctuated by burning cars – never happened, thank God.

West Country poet-novelist **Thomas Hardy** (1840–1928) writes of a time, more than a century before, when it was a rough area known for prostitution and disease caused by poor sewerage. The hero of his Oxford novel *Jude the Obscure* comes to live in the cheap district of Beersheba, where poor lodgings abounded: he means of course Jericho, just as he renames Oxford Christminster.

'How dare Hardy rename everything,' cries Boswell as we roll out of the Eagle and Child to conquer Jericho.

'Quite right, it's infernal cheek. Let's call him Adolf G Snotgobbler for the rest of this walk and see how he likes it,' I answer.

On the left see the stately enormity of the **Oxford University Press**, a building that could be a Ministry of the Interior in some Stalinist European state, or a massive pompous railway terminus or a not very good French museum rather than the print works it in fact has been. My Boswellian companion points to the garret window where he once toiled in the days of metal fonts and flat-bed presses. The paternalistic superintendent of the Press in Victorian times, he tells me, Thomas Combe, was a key figure in cleaning up the moral morass round here that Adolf G Snotgobbler described. He taught at Sunday schools, pressed for improvement to the drainage, and paid for the St Barnabas Church to be built with its elegant Italianate campanile, which still dominates Jericho.

Up in these gloomy garrets faceless functionaries perhaps ponder punctiliously over words that should or should not be included in the *Oxford English Dictionary*, although the decisions are no longer made mainly by mad American murderers from Broadmoor Asylum for the Criminally Insane. (See Simon Winchester's entertaining book, *The Surgeon of Crowthorne*, for how this happened, by post and thus without the authorities realising who the contributor, a Dr W C Minor, was, at the creation of the first Oxford Dictionary.)

Soon on the right is another grand building with vast fluted pillars and pediments, but a closer look shows this former **St Paul's** church is now a bar-café-music venue called **Freud**, an odd mixture of coffee stains and stained glass. It seems the wrong proportion for its present daytime use, not intimate enough. Designer makeovers have ruined many a good pub, but this place seems to be crying out for one. As it's turned out, Combe need hardly have bothered building Barney's, as the locals call the other church. They could today have fitted in here. The name Freud over the door kind of epitomises the triumph of one faith over another, and you expect a font filled with lager. Freud's is much better in the evening, Boswell tells me, when they do cocktails. 'I could do with a good screwdriver,' I reply looking around, 'and a paint roller, some brushes and a pair of steps.' This may have been done since, of course.

Further up Walton Street are a few pubs – **Jude the Obscure**, named after Snotgobbler's book, on the left does economically priced good simple food. It used to be one of at least four Oxford pubs called the Prince of Wales but is now probably the only pub in the world with this obscure name. It can get quite busy at weekends, which is probably why they didn't choose his book *Far From the Madding Crowd* as a name (but a central Oxford pub did, see page 246). Peaceful beer garden (well big yard really).

As if all pubs in this road have to begin with 'J', there's also the **Jericho Tavern**. Many an 'Oxpop' band has started life here including Radiohead and Supergrass. Frequented by those visiting the nearby **Phoenix Picture House**. Plus around here are rather pricey eateries that suggest the upper middle class are here to stay in Jericho. There's **Brasserie Blanc** (as in Old Marston master chef Raymond Blanc – well at least they didn't call it Blanc Mange) and **Loch Fyne**, an upmarket seafoody place. We soon go left down Walton Well Road which rapidly becomes quietly residential.

On the right is that well – or rather a replacement drinking fountain – urging us to:

Drink and Think of Him that is the fountain of life.

It, of course, doesn't work and probably hasn't much since being put up in 1885 'with the consent of the Lord of the Manor' (phew, that's all right then). Actually, well worship is a very old and interesting part of British folklore, and even here in intellectual Oxford we have Holywell Street and another equally useless fountain at the Plain which was, centuries before, an alleged source of miracles. And we are heading for the village of Binsey, source – literally – of the most miraculous well of the lot. 'The third font in less than a mile,' ventures Boswell dryly with his dictionary-like mind.

Onwards and upwards over the **Oxford Canal bridge** (more on the impact of this 18th-century technology on page 37) and the parallel **Castle Mill Stream** which would have once diverted enough of the Thames to run watermills. You can walk back to the city by the canal, possibly encountering bohemian narrowboat-minded canal dwellers en route.

But press on for much more interesting views. Over the railway with its hooting trains. In the distance to the left (south) can be seen Oxford station (if you are taller than Boswell and can see over the parapet).

To the right the railway heads for the industrial Midlands (as the canal did before it) up the Cherwell Valley, but the railway also has a left turn for Worcester and the Cotswolds and a right turn for Bicester just north of here. So it's a busy railway, but thanks to the bloody-minded independence of the Great Western and its successors, only now being electrified. Or as a railwayman put it: 'After the opening of the Channel Tunnel, you could go all the way from London to Vladivostok on the Pacific coast of Russia by modern electric railway, but not to Oxford.'

Down to **Port Meadow** at the end of the road, and a great view over the enormous length of this marvellous open space to the right. The extreme end is the village of Wolvercote and the Trout pub, although I'm not suggesting hiking that far today – it's a great 5-mile circular walk round Port Meadow, with inspiring views of Oxford at times.

Ahead and much closer is the path ahead across the meadow to **Binsey**, with bridges over the Thames. Boswell reminds me that it was of the felling of the poplar trees at Binsey that Grievous Bodily Hopkins (or was it Gerard Manley Hopkins?) wrote his mournful stuff about:

After-comers cannot guess the beauty been.

I'm not in the mood, as we're getting tired, the Eagle and Child's beer taking effect.

'Of course they can guess, because the flaming poplars have grown again. In fact even if they hadn't, they could still guess. That's what a guess is. Stick to windhovers, Grievous, old boy, you do those rather well. People do get so soppy about trees being felled (poplar or not poplar). They're just a crop like anything else. Get a grip.'

What, then, Boswell demands, about Balliol boy Hopkins's other famous poem about Oxford with the line:

Towery city and branchy between towers

'Towery? Branchy? Yes, Grievous, dear, nursey wursey will be along with your injectiony in a minute. Quick, back out quietly while he's calm. Hopkins also puts grave and acute accents on his poems, poncy git, it's not flaming French, is it? Let's get Anthony Hopkins to do the rest of the poems.'

Back to the walk. The low area to the right as we walk across the bridge often floods in the winter (as flood meadows are supposed to do, and as thick councils find when they allow building on them, the new homes get en-suite swimming pools). Once in a while this freezes enough for skating (although I'd be on thin ice if I told you it was safe, it's clearly shallower than the river).

197

The first bridge over the river seems to be a World War II-vintage **Bailey bridge**, those things the Army would put across a river while under fire from the other sort of Jerries. There's a funny scene in the movie *A Bridge Too Far* (not all that funny otherwise) where Michael Caine is told by an American officer the hold-up is for some Limey contraption called a Bailey bridge. If I remember rightly, Caine retorts in his British officer voice: 'You mean that miracle of British engineering that is the envy of the civilised world?'

Further on, past a marina in mid-river (we are now on an island) and strange notices about Bossoms (which turns out to be a boatyard), is an arched bridge over the main channel of the Thames. This is known as the **Rainbow Bridge** (although not as well known as the one of the same name and shape over the Cherwell). Boswell stops me halfway across and tests me on a word that is cast in iron on a notice on the bridge as surely as it was once cast in metal at the Oxford Dictionary. 'There,' he says in triumph. 'The shrievalty. What do you make of *that*?'

'Easy,' I bluff, having just noted at the road end something about how the Port Meadow is run by the Sheriff of Oxford. 'It means the tenure of the sheriff. This bridge was put up in this chap's shrievalty. Like mayoralty.'

Boswell, recovered from my unfair slighting of his favourite poet, is generously delighted with my wild guess – phew! – and we ignore an obvious mistake on the notice and walk the few hundred yards beyond to the excellent Perch pub in Binsey village to discuss other words you don't use every day over some pints and cigars, while Old Father Thames rolls past on his unhurried stately route to London and the North Sea, as he has done through many a good shrievalty. (For Binsey's miraculous treacle well, see page 221.)

Options for a return from the Perch at Binsey

Spry mountain goat with pukka boots, anorak and map in see-through plastic tied round neck who wants a proper day's walk: Go on north alongside the Thames to the Trout at Godstow and round through Wolvercote (across the river to the right, two bridges) and back down the other side of Port Meadow.

Tired but happy chappy, could manage a bit more: Don't walk down the long road on this side of the river, Binsey Lane to Botley Road. It'll seem an eternity and Botley Road isn't too great when you get there. Instead return the way you came, except stay on Walton Street right down into the centre of Oxford, past **Ruskin College**, the 'working-class Eton'. You could visit **Worcester College** at the end on the right, with a surprising lake and some great cloisters with quadripartite vaulting.

Same as above but frankly had enough Oxford people: Go back over the Rainbow Bridge but not over the Bailey bridge, heading on south down the narrow island that divides the streams. This is by far the most pleasant and shortest route and brings you out near the station (when the path emerges on Botley Road, turn left).

Totally knackered and/or booze-befuddled complete slob: Get a taxi.

NORTH OXFORD: PLAIN LIVING AND HIGH THINKING

North Oxford isn't just a place, it's a sociological phenomenon. For years the former bluestocking (that is, female undergraduate) has been its principal inhabitant, a doughty dragon of an old battleaxe who was once, maybe 60 years previously, one of the undergraduate young gels on a bicycle coming up St Giles with a wicker front basket stuffed with books.

They are fearless, these dragons of academe (a local school is called the Dragon, after all), and have been known to dress as men to tramp fearlessly into forbidden cities of the world, to face down brigands in remote corners of the Empire, to master and lead head-hunting tribes and above all to nurture their eccentricities without regard to what anyone else thinks. They can cripple would-be burglars with their umbrellas even in their 90s. They show no undue deference to rank or titles and they are often but not always the Fabian sort of socialist, independent and radical to their dying days. Not for nothing have a great number of charities such as Oxfam started in this city. When one of these eccentric old biddies rattles a collecting tin in your face, you dare not refuse.

They waste nothing, using scraps of paper for shopping lists, measuring the right number of cups of water into the kettle as if the war were still on, saving bits of string for God-knows-what.

Some don once wrote brilliantly: 'It has been discovered that plain living and high thinking can be combined in Oxford more easily than in any other provincial town.' Nowhere has this been more true than in North Oxford, where Lefty fads and sects and earnest pamphleteers have thrived among a population who seem all to be great academics, writers or artists or be related to one such.

North Oxford's paper of choice, besides the *Guardian* or *The Independent*, *New Statesman* and socialist or intellectual periodicals, that is, is the relatively cerebral weekly *Oxford Times*. Not the oikish *Oxford Mail* which rolls off the same presses daily and uses much shorter words, or as they might as easily understand it, eschews sesquipedalian circumlocution.

Hopeless generalisations, of course, but anyone with a long history in Oxford will recognise the fearless old bats described. They are now endangered and, like the other kind of bats, ones that live in belfries, they should be protected by law from interference in their eccentric ways.

SUMMERTOWN

Yet again a bit of Oxford with entirely its own character. Don't assume the main road, **Banbury Road**, is all there is. An interesting road sets off west from the top of that stretch of shops: **South Parade** which reaches rather dull Woodstock Road (the other arm of the Y that started back at St Giles) after about half a mile. There's a lot of interesting shops/bars/caffs along here, and a library with a sculpture garden at the back, and an arts centre. Eccentrically, while the women's bogs are sensibly near the library, the gents are way round the corner on Woodstock Road (run north about 200 yards, if you can do that cross-legged). And pretty primitive.

North Parade, as I mention elsewhere, is way south of South Parade and not really in Summertown, as it's almost back at St Giles. But it is a really interesting little road with its own shops and pub called **The Gardeners** (like the one very nearby in Jericho, which must cause the odd mix-up). I imagine inhabitants of North Parade feel they are Oxford's best kept secret, so unlike them, I won't dwell on it. By the way, locals will explain the geographical contradiction by telling you that one was the south parade ground for the Parliamentary besiegers in the Civil War and one the north parade ground for the Royalist defenders of Oxford. Tosh! They are only a cannonball apart. I think North Parade is north for part of Oxford, and South Parade south for part of Summertown. Probably.

ECCENTRIC THINGS TO SEE OR DO

PUNTING: PLEASURE OR HUMILIATION?

Punting if done well is a supremely elegant and efficient way of getting along the Cherwell or the Isis, as the Thames is perversely called in Oxford. It is Oxford's answer to the gondoliers of Venice. In the idealised image, a lady in a pretty summer dress reclines on the cushions holding a parasol, for the sun beams down and flowers nod over the water. A man in blazer and straw boater stands on the curved end making the punt glide along with minimum fuss (the flat end is for Cambridge cissies, after all). A wind-up gramophone warbles in the middle, next to an ice bucket with a bottle of champers. A wicker hamper contains elegant sandwiches with the crust cut off.

The reality is often somewhat different. The geeky tourist goon drives his pole into the mud and pushes. The boat moves away from under him. The goon clutches panic-stricken to the pole now locked in the mud and is left stretching out over the increasing span of water until he is doing a bad impersonation of the Golden Gate Bridge. The boat either shoots away or the pole begins to come out and the inevitable splash is greeted by wild cheers from onlookers. The water feels freezing at almost any time of the year, and the mud is vile.

Here is the average punter's guide to avoid total humiliation:

- Do not overcrowd the punt.
- Do not get drunk first or during the trip.
- Do not take non-swimmers without buoyancy aids.
- Do not stand up in the boat unless punting.
- Check that the pole is smooth and splinter free before you leave. It needs to slide through your hands hundreds of times, so change it if it isn't. Make sure you also have a paddle, or something to paddle with (see below).

How to punt

Now, facing the direction you wish to go in, with the punt in front of you, raise the pole until it is pointing up in the air at perhaps an 80-degree angle, that is tilting slightly from the vertical at the top in the direction of travel. Allow the pole to drop through your hands until it hits the bottom of the river. Push so the punt goes forward and your hands climb up the pole. As you reach the end of the pole, free it with a slight twisting movement and repeat. Steering is achieved by using the pole as a rudder while passing it up through your hands again to the starting position. It should stay on the same side of the punt, however. Swish its end in the water to the side you wish the front of the punt to turn. It is extremely satisfying if well done. And extremely funny if not.

INFREQUENTLY ASKED QUESTIONS

WHAT IF YOU CAN'T FIND THE BOTTOM?

You have gone too far, and are in the North Sea. Don't panic. Switch on navigation lights and practise your Dutch.

WHAT IF THE POLE GETS STUCK?

If you're a complete twerp or having a laugh, hang on. Otherwise, let go and paddle back. They never stay stuck.

WHAT IF I CAN'T RAISE THE POLE?

You may be under a bridge.

WHERE'S THE BEST PLACE TO GO?

Along the river, it's harder on the road.

NO, SERIOUSLY.

Well if you want rural peace and quiet and no stink boats (those with motors) start at the **Cherwell Boat House** and go up through a romantic, willow-hung stretch to the **Victoria Arms** at Old Marston, where booze and reasonable

food may be had and the lawns slope down to the river. You can see the jetty for the little ferry that worked across the Cherwell here before the bridge you have just gone under was opened in 1971 (the road is still called Marston Ferry Road).

John Betjeman talks in *An Oxford University Chest* (1938) of the most romantic approach to Oxford as coming down from the north through Elsfield, down to Marston, which is on the east bank here.

> *Here you take the footpath to Marston Ferry. At the ferry you board a punt or canoe or rob roy and paddle down the stream of the Cherwell to Magdalen Bridge. The Cherwell is as romantic as it ever was...*

So what's a rob roy?

Damn, I hoped you hadn't noticed. Haven't a clue. Any passing Scotsman I suppose. Their kilts must keep them afloat. Anyway, do you mind? I was talking about Marston.

Fascinatingly, this wasn't the first bridge here. During the Civil War the Parliamentary Roundheads besieging Oxford were based in **Marston** while the King's Cavaliers holding the city faced them downstream. Guns were fired from St Nicholas church tower in Marston.

In order to make a sneak attack possible, a bridge was thrown across just here by General Fairfax in 1646. Evidently the engineering decision was correct, because it was still the best place for a bridge in 1971. (Just like one of Hitler's engineers, invading Russia and choosing a spot for a bridge, found Napoleonic-army bridge foundations, and realised at that moment that they were doomed. Well, not *just* like that, as they don't speak much Russian in Marston and they weren't doomed.)

But in this case a peace treaty was signed, saving the city from destruction, and the King fled. In fact, if you wander up the lane from the pub and turn right into Old Marston you can see **Cromwell's House** where the treaty was signed, and on the way notice the humps in the field to your right. These are the 1,000-year-old remains of medieval strip cultivation. And there are a few pubs and a good church in Old Marston.

The ferry – villagers tell me it was a penny a ride – which Betjeperson mentions was a simple platform that the user pulled across on a chain, carrying his horse (the platform, not the user). No great navigation skills in getting a few feet across, so not much chance for a mishap you may think. That's not, sadly, allowing for the stupidity of pompous local bigwigs.

In the 19th century the Mayor and Corporation were riding round inspecting their franchises in all their robes, with the city's gold mace carried in front of them. They came to the ferry, and as they had also inspected a good number of pubs on the way, there was a lot of jostling. The whole lot tipped into the river. The gold mace went in too, and although most of it was recovered along with the bigwigs, a sizeable chunk of gold is still down there in the mud.

BLIMEY, THAT WAS A LONG ANSWER, WASN'T IT?

Well, I used to live in Old Marston, so do you want the interesting stuff or not?

ALL RIGHT, KEEP YOUR HAIR ON. OTHER PUNTING POSSIBILITIES?

What hair? The disadvantage of Cherwell Boat House is that it's out of the city centre (see below) and the rural route means you don't see that much of Oxford. You can go downstream from here, in which case you might see more than you want at Parson's Pleasure, once a nude bathing area for dons.

Other starting points include **Magdalen Bridge** (in which case you can punt down to the junction with the Isis (Thames) and up to Folly Bridge, or Folly Bridge and do the reverse. There are excellent views of the city across Christ Church Meadow along the way. Going downstream to Iffley Lock is a possibility but check how strong the river is flowing and how many hours you want to punt back before letting the punt drift too far, and ask the punt people for advice. You will find holes in the river where little if any of the pole is usable.

Iffley weir itself is deadly dangerous, so keep well away and along the right (southwest) bank. A rowing eight went over the weir here in the 19th century and all nine (that is, including the cox) were drowned.

WHAT ABOUT MAKING LOVE IN A PUNT?

Making love in a punt – which Graham Greene's chum seems to have done (page 187) – needs cushions and privacy, both usually in short supply. Keep clear of weirs etc and be careful where you put your pole (it can drift away). Actually, 'making love in a punt' was a nickname for an unpopular beer when I was a student. No, I'm not going to spell it out for you.

OR MAKING WAR?

Rumour has it that during the last war the upper Thames saw an armoured punt on Home Guard duty. It seems Dad's Army ludicrous – 'It's sinking, Captain Mainwaring': 'Stupid boy, Pike' – and about as dangerous to the expected German *blitzkrieg* as the Romney, Hythe and Dymchurch Railway's miniature armoured train of the same era, which could have been derailed with a German army sausage.

On the other hand, punts have for centuries been armed. Massive punt guns were installed and things looking like miniature one-gunned warships crept towards flocks of birds in boggy marshes, a cartridge more like an artillery shell in its breech, the gunner prostrate to avoid alarming the birds. A huge boom rent the air amidst much squawking, leaving a cloud of smoke, hundreds of dead and dying fowl, and the punt and its stunned, blackened

Punting locations

CHERWELL BOAT HOUSE (Signed to the right, going north, off Banbury Road, north of St Giles ☎ 01865 515978)

MAGDALEN BRIDGE (One end of the High Street ☎ 01865 202643)

HEAD OF THE RIVER (By Folly Bridge on St Aldate's (south from Carfax), Salter's ☎ 01865 243421 ▨ www.salterssteamers.co.uk). Costs around £10 per hour plus a large cash deposit to ensure you don't make for the Caribbean. Salter's also do motor boats, electric boats, rowing boats (you can pretend to be Lewis Carroll) and run scheduled trips to Abingdon, as part of a network of services the whole 76 miles down to Staines on the edge of London.

and deafened occupant shooting backwards, if not sinking. Not very gentlemanly. Don't try it under Magdalen Bridge.

THAT SOUNDS FUN. ARE TORPEDOES ALLOWED IN INTER-PUNT WARFARE?

They aren't specifically banned but all Royal Navy torpedoes run too deep to hit a punt. If you want to mess around in this way – and I'm not at all recommending it – then high-powered water pistols and water bombs (small balloons from toy shops) are a possibility. You will need to fill those from a tap and carry them in a carrier bag, not that I've ever been so childish of course. However, it might be regarded as environmentally unsound and might annoy not only other punters but also the monster Oxford mallards, which we know from the bizarre rituals devoted to hunting them (see page 21) can indeed be huge.

CHILDREN'S STUFF (OUTDOORS)

- Punting. The Parks. Walk round Christ Church Meadow. Walk to Elsfield church or across Port Meadow to Binsey.
- Climb St Mary the Virgin Tower in the High and make gargoyle faces at the students far below and enjoy cosmic views (see page 145).
- Hire bikes and cycle round Otmoor (see page 218).
- Get a train to Didcot and check out the steam railway at that station.

- Visit the Rollright stones, a magic circle of ancient stones just west of the A3400 Oxford–Stratford-upon-Avon road, helpfully between the villages of Little Rollright and Great Rollright. Unexpected, somehow, these stones lie in a less bleak setting than usual, and are full of legend. For a start there are said to be 77 stones, but they have never been counted to the same number twice. You try it.

OTHER IDEAS (INDOORS)

- The Covered Market (see page 263).
- The museums (see below).
- Partymania shop in Walton Street, Jericho (*179 Kingston Road, OX2 6EG ☎ 01865 513397*), which is a cornucopia, a plethora, an Aladdin's Cave, a treasure trove, a Diagon Alley of all things party-related. Here you can get every silly thing you could wish for. Hats, balloons, streamers, musical wotsits, even the things that go bang inside crackers so you can make your own. Brilliant. Good for outdoor, indoors, old, young, medium.

MUSEUMS (AND NOT JUST FOR CHILDREN)

MUSEUM OF THE HISTORY OF SCIENCE Small and free, great advantages in a museum, but interesting too, as is the building itself. Not much hands-on stuff, though.

Amazing 300-year-old intricate door locks still in use; a medieval computer. Fascinating stuff, worth an hour of anyone's time.

Inside you can see the first purpose-built science laboratories, ancient calculating devices for 'Far Things' (which puzzled me for a second, but turns out to be farthings, the old coins, with a calculating wheel in the middle of the word!), as well as many telescopes, etc for really far things. There is also Einstein's blackboard with his chalk equations, baffling to anyone with an IQ of less than around 200. And an amusing detail for anyone aged over 50 is, among the archaic obsolete calculating devices, the first LED electronic calculators and slide rules, both younger than those peering at them but both decidedly on technology's scrapheap.

Broad Street ☎ 01865 277280 💻 www.mhs.ox.ac.uk; closed Monday. Admission free.

UNIVERSITY AND PITT RIVERS MUSEUM To get to Pitt Rivers, you go through the first Natural History Museum (which itself features some spectacularly good carvings). PR is my favourite because it is one of those collections of obsessive eccentrics, and the building's pretty odd too, with each pillar of a different stone, that kind of detail.

The general angle is **anthropology**, but where else will you find: shrunken heads; a magnificent Tahitian mourner's costume collected during Captain Cook's Second Voyage; Hawaiian feather cloaks in brilliant shades of red and yellow; ivories from the Kingdom of Benin; wonderful ancient masks worn by Japanese Noh actors; mummified people; a witch in a bottle; sculpture from all over the world in wood, pottery, metal and stone; whole boats, ranging from full-sized sailing craft to model canoes somehow stuffed on the walls and ceilings; and American Indian skin shirts decorated with porcupine quills?

The place is crammed and many of the items are still labelled in the handwriting of the original curator. Pull open a drawer (under the display cases) and there may be magic objects including: amulets and charms; an intriguing collection of locks and keys; tools and weapons; voodoo dolls; weird musical instruments, mummified toads; or severed fingers. I was lost in reverie at all these unlikely magical wonders and suddenly realised where I seemed to be – in the shop in Knockturn Alley in *Harry Potter* where the hero buys his magic wands, etc. Note the opening hours at the time of writing are limited (noon–4.30pm) and they run some really good free events aimed at children, usually on the first Saturday of each month.

Parks Road – accessible on foot from St Giles through the Lamb and Flag passage ☎ 01865 270927
▨ www.prm.ox.ac.uk; open daily. Admission free.

MUSEUM OF MODERN ART Sorry, you are not going to get even a faintly reasonable review here. Personally, I can see enough unmade beds (featured posing as art at other such establishments) at home, and laughed heartily when a warehouse full of this stuff burnt down in 2004 (that may have been just a PR plug), or when a cleaner accidentally threw away one pile of rubbish that was supposedly a work of art. Even better when someone unplugged a freezer in which a head sculpture made out of the artist's own blood was being kept. Must have spoilt the ice-cream. Being in Oxford, one expects such tedious gimmicks to be eschewed here.

Pembroke Street ☎ 01865 722733
▨ www.modernartoxford.org.uk. Closed Mondays.

ASHMOLEAN MUSEUM Beneath the boring, pompous exterior lurks a boring, pompous interior. No, I'm only joking! There is a fabulous collection of world-class art and some real archeological treasures in Britain's first proper museum which many a national museum would envy. Not arranged to amuse children with the attention span of crack-crazed grasshoppers, however. For its unlikely origins, see page 184.

Beaumont Street ☎ 01865 278002

www.ashmol.ox.ac.uk; closed Mondays. Admission free.

ECCENTRIC DAYS OUT

FIND A REAL FOLLY

The last great private folly to be built in Britain, before the Disneyesque commercial fibreglass fakery of theme parks took over in their plastic parodies, was the fine **Faringdon folly** in Oxfordshire. Built by the truly eccentric composer-diplomat the 14th Baron Berners (1883–1950), the tower sits atop a landmark hill crowned with Scots pines and beeches just outside the small town. The 100ft-square brick tower's bulk is concealed by trees, leaving the octagonal neo-Gothic top poking out with its eight pinnacles and flagstaff.

The folly has generated as much controversy and legend in its short life as many of its much older brethren. The notion of building it received much publicity at the time and the local council voted against it, without benefit of details, purely on hearsay about Lord Berners's supposed plans to use the folly as a lighthouse, probing the rural darkness with a great beam, and to install a powerful siren on top. A public inquiry ensued, which gave Fleet Street diary writers the chance to record this exchange between the architect and crusty old Admiral Clifton Brown who objected that the tower would spoil his views:

Architect: *'But you could not see the tower from your garden without a telescope!'*
Admiral: *'Sir, it is always my custom to look at the view through a telescope.'*

As for legend, if there are some inaccuracies about the tower they were not exactly weeded out by the late Robert Heber-Percy, who died in 1987 having donated the folly to the community in 1983. He told how Lord Berners gave him the tower as a 21st-birthday present and how annoying this was as he had requested a horse.

He also recounted how Lord Berners wanted, once dead, to be stuffed and mounted in the belvedere room at the top of the tower eternally playing cheerful tunes on an automatic grand piano. Heber-Percy went on to say that he 'funked it' because of the impossibility of getting a grand piano up the narrow wooden stairs that cling to the tower's plunging and otherwise-blank interior.

The trust that now opens the tower to the public on the first Sunday afternoon of each month from April to October tries to bring down to earth some of the tall stories attached to the tower. It corrects books which claim a 140ft height and insists on a mere 100ft. It denies you can see six counties from the top and lists a mere five. It denies the claim – made about many a folly from Dorset to Sussex – that it was built to alleviate dire unemployment at the time. Only one extra man was taken on to the estate staff. It even points out that Mr Heber-Percy was born in 1911, so it would have been a late 21st-birthday present.

Some elements of the story remain unchallenged:

- That it was called Folly Hill long before the tower was built.
- That the fine trees were planted by poet laureate

Henry James Pye in the late 18th century.
(He built Faringdon House and wrote a poem
at Eaglehurst, which also boasts a fine tower.
He was such a lousy poet that the rhyme *Four
And Twenty Blackbirds* originated as a lampoon
of his corny style.)

- That the bones of Cromwellian soldiers
  were unearthed while building the tower –
  Parliamentary forces laid siege to an earlier
  Faringdon House.
- That the eccentric notices plastered by Lord
  Berners about his estate included one at the top
  of the tower stating: 'Members of the public
  committing suicide from this tower do so at their
  own risk.' Quite.
- That in another war – 1939–45 – the tower was
  employed as an observation post, soon thankfully
  returning to the uselessness which qualifies it as a
  true folly.

For more on the deeply eccentric Berners, see page 67.

Faringdon, Oxfordshire
☎ 01367 242191 🖳 www.faringdon.org
🚗 Reached from Oxford westwards on the A420 towards
Swindon.

BOARSTALL DUCK DECOY

A decoy duck is a well-known trick, a wooden one that
you float so that others come down in front of you and
you can blast the little quackers. A duck decoy, on the
other hand, is a bizarre tunnel-like contraption, set at one
end of a wooded lake, for capturing the birds alive. A rare

surviving example can be seen at Boarstall, two miles west of Brill near Oxford. It's owned by the National Trust who even show it working from time to time, and there's nearby 14th-century **Boarstall Tower** to visit separately – in fact a moated gate house with Civil War history. Nicest and slowest route by car: follow the Otmoor bike ride route (see page 218) and look for a bridge over the motorway marked Boarstall. The duck decoy must at least have been less noisy than the punt guns discussed earlier.

Almost unbelievable Brill trivia: Brill was once on the Metropolitan Railway (yes, the purple one on the Tube map), at the end of a rambling rural branch where one would pick up pigs on the way to market, a branch that hoped to reach Oxford but ran out of steam, as it were. It eventually connected with the Met into London and one could arrive in the city in a Pullman dining car, a far cry from today's Metropolitan. It must have been Brill.

Boarstall Duck Decoy: ☎ 01844 2374888

Boarstall Tower: ☎ 01844 239339

OTHER ODD OXFORD VILLAGES

See Iffley (page 224), Old Marston (page 206) and Binsey (page 221).

BIKE RIDE: SPOOKY OTMOOR

If you like bikes (and these are easily hired in Oxford), the city and nearby villages are flat and easily bikeable. But for a really different afternoon out (and this makes a pleasant car tour too), strike out north from the old part of Marston on the north of the city to visit the extremely odd and beautiful **Otmoor**. You get to Marston down Banbury Road north from St Giles, turn right down Marston Ferry Road, which has a bike path, and over the River Cherwell, then left into Oxford Road in Marston. Go through the

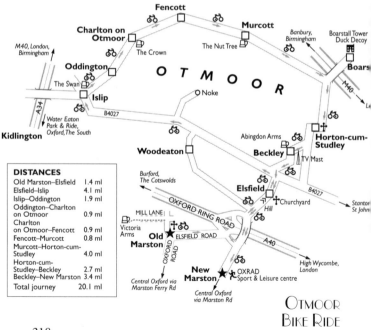

DISTANCES

Old Marston–Elsfield	1.4 ml
Elsfield–Islip	4.1 ml
Islip–Oddington	1.9 ml
Oddington–Charlton on Otmoor	0.9 ml
Charlton on Otmoor–Fencott	0.9 ml
Fencott–Murcott	0.8 ml
Murcott–Horton-cum-Studley	4.0 ml
Horton-cum-Studley–Beckley	2.7 ml
Beckley–New Marston	3.4 ml
Total journey	20.1 ml

OTMOOR
BIKE RIDE

village, with its sharp right turn, and past the church. Leaving Marston, do a quick right and left to cross the thundering ring road and turn right (north) towards Elsfield and escape the city completely. Here, after a lung-busting but short climb, you can see the wonderful view over Oxford from **Buchan's eccentric grave** in the churchyard (see page 125) and continue towards Beckley. Note the blue plaque on Buchan's large house on the left. At the junction about a mile on, turn left to join a circular route around the flat boggy ground ahead of you. This is Otmoor, a unique bit of Oxfordshire with fascinating **wildflowers**, **birds** and **insect life**. Its value is that it was left here after the Ice Age, and has never been ploughed because it's so boggy and difficult to drain. If you wish to go down and walk across from Beckley you can try at your own risk, but it is very squidgy and I ended up carrying a certain elderly lady who tried it once! If you wear boots, they will probably be sucked into the mire.

It is a wonderful place, with such wilderness just a gargoyle's spit from Oxford and its busy bypass, and has a lot of history, involving a legendary beast that supposedly seized cattle, a riot by the cattle owners when greedy landowners tried to enclose and drain it (they failed), RAF bombing practice on it, the threat of the M40 motorway right across it (defeated after a vehement campaign) and now its again-increasing wildlife population.

The view from Beckley is said to have inspired Lewis Carroll's imaginary chessboard landscape, for he stayed in the village for a while. There are some great little pubs.

Assuming you don't try to cross soggy Otmoor, go left at this road junction and enjoy a wonderful circular bike ride through the villages (known as Otmoor's seven towns), and rural peace. Basically, keep right (after turning left at the junction from Elsfield, that is) but don't take the dead-end turning to Noke or any other dead-end roads to the right marked as such (a T-shape on a square blue sign with the top bar being red). You go through Islip, Oddington, Charlton-on-Otmoor, Fencott and Murcott, in conditions of increasingly Cotswoldian charm and peace, after which you get a glimpse of the M40, and then Horton-cum-Studley, then Beckley.

Then you get back to your starting place, the junction where you turned left. You need to go more or less straight over. Back in Marston (see page 206) there are several pubs, including the riverside **Victoria Arms** down Mill Lane (the sharp bend we passed in the village at the start).

Otmoor's wildlife

For a superb and beautiful view of Otmoor's wildlife you couldn't do better than *Through The Garden Gate*, a DVD filmed by Otmoor resident Stephen De Vere. You'll never get as close to the big mammals and birds of prey as he does with his hides and incredible patience. De Vere is well known in the trade for his years spent in places such as Antarctica filming showpiece documentaries. Yet as this informative 49-minute film shows, shot over a whole year on Otmoor and close by, there's a whole world of natural wonders right on our doorstep, in walking distance of a busy city. Buy the DVD from Amazon.co.uk and www.stephendevere.co.uk.

OUT OF TOWN

BINSEY

Easily reached on foot from Jericho (see page 190), this is an ancient village somehow surviving almost in the middle of Oxford. The **Perch pub** is wonderful, although don't go mad with your cigar lighting: the thatch burned down at least twice in the last century. It is said to be haunted by a love-lorn soldier who threw himself in the Thames (and, oddly, still needs a drink). Binsey was, as the 'sey' ending implies, once an island in the Thames.

THE BINSEY TREACLE WELL

This is so unlikely that it reminds one of gullible tourists being directed to the treacle mines near St Albans and elsewhere. Lewis Carroll, who came here, takes the Binsey treacle well and puts it in *Alice's Adventures in Wonderland* where it is mentioned at the Mad Hatter's Tea Party as a place where children live. All suitably bonkers, of course, but it might come a surprise to find the treacle well exists and has a long historical provenance stretching back 1,000 years. That it exists can be seen at the west end of St Margaret's church. Many notable people have used its supposed curative powers, including Henry VIII, and some faithfuls still swear by it (I'd swear a bit further away from the church unless you want to be struck blind, if I were you, but you know what I mean). Treacle, I'm told, is an ancient word for a curative lotion, not that sticky black stuff. I did wonder (probably wrongly) if there is some link to 'trickle'. Must call in at the Oxford Dictionary on the way home.

Even more extraordinarily, the whole idea has a well-recorded source, as it were. As recorded in the history section, the 8th-century patron saint of Oxford, St Frideswide, was suffering the attentions of a Mercian king who wanted his wicked way with her. On reaching the city, he was struck blind by God for his sin. Fair enough you may think, and the parent of a comely daughter may respectfully wish God did a bit more of that nowadays. She, being a rather comely saint, was allowed to second-guess even God and called forth a well at this point that would cure the randy king's blindness. He went off (possibly chastised, but probably to rape, burn and pillage somewhere else – bloody Mercians never learn) and she set up the nunnery that became the most important institution in Oxford until the Reformation, 500 years later. Another 500 years later, roughly, a lot of water has flowed down the Thames past Binsey, but the well is still there.

BOARS HILL

This was the famous hill whence the all-encompassing view of Oxford was the genesis of great poetry including

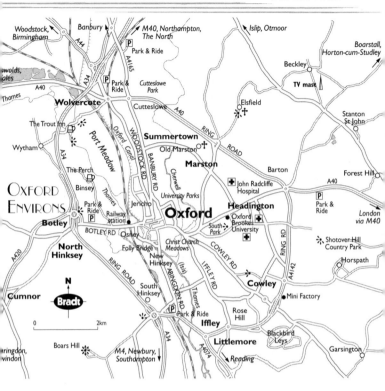

Matthew Arnold's 'dreaming spires'. The trouble is, sadly, that from the 19th century this once-bare hill with its cosmic views has been much built-upon, with fences, trees and hedges obstructing the once 360 degree sweep. You can, nevertheless, still enjoy those from certain angles, and of course the extraordinary poetry is still there too.

There is also an eccentric feature. You might think archaeologists should dig up interesting mounds in the landscape. Here one personally created a new one. **Sir Arthur Evans** (1851–1941) built **Jarn Mound**, in order to provide panoramic view across Oxfordshire and towards Warwickshire and Berkshire. It must have been wonderful.

223

But if Sir Arthur (famed for uncovering the Palace at Knossos on Crete, and starting us all off on minor tours) climbed the steps to this viewpoint today, he would be dismayed to discover how much trees and housing had radically altered the landscape, turning downland almost into a wealthy suburb. He'd also be dismayed that his house, Youlbury, with Minoan decoration, has been burnt down. (He may have said: 'It is a small thing, but Minoan.')

The hill has grown almost as many **poets** as trees. Arthur Hugh Clough visited and wrote here in the 1840s, followed by Matthew Arnold. Margaret Louisa Woods lived here in the 1880s, followed by two poets laureate – Robert Bridges and John Masefield, and then three First World War poets: Robert Graves, Edmund Blunden and Robert Nichols. Three of these (Arnold, Graves and Blunden) became Oxford Professors of Poetry. It's a staggering total, so there must be something special about the place.

Perhaps the best place for getting that glorious view of Oxford today is a stretch of Berkeley Road. Also see the Matthew Arnold Field while you're looking around.

He seemed to like the winter view:

This winter-eve is warm,
Humid the air! leafless, yet soft as spring,
The tender purple spray on copse and briers!
And that sweet city with her dreaming spires

IFFLEY

One of the odd things about Oxford is that the ring road is drawn so generously that acres of green countryside and whole villages are within its limits. Some of these former villages like Headington are swamped by suburbia, but one or two are remarkably well preserved, as at Binsey and Iffley. The latter is a gem with a charm normally associated with remote Cotswold crannies, and offering England's most perfect **Norman church**, a **thatched school** and a **riverside pub** with no road access.

It's easy to find, because Iffley Road leads down there from Magdalen Bridge, although soon after the Donnington Bridge Road traffic lights you must look out for a tiny sign marked Iffley on the left pointing across to a diverging road, usefully called Iffley Turn, on the right. If you come to a junction with a huge obelisk on the left before a rise, you've gone a little too far. If you're going by bus, catch a **No 4 from Carfax** and ask for the Iffley Turn. Even better, if you've got some time, is to walk from Folly Bridge on the south bank (not the north, the Cherwell will stop you), a fascinating mile-and-a-half on the level.

Assuming you've come down Iffley Road and turned into Iffley Turn, take the Church Way turn off the mini-roundabout, then Mill Lane, a downward slope to the right, parking where you can if motorised.

Walking down Mill Lane, the slope down to the river, you see **Grist Cottage** on the right with its millstones, but this is no longer grist to a mill, as it was burned down about 100 years ago. Crossing over the lock by footbridges and across an island or two, you see a **weir**, an ancient **disused pound lock** and the current **Iffley Lock**, which will be busy with boats in midsummer. Weirs maintain the depth necessary for navigation, provide power for mills such as the one that stood here, and make the river look full instead of a ditch, but, of course, paradoxically obstruct navigation too. The fascinating thing you can learn here is how the first primitive 'flash locks' worked. No massive gates. You paid the miller a fee, and he'd haul away a boat-shaped section of the weir. You surfed down the wave, although how much fun that was with 30 tons of grain or whatever aboard is hard to tell. Certainly more fun than travelling upstream: the boats had to be somehow winched slowly up the sloping torrent.

Max Beerbohm mentions in his novel *Zuleika Dobson*:

> *Over the closed gates of Iffley lock, the water gushed down, eager for the sacrament of the sea.*

Which was presumably the middle pound lock. Either that or the river was really high.

It all makes you want a drink, so head on over the ornamental bridge across the channel for rowing boats (note the rollers between here and the 'mathematical' bridge). On the right at this bridge are a few steps down to a monument which marks the start point of the Bump Races for the college rowing teams.

Further on is the former Isis Tavern, now the **Isis Farmhouse**, which I'm told does cracking good afternoons teas, etc, and has a lovely garden one can sit in.

The garden is, of course, crowded with spectators during Eights Week. The college boats speed past, but apparently this stretch isn't all that easy for a small rowing boat, as J K Jerome noted in that Thames comic novel *par excellence, Three Men In A Boat*:

> *We passed through Iffley Lock at about half-past twelve, and then, having tidied up the boat and made all ready for landing, we set to work on our last mile.*
>
> *Between Iffley and Oxford is the most difficult bit of the river I know. You want to be born on that bit of water, to understand it. I have been over it a fairish number of times, but I have never been able to get the hang of it. The man who could row a straight course from Oxford to Iffley ought to be*

able to live comfortably, under one roof, with his wife, his mother-in-law, his elder sister, and the old servant who was in the family when he was a baby.

First the current drives you on to the right bank, and then on to the left, then it takes you out into the middle, turns you round three times, and carries you up stream again, and always ends by trying to smash you up against a college barge.

Of course, as a consequence of this, we got in the way of a good many other boats, during the mile, and they in ours, and, of course, as a consequence of that, a good deal of bad language occurred.

If you return to Iffley (rather than going the mile-and-a-half up the towpath to Folly Bridge in the city), there are a few gems. Turn right at the top of the slope by Grist Cottage to go round the end of the village – spookily quiet when I was there, like some remote Cotswold hideaway – and you reach the parish church of **St Mary the Virgin**, built in 1170 and basically unchanged.

St Mary the Virgin

This church is well worth a look, with its fantastic original Norman carvings around the west door, featuring not only the Norman's favourite zigzag effect but very strange beasts, all remarkably sharp for stones carved nearly 1,000 years ago. I'm told by a villager that the reason the upper part of this is so remarkably preserved is that there was a porch above here for a few centuries, so it didn't weather as much, and now the porch has gone, it looks as its builders intended, in their Norman wisdom. If so, that's our great luck to find carvings nearly a millennium old so fresh, but possibly bad luck for our distant descendants who may see the whole lot worn away by rain, sun and frost.

Inside there are many of those little round-arched windows and blind arcades (that is rows of arches with solid walls) that the Normans loved. It is beautiful and mostly original, but I began to realise that its title 'best preserved Norman church' is a little strained.

Obviously the perpendicular-style windows (the big ones with shallow pointed arches) can't be Norman. They hadn't the technology for this wall of glass approach which reached its apex in places such as the Divinity School at the Bodleian. And the altar is altered.

When you think about it, even having rows of pews is a post-Reformation event. Norman and Saxon churches were strewn with rushes and you had to attend church and had to stand for up to four hours, much of it being burbling in Latin. There was a shelf-like ledge round the edge, hence we still say the weakest go to the wall, although the meaning has been reversed. And Roman Catholicism insisted on the separation of the laity from the priests, hence the need for a rood screen halfway down the church. Here at Iffley its location is charmingly indicated on the right before the arch of the tower, where a spiral staircase seemingly for dwarves disappears into the wall and reappears above our heads in a doorway to thin air – this is where the top of the wooden screen would have been. Wouldn't any child want to climb this staircase to nowhere?

Leaving the church, go on the level road opposite and you will loop back to your starting place. Note the thatched 1838 **village school** on your left. It's picture-perfect. Awfully Iffley.

ECCENTRIC FACTS

OXFORD AND CAMBRIDGE: STRANGE SIMILARITIES

1   Both have a Cowley Road, and both these are slightly disreputable, in a nice kind of way.

2   Both are named after a river crossing, strongly feature rowing and punting, and use blue as their colour (a different blue, true).

3   Both rivers change their names, some pedants say, near the city.

4   Both have Corpus Christi, Jesus, Magdalen, Pembroke, Queens, St Catharine's, St John's, Trinity and Wolfson colleges (any spelling differences being relatively recent distinctions).

5   Both also have a pukkah college virtually no one has ever heard of: Kellogg (Oxford) and Murray Edwards (Cambridge).

6   Both have a so-called Bridge of Sighs (as in Venice) and both are copies of the wrong bridge.

7   In neither town can you say to a taxi driver: 'Take me to the cathedral' or 'Take me to the university.' They don't exist in the usual sense of a separate location.

8   Both universities use a church called St Mary's instead.

9   Both could have had the railway station in the centre but snootily pushed it out to the edge of town to the annoyance of millions of passengers ever since, but both bus stations are a lot more central. Both have a redundant rail branch line – to St Ives (Cambridge) and Cowley (Oxford) – that should be used but isn't, and a cross-country route that was expensively modernised and then closed (to each other).

10 Both are bicycle mad, being in the flat basin of a river, both being reached through hills that are about 20 miles away from London. Both have had motorways built nearby in recent years, and both have a noisy dual carriageway down the other side. Both have a major airport between themselves and London and a minor one nearby.

11 Both were unimportant to the Romans.

12   Both have remains of pagan well worship.

13   Both were involved in the 1954 four-minute mile
     and the 1555–56 burning of bishops.

14   Both produced some of the world's greatest
     children's stories: *Alice*, *The Wind in the Willows*,
     The Lion, the Witch and the Wardrobe (Oxford) and
     Winnie-the-Pooh and *The Water Babies* (Cambridge).

15   Both have many towns named after them in New
     Zealand, the United States, etc.

16   Both have featured a key character called Morse:
     Inspector Morse in Oxford and Murray Morse,
     editor of the *Cambridge Evening News* until 2008.

17   Both are far away enough from London to be their
     own place, but near enough for a day out.

18   Both have a circus in the West End of London,
     which isn't one.

19   Both have a saint nobody has ever heard of who
     turns out to be a defiled virgin with miraculous
     powers (Frideswide and Rhadegund).

20   Both contain property belonging to the other
     university.

21   Both contain a place called Paradise.

22   Both had leper hospitals on the edge of town and
     both retain the chapels of these institutions.

23 Both have an evening paper, a weekly one, and a BBC radio station but not a morning paper.

24 Both have an eclectic mix of museums, some very odd, headed by one huge pile with a huge Neo-classical frontage (the Ashmolean and the Fitzwilliam), plus both have Botanic Gardens (see page 136). Both have a museum of calculators.

25 Both suffered strife through North v South riots in the Middle Ages, Catholic v Protestant repression and regular Town v Gown head-breaking ever since.

26 Both sets of colleges have long lists of men killed in World War I, both have famous war poets who died in that war, and both have members killed fighting for the Germans, often also listed on memorial plaques.

27 Both have famous university presses and massive bookshops, one of which is unique to each city (Heffers and Blackwell's).

28 Both had technical colleges in the mid 20th century which by 2000 had morphed first into polytechnics and then into the 'other university' in town.

29 Both struggled to cope with the motor car in the late 20th century, banning them from the centre with Park & Ride schemes, despite there being Morris Oxford and Austin Cambridge models.

30 Both have pubs called The Eagle and Child where great people have met and discussed huge ideas (Tolkien, C S Lewis, Crick and Watson). To those who point out the Cambridge one is called just The Eagle, I'd say yes, but only in the last 150 years or so.

31 Both have insanely tall chapels built by the same 19th-century architect who was obsessed by the same 13th-century chapel in France. Gothic revival nut Sir George Gilbert Scott was so knocked out by the Sainte-Chapelle in Paris that he built a soaring version of it here in Cambridge, at St John's, and also in Oxford, at Exeter College. You may think he was right: they're terrific.

32 Both have colleges called Ruskin that aren't part of the main university.

33 Both send choristers up a tower to sing to the birds once a year each spring. Ascension Day, St John's, Cambridge; 1 May, Magdalen, Oxford.

ECCENTRIC OXFORD STREET NAMES

ALEC ISSIGONIS WAY Not the easiest road name to say. Named after the genius designer who took the engine of the post-war Morris Minor, turned it through 90 degrees to save space, created the million-selling Mini and thus made the *Italian Job* possible. Appropriately, the new Mini is built within a gear-knob's throw of here.

ARISTOTLE LANE, ANDROMEDA CLOSE, OBSERVATORY STREET Other cities would make do with Shepherd's Mead or some such trite twaddle. Not Oxford.

BALTIC WHARF A few streets west of Folly Bridge, it may be reached across the Thames by a footbridge from Preachers Lane, but about as Baltic as Bob Marley.

BEEF LANE Needs extending into Pork Walk.

BULWARKS LANE Not so much the name as the look of this largely forgotten link from George Street to Bonn Square (just about). A spooky spot with canyon-like walls and ill-lit by flickering lamps, it would be great for scaring yourself silly about an Oxford Ripper. Or escaping if you were one…

CARFAX Sounds like an abbreviation for car factories, which Oxford has had for nearly a century, but being the crossroads at the heart of the city, the name is much older. Carfax, probably from the Old French for crossroads, which Carfax is. Think of the modern French carrefour, meaning crossroads (both literally and metaphorically, appropriate in Oxford, as in a crossroad in life), and also a well-known supermarket brand over there, and you are nearly there. Well, no you're not, you're in France. Never mind…

CATTE STREET Poshed up as St Catherine's Street for a bit and then, thankfully, restored.

CROTCH CRESCENT Makes passing puerile prats in Marston giggle. And me.

DEADMAN'S WALK A route to a Jewish cemetery.

DEVIL'S BACKBONE A path near South Hinksey.

DIVINITY ROAD Off Cowley Road. Very Oxford.

FOLLY BRIDGE Possibly named after the daft building or folly still alongside, or after the city gatehouse of early days.

FRIARS ENTRY Possibly named after the ... no, no rude jokes. This odd passage linking Gloucester Green with Magdalen Street is a remnant of pre-Reformation monastic Oxford.

HELL PASSAGE Not the most pleasant name for this path, no doubt paved with good intentions, down to the Turf pub from New College Lane, so it has been more recently known as St Helen's Passage. Frankly, I'm not sure if that's an improvement.

JERICHO STREET The area's name, linked to the earlier Jericho Gardens, mocks its remoteness from Oxford, probably.

LOGIC LANE Used, appropriately, as the title for a film about philosophy by Professor Michael Chanan. Connects High Street to Merton Street past University College and named after a school of logicians. A graduate who attended Oxford used to visit the philosophers gathered down here and also their infants whom they had left in Summertown, North Oxford. He reported that whereas one group made a disinterested search with open minds for the meaning of life, the other were self-centred, badly

235

A S WELL AS HAVING eccentric names, many things in Oxford are eccentrically mispronounced, seemingly in order to trap the unwary tourist, with a complete gay abandon of the written word that only a Frenchman would really appreciate.

The **Cherwell** river is said Charwell. The Thames is said Isis, bizarrely, but only within Oxford. Either side its name changes. **Magdalen** College is said Mawdlin. Nobody but a tourist would say Street after **High**, **Broad** or **Cornmarket** but you are allowed to prefix them with 'the'. Nearby **Bicester** is pronounced to rhyme with sister (as it does in some very rude limericks). If in doubt, put a silver spoon or plum in your mouth and just waffle.

Cuppers is the intercollegiate knock-out competitions in sports, or drama. The Oxford suffix '-ers' was much favoured early in the 20th century, and seems somewhat cringeworthy now.

I have heard **Martyrs' Memogger** used for the Martyrs' Memorial, but not yet the infamous **wagger pagger bagger** (waste paper basket). This rather soppy habit started at Rugby School, I'm told, which would explain why the game also from the school is known as rugger. Sitting here writing on the morning of April 1, I'd further advise you that to show how truly posh you are, you could ask for train tickets not to Didcot or Reading, but Dodders and Rodders.

Pronunciation and terminology: useless information

The meanings of some words are peculiar to Oxford, or flexible, Alice-in-Wonderland style. **Rusticated** (country-style) means the deliberately rough course of stonework in a building such as the Sheldonian or being temporarily expelled (sent to the countryside) in the case of a student – the link being the Latin for countryside, *rus*. To be permanently expelled is, if you live south of Oxford, to be **sent down**. Even if you live up north or up a hill, it's still sent down. Like trains going to London, up and down are towards and away. So Londoners come up by the down train, and go down by the up train. Clear?

Heads of colleges: virtually every college has a different title: Warden, Dean, President, Rector, Master. Being a **gentleman commoner** as a student meant you weren't common but were rich, usually idle and possibly not a gentleman at all: common or poor people who got into the university were **servitors** and the ones who actually did any studying, by and large. Dr Johnson was one of the latter at Pembroke and said: 'The difference between us servitors and gentlemen commoners is this, that we are men of wit and no fortune and they are men of fortune and no wit.'

Scouts are college servants, often rather well educated and right-wing, much valued by students and dons. In another university shivering amongst the boggy fens of Cambridgeshire, they have bedders, but they are a much inferior creature to an Oxford scout. Discipline was enforced by two **proctors** in charge of the **bulldogs**, or university police. The latter would enforce matters such as the curfew, although being Oxford this was not easy.

(CONTINUED OVERLEAF)

Pronunciation and terminology:
useless information

(CONTINUED)

On one occasion a student out late was asked to give his name by a policeman, and later was stopped by a bulldog and asked his name again. He said: 'I'm terribly sorry old chap, I haven't got one. I gave it to some other fool down the street.'

On another occasion a student was asked what his name might be and answered Caesar Augustus. On being told not to be so cheeky, the student replied: 'Well you asked what it might be, not what it is.' What larks!

behaved, narcissistic and demanded attention and support all the time. Yes, by the latter he meant the philosophers…

MAGPIE LANE Although magpies do play a role in Oxford's history – they were thought to be the souls of the dead hanging around so an abbey was set up here – this name replaced an extremely rude name for a road where one found prostitutes. Part of that name was Grope.

NORTH PARADE Eccentric in that it's south of South Parade.

PARADISE SQUARE AND PARADISE STREET On the opposite side of town, appropriately, to Hell Passage. More remnants of the monastic Oxford swept away by the Reformation, referring to a garden. I know an old lady in the city who still talks fondly of 'the times when monks used to walk in Paradise'. She must be older than she looks.

PENNY FARTHING PLACE
Named after the early bicycle?

QUAKING BRIDGE
Name sometimes given to the bridge over Castle Mill Stream in St Thomas Street. Quakers, on the other hand, are not posh ducks from Worcester College Lake but a religious group.

SEVEN DEADLY SINS LANE Now, disappointingly you may think, renamed New Inn Hall Street.

SOUTH PARADE North of South Parade

SQUITCHEY LANE Muddy once ... or friend of a late Princess?

TUMBLING BAY COURT What an utterly charming address. Sounds like an Aussie dry white.

TURN AGAIN LANE There's one of these in the City of London, where people popularly take it to be something to do with the Dick Whittington legend, whereas it has the much more prosaic origin of being a dead end or loop road.

War Street Because the two countries were fighting when roads were laid out off Cowley Road in the 1860s, three of them were named German Street, Denmark Street and War Street, not the most attractive name. Denmark was clearly acceptable, but the other two were later changed to St Mary's Road and Hurst Street.

12 PECULIAR MEANINGS OF THE WORD OXFORD

Oxford accent Doesn't really exist because it is correct, otherwise Queen's English and everything else is a deviation. Used to be *de rigueur* on the BBC. Now it's almost banned by the broadcaster in a tide of efnic yoofspeak.

Oxford bags Ludicrously baggy trousers once the thing in Oxford. However, when naive students went out and bought a pair, they were sometimes torn to shreds and the pieces hung all over the college in question.

Oxford blue Two meanings: the colour, which is dark blue as opposed to Cambridge's light, and also the honour of competing against that other university in sport. The most famous Oxford blue was Roger Bannister, whose life was utterly changed by six-tenths of a second on May 6 1954. This was the part of four minutes he didn't use to run the world's first sub four-minute mile on the Iffley Road running track, thus earning himself global fame (see page 171). One becomes a blue rather like one becomes an England cap for playing for the country. Some less important sports make you a 'half blue', which sounds a light mauve to me. Nice.

OXFORD COMMA A comma in a list before 'and', and particularly useful in a list such as this: you can eat sausages, bubble and squeak, and ice-cream. With the comma, delicious. Without, horrid. Possibly puzzling to Americans who use them freely all the time, I'm told.

OXFORD ENGLISH See Oxford accent.

OXFORD FRAME A typographical device where a box around a bit of text or picture has rules on the sides that go a little way beyond the corners.

OXFORD GROUP A group of idealists in the early 20th century who transformed into Moral Rearmament.

OXFORD MARMALADE Frank Cooper's. There is none better in the whole world. If Heaven really is England on a May morning, then there will be Cooper's Oxford Marmalade for breakfast.

OXFORD MOVEMENT A High Church 19th-century part of Anglicanism with incense, elaborate robes, etc.

MORRIS OXFORD A type of car built in Cowley through much of the 20th century in various models. A version is still built in India, called the Ambassador, and is much loved there, while causing spasms of joy among Brits of a certain age arriving in that country. The same company also made a version called the Austin Cambridge, which was, of course, rubbish.

OXFORD RAGWORT A form of the plant that escaped from the Oxford Botanic Gardens in the 18th century and took its time spreading along the railway lines to arrive in London perfectly timed to colonise the bomb sites during the Blitz. So there *is* something slower than the 11.18 stopping train.

OXFORD PAPERS The *Oxford Mail* (daily, evening, town bias, more suited to East Oxford) and *Oxford Times* (weekly, gown bias, more suited to North Oxford), but America's Oxfords by contrast boast the *Oxford Eagle* (Oxford, Mississippi), *Oxford Press* (Oxford, Ohio) and, wait for it, the *Oxford Eccentric* (Oxford, Michigan), where you may read strange headlines such as: 'Father finds quarter barrel of beer in teen's closet'. Only a quarter barrel? You've got nothing to worry about, mate. Let him get on with it.

ECCENTRIC LIVING

EAT ECCENTRIC

Coco's, 23 Cowley Road ☎ 01865 200232
This is a very happening café/bistro at the town centre end of Cowley Road, popular with both students and 'normal' people. Despite student tendencies to inhale weird stuff (not Bill Clinton, of course) you are *not* hallucinating if you see a clown soaping himself in a bath halfway up the wall. He is really there. And you have not partaken of the wacky backy if you see a full English breakfast served in a pizza. It's rather good. Good for brunch, crowded in the evenings with braying people who like being in the in-crowd.

Copa, 9 George Street ☎ 01865 246906
Good for lunches; affordable Mediterranean cuisine.

Edamame, 15 Holywell Street ☎ 01865 246111
Serves good Japanese food at reasonable prices but gets full up (as you will), so book.

BROWNS, 5–11 Woodstock Road – the St Giles end ☎ 01865 511995 🖥 www.browns-restaurants.com Famed Oxford café with a very pleasant location overlooking St Giles and posher student-friendly food (in terms of menu, if not price). It is actually part of a chain at many of Britain's more chic towns. Not to be confused with...

BROWN'S, Avenue 4, Covered Market ☎ 01865 243436 You can easily eat for less than a fiver at this good old-fashioned greasy-spoon caff. It seems to be run by a Portuguese family but the food is so resolutely English that Sergeant Lewis would have loved it. In fact, what with the rock cakes and scones, and the décor, it's as if one has returned to about 1955. Donkey-jacketed workmen mix with dons looking like Jim Dixon in old corduroy jackets with patched elbows, and bleary undergrads try to settle their stomachs after a night of carousing.

BRASSERIE BLANC, 71, Walton Street, Jericho, OX2 6AG ☎ 01865 510999 🖥 www.brasserieblanc.com Yes, this is Blanc is as in Raymond Blanc, Oxford-based proprietor of Le Manoir Aux Quat' Saisons at Great Milton near Thame, the famously poshest if not priciest place you can eat near Oxford. Blanc said in 2003: 'I've lived in England for 30 years and I'm a much better Frenchman for it.' Absoluement, mon vieux fromage.

CHIANG MAI KITCHEN LTD, 130A High Street
☎ 01865 202233
This top Thai restaurant which is in a side alley off
the High in an impressive medieval or Tudor building
spoiled only, some may think, by the over-obvious air-
conditioning units. Still, what do you want – a perfect
Thai-food experience or Bangkok-style all-year-round
sweatbath? One of the best Thai eateries with a very cheap
and reasonable lunch menu.

CHERWELL BOAT HOUSE, off Bardwell Road
☎ 01865 552746 ▨ www.cherwellboathouse.co.uk
Right off Banbury Road going north from St Giles before
you reach Marston Ferry Road traffic lights – left and after
the lights coming in from by-pass.

This is a bit off the beaten track (go to the end of
Bardwell Road and turn right down a track where it
swings left, but best to leave the car, if you have one, in
Bardwell Road) but a real gem, a superb find. I prefer
places that have a very restricted menu, as this did when
I went there (three choices), because it not only makes
choosing very simple but removes one of the problems of
places that offer maybe 100 dishes. Either those places
will be really slow, or they will be microwaving stuff that
was made in a factory in Scunthorpe and sticking a bit of
cress on the side to make it look home-prepared. No such
problems here where the atmosphere was rather as if I'd
invited people round and said: 'Look, I've cooked this,
that and that, which do you want?' Except that the
modern English cooking is miles better, such as crackling
pork belly with a damson sauce or smoky mackerel tart.
Now has a bar as well. My Oxfordshire chum John Price
writes:

In my view the best place to eat is the Cherwell Boat house (near the Dragon School) – preferably in summer, outside on the balcony or on the decking, watching people taking their punts out onto the river. One of the great entertainments is watching people punting with no idea which end of the boat is which and the river traffic jams that result.

FURTHER CHOICES: See the pubs and hotels in this section for comments about their food.

DRINK ECCENTRIC

There are a great many real Oxford pubs in fiction, from Inspector Morse to Jerome K Jerome, but then few cities have had so many great authors propping up their bars. Not that they were stuck for choice: there were 370 taverns recorded in Oxford in the 1660s, which of course was a good deal smaller than the city we know today. Here's a selection of the eccentric and interesting ones in the city and nearby.

FAR FROM THE MADDING CROWD, 10–12 Friars' Entry
This is a newish pub, but none the worse for that. Good beer, nice staff and a respite from the melee (as the name, pinched from Thomas Hardy's novel, suggests). Pub of the Year recently. Perhaps the antidote to the nearby giant Wetherspoon's effort, **Four Candles** (surely a reference to Ronnie Barker's great joke confusing them with fork 'andles) in George Street. To be fair, that pub does a decent pint and reasonably priced food in pleasant enough surroundings, and nothing wrong with that, if you don't mind being in a theatre-sized place rather than a cosy pub.

THE NUT TREE, Main Street, Murcott, not far from Kidlington, and also on the round Otmoor bike ride, OX5 2RE ☎ 01865 331253

Regulars have been immortalised in strange gargoyles – or rather grotesques – found in the undergrowth of the garden. They were carved by a Canadian sculptor who regularly drank here. Rather a lot, obviously.

THE OLD TOM, St Aldate's

A small town pub, not hugely eccentric, but a friendly fixture in the city centre, and after all named after a bell that changed sex in a street named after a saint that never existed. Worth pondering over a pint.

THE BOOT INN, Barnard Gate, just before Witney on the A40 west from Oxford, OX29 6XE ☎ 01865 881231

Bonkers for its bizarre collection of celebrity footwear, donated from personalities such as Ronnie Barker, the Bee Gees, Clive James and the famously boozy footballer George Best. Presumably if they got legless, they didn't need the footwear. I'm just glad their withered old socks aren't around. No cheese 'n' bunion flavour…

THE PRIORY AND ?, Priory Lane, Littlemore

A friendly enough country pub, but no explanation for its name.

THE KING OF PRUSSIA, Rose Hill, along Iffley Road

It would be deeply eccentric indeed to tell you about a pub that isn't there any more, but as the story is better than the pub ever was, here goes. It might be reopened by the time you get there, of course. It shows the perils of naming a pub after a political entity. Opened in 1809, and doing a good trade in 1815 when the Prussian (German) army was on our side and saved the day by turning up late on the day against the French at the Battle of Waterloo. A century later and things were somewhat different: a bunch of German workers were staying in the pub and sang anti-British songs, which didn't go down as well as the Morrell's beer. Not long afterwards a group of British soldiers pulled down the sign showing the German king and destroyed it. The name was hurriedly changed to the Allied Arms. The sign depicted British, French and Belgian soldiers with no Prussians (or Germans), and later, after the second war with Germany, showed Churchill, Roosevelt and Stalin. Only in 1996 was it deemed sufficient time had passed for the name to revert to the original King of Prussia.

There is a website which I recommend called www.oxfordpubguide.co.uk which rates the various pubs and will update you on changes. Its one-star rating, which was given to the King of Prussia, was explained thus in the key of star ratings:

> *Abysmal. Shoot landlord, burn down and run away.*

Sadly, that's what then happened to the KoP. Well not the shooting bit, but I wouldn't be surprised. In July 2006, the website ruefully recorded:

> *The empty building has just recently been torched. Somebody obviously took my one star rating too literally!*

None of this is a comment on anyone who may or may not have reopened the pub in the meantime. Good luck to them – they can hardly do worse.

THE BEAR, Blue Boar Street and Alfred Street
A cosy, charming and creaky pub, of the duck-your-head

variety, which sits conveniently close to the city centre yet in a quiet back street. There's sitting outside when weather permits. On two sides it says 'a historic inn since 1242'. As a pedant, I'd disagree. Not that it should be an historic – how pretentious, as if anyone ever pronounced it French-style – but that it wasn't historic in 1243 or 1244, was it? It was virtually brand new. But does the 'oldest pub in Oxford' title sometimes given to the Bear bear examination?

Not really, and if you like history, the story's fascinating. There *has* been a pub, sometimes called the Bear, hereabouts in Oxford since 1242, but it wasn't exactly this one. The Great Bear Inn was a coaching establishment on the High. These airport-terminals-come-hotels of the day were big and rambling. Behind them were stables and yards for carriages and horses, quarters for coachmen, and beyond that, at the back of the site – it could be a quarter or half-mile away – a more rough-and- ready pub, far less grand than the big hotel or inn, for the coachmen, footmen, farriers and ostlers to drink in. I have known the parent grand inn and its humble satellite pub become so separated by other buildings and roads (as with the White Hart and White Hart Tap in St Albans) that no-one would imagine it was once all part of the same giant enterprise. This is what happened here, but more so.

The Bear Inn facing the High, at the other end of Alfred Street, was a massive operation with 30 rooms, stables for 36 horses and accommodation for all the coachmen and staff. It had indeed been built and rebuilt since early days (in medieval times being called Le Tabard), and took the Bear name (or rather the Bear and Ragged Staff, as depicted on one side of the present pub) as the emblem of the Earl of Warwick back in the Wars of the Roses days. By the 18th-century heyday of the mail coaches and turnpike roads, before the railways took their passengers away, the famous 'Oxford Machine' coach was based at the Bear Inn (today a coach service to London is called the 'Oxford Tube': not much difference, apart from the horse-power). Alfred Street was known as Bear Lane as it was lined by this great inn, which shut for redevelopment in 1801. This left just the little ostlers' pub at the bottom of the site, by then known as the Jolly Trooper, as the sole remnant of the original inn. So they gave it the name the Bear. An ostler, if you didn't know, was a chap who helped with the horses and was originally a hosteller, a hostel being what most of Europe called a hotel until the trouble-making French thought of leaving the 's' out. Which brings us back to that other question – is it 'an hotel' or 'a hotel'?

Drinkers at the Bear have been known to have their ties snipped off by the landlord for his collection which lines the walls and ceiling. You get a pint in exchange, which seems fair enough, plus the immortality of your tie and name being on the pub wall for ever. Although there is space left in the displays, there don't seem to be that many customers wearing ties nowadays.

THE CROWN INN, Cornmarket Street

It was here that a certain Will Shakespeare used to indulge in a bit of romantic comedy on his way between Stratford-upon-Avon and the Globe Theatre, London. His wife was called Hathaway, you'll recall, and he did hath it away here too, allegedly, but not with her.

THE MITRE, High Street

This is a hugely historic pub and inn, now more of a restaurant, that has seen more blood shed than some Wild West saloons and well deserves its ghosts. An Oxford don once fell dead here with a bottle of brandy in his hand, as you do. More: page 143. There is a straightforward bar round the back, the Turl Bar.

THE OLD BOOKBINDERS, Victor Street, Jericho

You may have seen this pub in *Inspector Morse* on TV, starring the late John Thaw. The pub name itself is said to be unique, although it is a common enough idea to name a pub after a trade: The Waterman's Arms, for example.

THE CAPE OF GOOD HOPE, 1 Iffley Road

Located on the bit of land at the end of Magdalen Bridge which is known as The Plain; it divides quickly into the diverging Cowley Road, Iffley Road and St Clement's. The pub between the Cowley and Iffley roads was known as the Cape of Good Hope because of its site at the end of a tongue of land like the southern tip of Africa. By that logic, the end of the buildings between Cowley Road and St Clement's should be Cape Horn (and be very difficult to get round) and Magdalen Bridge should be Antarctica. This pub has always been a great live-music venue, so its isolation from neighbouring buildings could have been an advantage.

The present building, which uses as a signboard a copy of Edvard Munch's painting *The Scream*, was designed by the ludicrously inaptly named Mr Drinkwater. Talking of which, roughly where the fountain is in the middle of the roundabout on The Plain was the miraculous **St Edmund's Well** (in the yard of the long-gone St Clement's Church), which operated until 1290 when it was banned by the Bishop of Lincoln. If by some miracle you can get the fountain to work, you could have a go but I'm not promising anything…

THE TURF, Bath Place

Formerly the Spotted Cow, an exceptional pub with some

great stories attached to it. Absolutely not to be missed if you like beer, food, history, atmosphere or people (see page 154).

THE EAGLE AND CHILD, St Giles
Also known as the Bird and Baby or even the Bird and Bastard. Where C S Lewis and J R R Tolkien met as the Inklings (see page 188).

The **BULLNOSE MORRIS**, Watlington Road, Cowley
Named after the first car that William Morris built. For more on him, see page 40.

THE ISIS FARMHOUSE, Iffley
Previously known as The Isis Tavern, this is well situated beside the Thames. No road access, pub food (page 226).

STAY ECCENTRIC

THE ROYAL OXFORD HOTEL, Park End Street
☎ 01865 248432 💻 www.royaloxfordhotel.co.uk
A short walk to the centre, this hotel is handy for the station, although parking cars is a problem (ask staff). Nice clean luxurious hotel, good spacious rooms, charming staff at front desk, cool cocktail bar and restaurant downstairs. Breakfasts excellent, but rather disdainful waitresses frankly could have been a lot more attentive and helpful on our visit. Perhaps they're just being cool like the building, but it must be confusing for Americans who are used to people actually wanting to bring you more coffee, etc. If you're going to have a buffet breakfast, you should refill the bowls of stuff. The chef-cooked breakfasts are, however, of a quality that far surpasses your average

B&B. Location is less than charming with busy traffic, but surprisingly noise wasn't a great problem when sleeping. Must have been the excellent cocktails in the bar. *Singles from £131, doubles from £131, room only.*

MALMAISON, Old Oxford Jail, Oxford Castle, 3 New Road, OX1 1AY
☎ 01865 268 400
💻 www.malmaison.com/hotels/oxford
This is deeply eccentric – getting people to pay good money to stay in what was until recently Oxford jail. Admittedly this wasn't the worst nick in Britain, not by a long stretch, being at the old castle and banged up bang in the middle of Oxford. I'm told the rooms aren't that bad as they have knocked three cells together for each room (presumably this was done by a bloke with an icepick over 40 years and covered up with a sexy poster on the wall when the screws came round, the debris being shaken out of his trouser legs in the exercise yard). You don't even get the 'slop bucket' with 'slopping out' (that is removal of waste) at 6am, so what kind do you get – ah yes, 'integral sanitation'. Normal for hotels but worth pointing out here. No bars, except the one you drink from, and cell phones in the rooms, no doubt.

Actually the hotel's line in such jokes (*'is that what they were?' – Ed*) is quite good. They say in their blurb:

> *This time we are taking no prisoners in our war on bad hotels.*

Good line, that. Well done, chaps. Not sure about the rest. 'You've been bad.' (dang, you thought no one knew about that night out in Penge). And 'You're doing time at the Mal.' (Frankly, better than doing time at the Mall, I'd say).

My Oxford prison insider tells me: 'This prison was built in the late 18th century by George Moneypenny. It was a local prison much-loved by cons as nice small cosy nick and you could "work out" in Oxford. The North Oxford old dears [do-gooder bluestockings, I think he means] loved visiting the poor old lags. It closed in the late 1990s as it was too costly to modernise. A double room now starts at £190 per night which for two, is considerably cheaper than the cost at our local prisons!'

Are you listening, right-wing newspaper columnists? It would be cheaper to check the old lags back into the gezillion-star Malmaison than to keep them there as a prison.

I do sometimes wonder about the similarity between our prisons and hotels. I mean how much worse than a cheap lodgy thing can it be? I suppose the key difference is that you can't walk out, but apart from that you get colour TV (Tory newspapers always complain, as if it were a sin and someone should find a now more expensive black and white one), clean sheets, porridge, freedom from worries about bills and mortgages... doesn't sound that bad. Couldn't we introduce just a teensy bit of pointless suffering, loads of self-financing hard work and occasional random humiliation? It'd prepare them for real life outside.

The other scandal about this was the price. I'm told the prisons department sold it for £9,000 to Oxford City Council. Well, it'd be worth what now – a top cool hotel in a great city – £30 million? That's public sector management of our money for you. Someone ought to be sent to – now where did we put that prison?

Not that any of it is Malmaison's fault. All credit to them for making such a splendid go of it. That name – doesn't it mean Bad House? Perhaps not so much House of Evil, which would be apt here but not as their other equally peaceful hotels, but Wicked (which means not bad, but cool, if you are under 200 years old, and cool means not chilly but ... oh, never mind.)

Probably unique in being a hotel ex-prison, but as my book *Eccentric Britain* says, you can stay elsewhere in plenty of lock-ups (and a brothel, lighthouse and onion store) on a B&B basis.

Back to the Malmaison Oxford. I've had nothing but good reports about it as a hotel and also about the brasserie. Best *steak frites* in the world, says my nephew. *Standard double room only, from £99.*

THE RANDOLPH, Beaumont Street ☎ 0870 4008200
This is *the* Oxford hotel. Properly The Macdonald Randolph, it could be described as baronial in style, and the great thing about that is that it can never go more out of date because it is by definition totally out of date. Or perhaps Mock-Hogwarts. One expect the immense staircase to creak and groan and move sideways: the staff who were immensely friendly and efficient included a couple of Hagrid-like characters (this is *Harry Potter* if you're puzzled). Of course it's not cheap, but it's right in the middle of Oxford opposite the Ashmolean and unless you're a student backpacker it's not that horribly expensive. I mean, if some tight-fisted grumpy old bat in a B&B charges you £65 for not being able to use her house during the day (and most of them aren't like that!), why not pay around £100 per person per night (which is what our bill worked out at, booking bargain on the internet) and have freshed starched sheets, those wonderful huge bath robes, really high-ceilinged large rooms, sumptuous bubble baths, CDs and huge TVs, nubile Nubians waving palm fronds. Well, OK, not the Nubians, but the rest was pretty good. Room service sandwich on Christmas Day cost £6.50, but then a beaming giant – it could have

been Hagrid shaved and in a suit – came to the room and delivered it cheerfully with a fresh cut rose floating in a cut glass bowl, and free munchy things alongside. It might be luxury and expensive, but I'd want a lot more than £6 on Christmas Day for such a job, and I couldn't provide a fresh rose.

Breakfast is extra – about £20 when we were there – and the best you can imagine, served beautifully and perfectly in a room hung with a mirror in a fantastical frame the size of a swimming pool, and decorated with the shields of all the colleges. I thought Kelloggs College would be particularly apt for the time of day.

We're talking preppy quality here. Posh New York country club. Or the club in *Trading Places* where the scheming millionaires hung out before Eddie Murphy arrived.

We asked for whisky and it was Tallisker single malt in the Morse Bar. It came in crystal cut glass. It came with peanuts, but not the common ones: the ones with brown skins and sea salt. A live church choir was singing carols in the dining room, not canned Muzak. At Midnight Mass we went round the corner to candlelit St Michael Northgate and had a good old go ourselves. Magic. If that's what it's like being well off, I could manage it. As American actress Sophie Tucker said about the trendy poverty of artistic types: 'I've been rich and I've been poor. Believe me, honey, rich is better.' *Singles from £134, room only. Doubles from £144.*

THE OLD BANK HOTEL, High Street ☎ 01865 799599
🖥 www.oxford-hotels-restaurants.co.uk
As central as the Randolph, even more so for the best bits of Oxford, and far more trendy. Excellent brasserie restaurant, the Quod. A former Barclays (do you cheque-in and cheque-out?), good modern art throughout,

luxurious bedrooms and bathrooms. *Doubles from £165, room only. Dinner in the Quod about £40 a head.*

THE EASTGATE, 73 High Street ☎ 01865 248332
🖥 www.accorhotels.com
This is a former coaching inn on the corner of the High and Merton Street, along towards Magdalen from the Old Bank. *Doubles from £105 including breakfast.*

THE BATH PLACE HOTEL, Bath Place ☎ 01865 791812
🖥 www.bathplace.co.uk
A little gem, little known-about but with little need to advertise, tucked away in the lane of that name leading towards the Turf pub from Holywell Street. Not a conventional hotel, but a group of 17th-century Flemish weavers' cottages around a stone-flagged courtyard, in a very quiet location right in the middle of Oxford (well some rooms might have the hum of voices from the nearby Turf Tavern on a summer's night). The rooms are therefore all different, and all individual. If you love Hiltons and Holiday Inns, don't even think about it. If you like quirky old inns with creaky floors, character and crooked walls, this is a gem. The hotel says it will arrange parking if booked in advance (a real problem round here, so do so) and there's a bar, but with the inimitable Turf, Inspector Morse and Bill Clinton's fave pub, right there, why bother? *Doubles from £118 including breakfast.*

ISIS GUEST HOUSE, 45 Iffley Road ☎ 01865 613700
🖥 www.isisguesthouse.com
Run by a college, this is available in student vacations only. There are innumerable other guesthouses on Iffley Road, Banbury and Woodstock roads. *Singles and doubles from £37, including breakfast.* See page 271 for Tourist information.

THE BACKPACKERS' HOSTEL, 9A Hythe Bridge Street ☎ 01865 721761 💻 www.hostels.co.uk
On the way to the station, this is very cheap with 92 beds in dormitories. Just hope you don't get a big snorer or 4am partygoer (unless you are one, that is). Internet access, bar, pool table etc. *Dormitory beds from £15.50.*

CENTRAL BACKPACKERS, 13 Park End Street, OX1 1HH ☎ 01865 24 22 88 💻 www.centralbackpackers.co.uk
This road is also on the way to the station from the city centre (so two mins from the bus station and railway station), but is the road south of the Royal Oxford Hotel, where the two street join. Both hostels include light breakfast and internet access. *Dormitory beds from £19.*

SHOP ECCENTRIC

Oxford is just great for eccentric, individual, idiosyncratic or just plain batty shops. True, there are the usual probably useful chain stores that could be in provincial cities anywhere in the Western world (mostly in Cornmarket, Queen Street and the malls off those roads) but they are not what Oxford is really about. Try **Magdalen Road** in East Oxford for a few way-out shops you could not predict (see page 165).

Try, above all, **Cowley Road** (see page 176) where

you can get Russian groceries, tattoos, Polish food, Bengali spices, Pakistani snacks, Greek deli at Meli's (I think it means honey in that language) – just about anything – mixed up with weird art shops and strange bars full of even stranger people. Try the brilliant bookshops all over town, and all offering something unusual (for the eccentricities of the greatest, **Blackwell's** of Broad Street, see page 163).

Walton Street, which goes north from the city at the west end of Beaumont Street (that's the street with the Randolph and Ashmolean in, so you want the other end where it hits Worcester College bang-on and just gives up), is a total gem for shopping and browsing: boho chic, delis, cafes, book shops, great little bars and restaurants, quirky clothes and jewellery. The antidote to awful chain stores and shopping malls. I love it and think you – having had the good taste to buy this book – might too.

And the point is that these are almost entirely independent and interesting, although given the money around here, not always as dirt cheap as Cowley Road, or rather offering different things (upscale posh interior design, expensive deli stuff).

Of these, here's a taster of Walton Street. **Liscious** offers achingly cool interior stuff and linen. Or a ridiculously expensive second-hand shop. You decide. There are an awful lot of people out there – as with cosmetics and women's handbags – who are greatly reassured by high prices, of course, and prefer them to low ones. But here are lovely things in a *Country Living* kind of way. Also at 12 South Parade in Summertown.

Just north of Little Clarendon Street's junction (near the south end of Walton Street) is one of these bargain remainder shops, **The Last Bookshop**, (£2 for anything at the time of writing) which is OK if you actually want the book concerned or don't like the relative for whom it

Oxford's bookshops, new and secondhand

Antiques on High, 85 High Street ☎ 01865 251075. Both affordable secondhand and pricey collectibles. Art and children's, first editions, history, philosophers.

Albion Beatnik, 34 Walton Street ☎ 01865 511345. New: speciality 20th-century fiction Marvellous.

Blackwell's Music Shop, 23-25 Broad Street ☎ 01865 792792. Music-related titles.

Blackwell's Art & Poster, 27 Broad Street. What it says on the tin.

Blackwell's and Blackwell's Rare Books, 48-51 Broad Street ☎ 01865 333555. One of the world's great bookstores and always worth a browse. For their story, see page 163.

Arcadia Booksellers, 4 St. Michael's Street ☎ 01865 241757. Secondhand paperbacks.

Booklover Oxford, 1 Woodins Way, Paradise Street ☎ 01865 247356. Secondhand books and comics. Crime, science fiction, history, military history, transport, etc.

St Philip's Books, 82 St Aldates ☎ 01865 202182. Rare and secondhand. Plus new theology.

The Inner Bookshop, 111 Magdalen Road ☎ 01865 245301. Mind, Body, Spirit, Health and the Unexplained.

The Last Bookshop, 107 St Aldates. Remainder bargains at staggeringly low prices, if you want them.

Waterstone's, William Baker House, Broad Street ☎ 0843 290 8537. Massive general bookstore. The last such big chain standing fighting off the onslaught of internet and ebook with commendable enthusiasm. Good luck to them.

WHSmith, 22 Cornmarket Street ☎ 01865 248698. They do have some popular books but this descendant of the old railway bookstalls is really more useful for magazines, newspapers and stationery.

will be a gift. I found something I loved and saved about £15, but I quipped to the friendly chap inside: 'This is the only bookshop which I hope never sells my books!'

But across the road, what a treasure: The **AB Albion Beatnik bookstore** (*34 Walton Street, OX2 6AA* ☎ *01865 511345*) is a book-lover's bookshop. The theme feels mid 20th century American intellectual, with cool jazz and lots of books from that era, but of course it covers all periods of English books. There are free leaflet guides to the Great American Novel of the 1940s, for example, which made me realise I should read a few more. The enthusiasm and friendliness of the place – there's an integral cafe – makes it great for browsing. They have poetry readings, book debates, music etc in evenings, some so popular that people crowd out of the door onto the street.

This is what good indie bookshops were once like and they were great. Give them your support (no, not your surgical appliance, buy a book!).

And look at **Raoul's** next door. Oxford's only cowboy/musician/hairdresser.

Try side streets for exploring the unexpected – **Little Clarendon Street** off St Giles, for example, for retro furniture and other curious little shops, or **Ship Street** between Cornmarket and Turl Street where there is an amazing second-hand clothes shop called Unicorn. This is more like a treasure chest with reasonably priced second-hand clothing scattered all over the floor and draped over every inch of the walls. Thirties style, '40s glamour, '50s ballgowns, swinging '60s excesses, elaborate fashions absolutely redolent of past decades. Might even be some '80s shoulderpads in there somewhere.

Even the **High** (Street), at the very centre of the tourist honeypot that is the colleges to the north and south of it, offers quirky little shops. To the oft-criticised Oxford authorities, I'd say whoever decided that the international chain stores wouldn't be allowed to put their ghastly glass frontages and bland merchandise such as mobile-phone stores (how fascinating – not!) all the way down this street deserves a gong of some sort. Just a knighthood, damehood, or sainthood. Nothing excessive.

The result is a deeply odd set of shops, very much second fiddle to the colleges, that couldn't be anywhere else.

Even here amid the hubbub of buses and bicycles, and students and tourists rushing back and forth, it is worth examining the shops for their quirky details above them. The dog holding a watch above a jewellers near Carfax, the tobacconist with the politically incorrect sign thanking you for smoking, that kind of thing.

And the **Covered Market** between the High and Market Street offers quirky individual shops *par excellence* without one single tedious multiple chain store in sight. All of these are individual traders, with a heavy emphasis on game and butchers dating back to the days when the old street market was cleared away because of the offensive shambles (this is the original meaning of the word, after all) that the slaughter, the blood and the offal made.

Today things are much more hygienic and much more varied. Try the superb delis and tell me you're not impressed. Well, actually don't, it's just a figure of speech. And there are many non-foodie outlets, such as the remarkably creative **Hat Box** boutique, a must for eccentric headgear if one is orf to the regatta or Ascot. A mad hatter, as Oxford's Alice had it, in a positive sense.

But the butchers and game side is still strong in the market, as are the well-hung pheasants sometimes.

Feller, Daughter and Son (or Son and Daughter or Daughter and Feller but possibly not Son and Feller, I can't remember which) do absolutely superb bacon – dry cured, smoked streaky is best – that is just like it were when we was nippers before factory farming and hormone treatments and giant bland pigs came along. Wonderful. Do not cook while passing vegetarians or rabbis are around, the temptation may be too strong.

Which reminds me of a rabbi and a Catholic priest in a train, a story told to me by a Jew who became a Catholic (which makes it doubly OK).

Priest: *'Tell me, Rabbi, did you ever try bacon? In complete confidence, of course.'*
Rabbi: *'Well, just the once, yes. I admit it, I did.'*
Priest: *'Good wasn't it?'*
Rabbi: *'Yes.'*
Long pause.
Rabbi: *'Tell me, Father, did you never, ever sleep with a woman?'*
Priest: *'Well, as you've been honest with me, yes, when I was 17, I strayed, with a young nun who looked rather like Sophia Loren. Wonderful girl.'*
Long pause. Train goes into tunnel. Comes out into the sunshine.
Rabbi: *'Better than bacon, wasn't it?'*

Well, this is the bacon that could make them both think again.

NUTS AND BOLTS

HOW TO GET TO OXFORD

Oxford is very well connected to national transport networks, being pretty well central to England. Any fares quoted are 2011 prices, adult return. There are discounts for children. Details subject to change.

By car

From London or the Midlands: The main route from London and the Midlands is the **M40 motorway**: two hours from Central London off-peak. At the London end the A40 which leads to the M40 is a continuation of Euston Road (which crosses the top of the West End) westwards, and has a spur down to Shepherd's Bush.

From Heathrow Airport: You need to get on the London orbital M25 (which will mean getting on the M4 westbound briefly if starting from terminals 1–3).

Turn north (clockwise) on the M25 for a few miles before turning west again on the M40. Journey time: one hour on a good day.

FROM GATWICK AIRPORT: Take the M23 in towards London (north) and pick up the M25 westbound and follow it round to the M40. Journey time: two hours on a good day.

FROM DOVER AND FERRIES: Take the M20 motorway towards London and pick up the M25 westbound as above (three hours or more).

FROM SOUTHAMPTON AND PORTSMOUTH FERRIES: Take the M3 northbound towards London (M27 westbound a while first from the latter) and then at Winchester look out for the junction with the A34 which will take you directly to Oxford (two hours or more).

Having said all that, the cross-country routes off the motorways near Oxford really repay the effort if you've got a good map and bags of time.

RECOMMENDED FOR SCENIC BEAUTY AND LOVELY PUBS: From the south, turn off into Newbury and take the A4 west briefly, turning north past Donnington on the road for Wantage. It's achingly beautiful. At Wantage turn east and pick up the A34 into Oxford. If starting from Reading city centre, go through the town over Caversham Bridge across the Thames and turn left to pick up the A4074 for Oxford.

PARKING

Access is deliberately awful in Oxford. If you come from Vulture Gulch or somewhere where you drive up and park outside Hank the trapper's store with no restrictions, you've got a real shock coming. You cannot drive up the High (Street), making it almost impossible to go from the west of the city centre (near the station) to the east (Magdalen Bridge) except on a bus or by canoe. North to south isn't much better, although just about possible. You are bound to spend some time in queues. Instead use the ring road that encircles the city or, if you have a street map, suburban cut-throughs such as Marston Ferry Road and Donnington Bridge.

Plus it's almost impossible – really – to park a car in the city centre. Any promising side streets at the city end of Cowley Road, for example, or near the station will be residents only.

So you have to use **Park-and-Ride** facilities, which are located on all the major routes into town, or make up your own by parking in a suburban street and catching a bus in. The buses are cheap and frequent on the main roads and from the Park And Ride locations on all four points of the compass (on the A34 from the north, A420 from the west, A4144 from the south and A40 from the east), or just park in a side street on Cowley Road to the southeast, or Banbury or Woodstock Road to the north, and take one of the many buses heading for the town. It's that simple.

You can park for a while if you're very lucky at St Giles, the wide thoroughfare in the north of the city, and in the west a hotel manager advised me to use the signposted railway long-stay car park at £5.60 for 24 hours, and gave me the cheapest-possible train ticket dated for that day (child single to Islip, 65p) because you apparently need one to get out (I didn't). I don't know if it's advisable or legal, but it was interesting that a hotel was driven to such lengths by the city's parking fascists (yes, I know, they're not really, it just feels like that).

SECURITY: If possible, park under a street lamp or in a car park with CCTV, and don't leave valuables in your car or anything that might lead some scumbag to break in. I've suffered in Oxford (just once in many years). A break-in could really spoil your holiday.

BY RAIL

Oxford is well served not only from **London Paddington** (one hour; £21.50 off-peak day return, £22.50 return advance off peak, £52 anytime including rush-hour, note web has advance returns for £10.50 on a few trains) but also directly from many provincial cities such as Southampton, Birmingham, Brighton, Edinburgh, York and Manchester. The ride out by train from Reading to Didcot is delightfully smooth along the beautiful Thames Valley because Brunel laid out the track like a billiard table and insisted on his own eccentric wide track gauge.

If coming from Heathrow, there is the **Heathrow Express** link into Paddington but for a family it's not cheap (22 minutes; £18 single; every 15 minutes – expensive for something going the wrong way and slower than it was to start with). Why some durbrain didn't make it possible for westbound trains from London to call in at Heathrow en route to places such as Oxford, I don't know. I hope when the Oxford rail electrification happens, this will be done at long last. Imbeciles!

If coming from Gatwick you can either take the **Gatwick Express** into London (30 minutes; £17.90 single, but you can get to London in about the same time with other train operators for £9.40, so do check) and battle round on the Underground to Paddington, or (better) take the cross-country Gatwick–Reading trains, a pleasant ride, avoiding most of the hassle. Then Oxford is only a few stops out from Reading (two hours or more; £31 off peak return, £59.40 anytime). Oxford railway station is a little out of town – a walk of over half a mile up New Road to Carfax. If you are carrying huge suitcases, tiny children or have difficulty walking, you will need a local bus or taxi (outside station on city, east side). It is worth researching the best train fares and times in advance. Nothing is fixed in railway prices. ☎ *08457 484950* 🖥 *www.nationalrail.co.uk*

By bus

Preferred mode for students and many other people because although slower than the train, it goes more to the city centres at each end, is cheaper and more frequent. The bus station in Oxford is at **Gloucester Green**, west of the town centre between George Street and Beaumont Street.

Three competing companies offering luxury coaches from London, 1hr 40min–2hr, £14/£20 approx, pick-up points en route, including the High (Street) and Headington in Oxford and Marble Arch and Hillingdon in London:

X90 Oxford Espress
🖥 www.oxfordbus.co.uk/london.html
From Victoria Coach station in London.

The Oxford Tube ☎ 01865 772250
🖥 www.oxfordtube.com
From Victoria Grosvenor Gardens in Victoria, London

Megabus ☎ 01738 639095 🖥 www.megabus.com
Very low fares – as little as £13 last time I looked – for advance bookings on internet. From Gloucester Place in London.

NATIONAL EXPRESS: ☎ 08717 818181
🖳 www.nationalexpress.com
Check for buses from other British cities.

There is also a very useful direct airport service, **Airline** (☎ 01865 785 400 🖳 www.theairline.info), with departures every 30 minutes for Heathrow (70-minute journey, £18/£26) and every hour for **Gatwick** (two hours, £27/£36). You can pick these up from stand 14 at Heathrow central bus station, Heathrow Terminal 5, stand 18, stand 8 at Gatwick South Terminal coach station, and stand 4 at the Gatwick North Terminal. You can pay on the bus in sterling, euros or US dollars, but you need cash not cards. All services, calling points and fares liable to change.

IN OXFORD

ABC TAXIS ☎ 01865 770077
RADIO TAXIS ☎ 01865 249743 or 242424

AIRPORT CARS

OXICARS ☎ 01865 875900 🖳 www.oxicars.com
From Heathrow £85, from Gatwick £145, per car one-way, less on return from Oxford because of parking and waiting. For a family group this may work out cheaper one-way if not return, and certainly easier.

AIRPORT ACCESS

See under relevant headings for modes of transport above. Choose Heathrow first.

TOURIST INFORMATION

15 Broad Street ☎ 01865 252500 ▦ www.visitoxford.org

WHEELCHAIR ACCESS

Oxford is in many ways far better for wheelchair users than, say, up-and-down Edinburgh because it is flat and on river levels. But of course many of the buildings are not adapted for wheelchair use. The city council's *Accessible Oxford Guide* is a free publication available from the Oxford Information Centre, the Oxford Town Hall and most council buildings. There's also an excellent self-guided wheelchair-friendly tour on the web. Go into the website (above) and look for accessibility and you can find it there.

PHONE NUMBERS

If phoning from abroad, you need to dial whatever your country's code for international calls is (011 from the USA, for instance), then the country code for Britain (which is 44), then the area code and local number leaving off the initial 0. So from the USA, an Oxford number such as tourist information on ☎ 01865 252200 becomes ☎ 011 44 1865 252200.

Area codes are included in this book – these only need to be dialled when calling from outside the area. The code for Oxford is 01865.

Emergencies 999
Directory enquiries 118 500 (and various similar numbers)

Oxford's oddest relic

IF you were told that Oxford's oddest historic relic is around 20ft wide, 100ft long and weighs 200 tons, is made of iron and steel, is in full open air, that nearly everyone in Oxford has passed within a few feet of it, yet no-one knows it is there, you might be puzzled. Is is true, however. Well, almost no-one, and yes, I'm guessing the weight. Just north of Oxford railway station, a useful cut links the Oxford Canal with the Thames. You can reach this on foot by walking up the towpath of the river north (right) from the first river bridge on the Botley Road west of Oxford station. You cross the channel on an arched footbridge, then turn right and for goodness sake duck your head as you pass under the main line tracks close to the platform ends. You then come across the relic: an entire railway swing bridge, which clearly connects nothing with nothing, yet is still there, in the open-to-boats position. Why was it built?

Well thereby hangs a classic tale of those who do not study history being doomed to repeat it. In the 19th century, the Great Western Railway reached Oxford from the south. Soon the townsfolk were fed up with the monopoly's poor service, and the rival London & North Western decided to approach from the northwest, through Bicester, to give Oxford a choice. This bridge linked the new line to Oxford Rewley Road station, which was where the Said Business School now is on Frideswide Square. After nationalisation, there was no point having two stations, so it was closed 60 years ago.

In recent denationalised years, however, First Great Western has enjoyed a similar rail monopoly and guess what? People again feel that a choice would be a good thing, and a new line linking to the Chiltern Railway route down from Bicester is being built to repeat what was done more than a century ago and then forgotten.

ECCENTRIC GLOSSARY

Your guide through the eccentric linguistic jungle of Oxford University's deeply tangled terminology. Anything not in English is probably Latin. Talking about which, we use *QV* in here, which you probably know means *quod vide*, literally see which, or in practical terms – it's got its own entry.

AEGROTAT He (or she) is ill, literally. A type of degree awarded to someone who was too ill to sit the tripos exams. Several of them would be *aegrotant*. You have to have done or caught something pretty dreadful.

ASHMOLEAN Oldest museum in Britain, created by Edias Ashmole; see page 183.

ALUMNUS Pretty well-known word for a graduate, thanks to endless American college films, but actually means in Latin nursling, one who is nourished. In English it means a student who has matriculated, but not necessarily graduated. Plural *alumni*, feminine *alumna* and *alumnae*.

ANOTHER PLACE The evil entity that is Cambridge, a college-studded swamp somewhere in the backward swamps of fenland. This aversion to naming your arch-rival is like that in the House of Lords where they traditionally refer to Another Place, not the Commons (or is it the other way round?).

ARSE-FREEZER Short gown.

AULARIANS To do with a hall. Before they invented colleges and collegians, everyone was Aularians at Oxford. Teddy Hall members still are.

BATTELS Charges made to college members for rooms, grub, booze, etc.

BEDDEL Bigwig in official processions. Probably related to Beadle. There are four of them.

BLUE Two meanings, the colour Oxford Blue, which is dark blue (Pantone 282 on a computer, I'm told; don't order panettone 282 unless you're starving) as opposed to Cambridge's light, and also the honour of competing against that other university in sport. One becomes a Blue rather like one becomes an England Cap for playing for the country. Also some lesser sports (may I suggest, by the way, dwile flonking, bog snorkelling or conkers?) earn a half blue, which sounds like a mauve grey. The people concerned, if multi-talented, can become one and a half blues, an even more peculiar concept. Deep purple, possibly.

BOATER Not, of course, a boater. A hard straw hat that might be worn by one, liable to be set on fire by oiks (this happened to me!), thus becoming a blazer.

Blazer Not, of course, a blazer. But rowing club members of Another Place had bright-red jackets once, which were nicknamed blazers, now it's all of them.

Bodleian The splendid, ancient, huge and brilliant library.

Bulldog Much-feared bowler-hatted university police who used to enforce rigorously wearing of gowns, curfews, etc. Good sprinters, often, so 'Here come the bloody bulldogs, the ********, run!' only worked if you were Roger Bannister. Known to drag students half out of windows back by the heels.

Bumps Boat races where you overtake a crew ahead by not always literally bumping them, but drawing level, except in Another Place where they don't have a proper river so do sometimes literally bump them, with, in at least one case, fatal results.

Buttery A kind of cafeteria/tuckshop attached to college kitchens where one might eat something other than the formal college dinners. Having had one at school, I'd always assumed it was something to do with butter, but learned people point out that, like butler, its origins are probably to do with bottles.

Chancellor Ceremonial head of the university. Mostly flummery. A title given to someone already rich, powerful and famous to do not much.

Cherwell The other river coming down from Marston to Magdalen, much better for perfectly peaceful punting. Pronounced Charwell.

CLERK OF THE MARKET Official appointed to not set the price of grain in Oxford. He once did this, now he doesn't, but still gets appointed.

COD Concise Oxford Dictionary. If you think 240,000 entries and 1,728 pages is the meaning of 'Concise' they had better look it up. They mean compared to the parent Oxford English Dictionary with 21,000 pages.

COFFEE Rather boringly, the drug of choice for today's so serious students. In fact, such is Oxford's obsession with the beautiful, brown-baked berry (not really a bean) that one suspects agents of the Coffee Marketing Board have got together with the spies from Another Place (see above) and hijacked one of the University physics labs to build a Coffee Bar Duplication Ray-Gun, no doubt controlled by some evil bald git in a rotating black leather chair stroking a white cat.

I mean, you go into a bookshop and what's there? Coffee bar. College, Coffee bar. Church, Coffee bar. Museum, Coffee bar. Station, Coffee bar. In between these institutions that would make a visiting Costa Rican dance with joy, there are more coffee bars in case you can't stagger 40 yards without another shot. In my day we didn't have *mocha latte gran turismo in excelsis gloria* (is that decaff? With Peruvian goat's milk? Skimmed or semi? And unrefined demerara organic sugar or Bolivian natural cane?). We made do with honest, simpler stuff: cannabis, Speed, scrumpy, LSD, opium, brass polish, revolting home-brew goat and parsnip wine, vodka stolen from grown-ups, etc, etc. Maybe that's why students are so damned studious nowadays and fewer of them are in mental hospitals.

Not that coffee is all good, of course. There was a report

when I lived in Another Place of an undergrad who had not revised much. She sat up all night and ate spoonfuls of dry instant coffee (yeuch) from the jar until she was buzzing. The whole jar! She walked into the exam the next day, scored the highest mark of her life and then dropped dead.

COLLECTIONS Termly examinations. Or a charity nitwit trying to save the albino dolphins of Chad from sunburn.

CONGREGATION About 4,000 senior bods such as fellows and professors who are the legislative body of the university and the nearest thing it has to existing at all (as opposed to being a federation of colleges). Not to be confused with…

CONVOCATION All graduates plus all members of congregation (above), who elect a new Chancellor and a new Professor of Poetry. The latter appointment, which you could think the most polite and civilised thing on the planet, was in fact accompanied by a barrage of back-biting bitchery (no reflection on the excellent people concerned, of course) connected with the 2009 election (which was put aside after awful alliteration angered alumni, onomatopoeia sizzled, hyperbole went absolutely galactic, tautology climbed up to a high peak, oxymorons were terribly kind, euphemism hit the air conditioning and simile was like a bloodbath in a metaphorical dungheap).

COMMONER Nothing to do with being a pleb, lout, yob, oik or chav. In fact many Oxford commoners are posh, and could be aristocrats or Eton scholars. It simply meant those who paid for their own food (as in 'short commons') rather than exhibitioners and scholars who didn't. They wear shorter gowns, known commonly as arse-freezers.

CREWEIAN ORATION Delivered at Encaenia (qv) often by the Professor of Poetry. A summary of the year's achievements. Named after the old buffers at Crewe railway junction. Or possibly Lord Crewe who first thought of it.

QUAD Used instead of *court*, a term from Another Place, for the large square spaces surrounded by buildings. The large square space surrounded by teeth, however, may be Andy Murray or his mum on a flying visit.

DAILY INFORMATION Oddly for Oxford, does what it says, in paper or online. Tells you what's going on.

DESMOND Studentspeak for a 2:2 degree, after Bishop Desmond Tutu of South Africa. Similarly – and you can have fun guessing the rhymes – a first is similarly a Damien; a 2:1 an Attila; a third a Douglas; a fail a Dan.

DONS Slang name for all tutors, professors, master, fellows, lecturers, etc.

EIGHTS WEEK Inter-college rowing regatta in mid-summer, Pimm's, blazers, boaters, fit young manly types slicing ludicrously thin boats past ludicrously thin gels. The really, really thin boats compete in After-Eights week.

ENCAENIA Multiple choice – (a) the beneficial bug that makes yoghurt good for you, (b) a forgotten Baltic state or (c) the ceremony where Oxford degrees are conferred and the Creweian Oration (qv) is delivered.

EXEAT Boarding school types may remember this term, being permission to leave, or he may leave. Plural is, illogically, *exeats* but, hey, that's what happens when you mix two incompatible languages.

EXHIBITION In an academic sense, means a particularly high-scoring student who gets a money grant to help him/her being at Oxford, becoming an exhibitioner, not necessarily an exhibitionist. Related purely to brains, not need. My Oxford Boswellian companion in this book was one such. Not quite as good as a scholar.

FELLOW Member of the governing academic staff of a college. Gender neutral, (helpful as gender is not always clear or fixed in Oxford).

GAUDY Formal nosh-up at college, often for alumni.

GREATS Classics, *id est* Latin and Greek.

HEAD OF THE RIVER Winning crew in Torpids or Eight Weeks. Or the pub named after them at Folly Bridge.

HIGH TABLE The master and dons usually sit at a table in the college hall set at right angles to the main ones, and raised on a wooden platform. Or the people who would sit at such a table.

HILARY TERM Most universities dishonestly call it Spring Term (January–March) although that is still winter.

HOOD Attached to academic gowns for various occasions, these denote rank and learning and are carefully distinguished by colour and design. Insanely, even though the Oxford canal freezes solid sometimes, they are never, ever worn. Perhaps to stop people looking like those dead chaps in *Lord of the Rings* all hood and no face. People actually wearing hoods, on the other hand, are those who the middle class fear are going to steal all their muesli (as if they would be interested) – argh, it's the hoodies!

Isis Name for River Thames while in Oxford for no reason whatsoever.

JCR Junior Common Room, the student social organisation of each college.

Long vac The long summer holiday. Or a Hoover job in Christ Church.

Michaelmas term The autumn term and possibly the nicest of Oxford's silly names for terms, maybe because we have Michaelmas daisies. If you know your saints' days, then it is September 29, Feast of Saints Michael, Gabriel, and Raphael, the Feast of the Archangels, or the Feast of Saint Michael and All Angels.

Mods Exams at the end of your first year. Or geezers on motorscooters with fur-trimmed parka coats and sharp-creased trousers.

Norrington table A league table of how colleges are performing.

Noughth week A rarely used adjective to denote the week before term. And we accuse the Irish of assembling unpronounceable words!

Oxford dikker of quotaggers Ox -er slang for the Oxford Dictionary of Quotations. Allegedly.

OUDS Pronounced 'owds', Oxford University Dramatic Society.

OUP Oxford University Press (see page 194).

PARSON'S PLEASURE Where male dons would sun-bathe naked and shock passing punters on the Cherwell. The female version, Dame's Delight, hardly seems to have got going.

PIGEON POST The free internal mail system, not involving pigeons, but possibly connected with...

PLUCK As an examiner, to fail someone at an examination. Shakespeare uses it.

PUBLIC ORATOR Makes speeches etc. One was appointed in a panic in 1564 when Queen Elizabeth I was coming and no one has noticed that you don't really need one since.

QUICHE A verb, to not try hard enough, particularly in rowing. They're losing because they are quiching. *Derivation:* Real men don't eat quiche.

PUNTING A ludicrous, tedious, expensive and accident-prone way of getting from A back to A again on a boat without steering, keel, sides, motor, catering, sails, oars, navigation, GPS, radio or liferaft, and thus extremely popular. Fun to try and a great way to see Oxford (see page 203).

RUSTICATE Has two apparently unconnected meanings at Oxford. A *rusticated* course of stone in a building is a layer of unfinished, rough-hewn stone in an otherwise smooth wall, for visual effect. A *rusticated* student is one who has been sent down for misbehaving, probably temporarily. The link is in the Latin *rus*, countryside. The one is to build as they do in rural country, the other to be sent back there.

SCHOLAR A superior grade of undergrad, who has won a scholarship. No need to wear a mere arse-freezer (qv) but can have a full gown. Therefore more protection when buns hurled about at formal dinners.

SCHOOLS Means anything except schools. To *take schools* is to sit exams in the *schools building*, which may be in a *school of philosophy*, academically. Clear?

SCOUTS A servant in the colleges for domestic cleaning etc. Used to be bedmakers and fetch hot water to pour down the students' backs, making up fires etc. Nowadays more of a cleaner. Once paid almost entirely in tips and unused commons (qv), which they would carry off in baskets and resell. The scout takes on a *staircase* in a college, that is the various *sets* of rooms off one stairway. In Another Place they are called Bedders.

STUDENT A tutor at Christ Church, so not, of course, a student.

SUB-FUSC Formal suit and gown garb for students and fellows, meaning in Latin dark brown, which, of course, it never is.

SPORTING YOUR OAKS A phrase that could mean something honours-related like resting on your laurels. In fact it means the equivalent of those notices on hotel door knobs saying 'Do not disturb'. Sets of rooms in colleges have two doors, one opening into the room, and one into the hall or staircase. If both are closed (leaving a small gap between them, that is), it means the occupant is away, studying hard and not wishing to be disturbed, discussing Uganda with a member of the opposite sex (or even, fwankly Wupert, the same one), or enduring a hangover from hell after unwisely downing 16 pints of Bogblaster's Old Disgusting at the Flatulent Ferret last night. A favourite request to departing guests is 'Close both doors, I don't want to be disturbed. Would you mind closing the outer door first please?'

TORPIDS Summer rowing races.

TRINITY TERM In the fine Oxford tradition of calling a spade a wombat, this means summer term.

TRIVIUM The only three ways (in Latin) to starts a degree in early times Grammar, Logic and Rhetoric. But it was elementary undergraduate stuff, hence our word *trivial*.

UP AND DOWN Let's get one thing straight. You go *up* to Oxford, even by the *down* train from London. Conversely, you'd catch the *up* train to go *down*. If you got sent *down*, it'd be *down* to what you got *up* to, and you'd certainly be *up* for a dressing *down*. If you went to study a further degree at Cambridge, you could be going *down* and *up* at once. You may of course be not *up* yet and feeling a little *down*, *down* to *downing* a few pints, which is *up* to you. It all makes perfect sense, like people going *up* the *Downs* in Sussex, or being *down* on your *uppers*, or cricketers who are *in* going *out* and then coming *in* when they're *out*. If you're foreign, you probably think by now I'm absolutely barking. Not literally barking ... oh, never mind. It's just the rather flexible English language where it seems a word, as the Red Queen said in *Alice*, means what I want it to mean.

VICE-CHANCELLOR The person in charge of vice. No, silly, silly ... this is the only really important bod who does anything round here. At most universities, he or she wields the real power while the Chancellor (qv) does little more than ponce about and eat vol-au-vents masquerading as canapés, sip getting-too-warm champagne and smile at twits, numpties and poltroons (it's called networking). Good thing this doesn't apply in the White House with vice-prez and prez, you may reasonably think...

VIVA An oral exam, from Latin *viva voce*, meaning live voice. Or a particularly poxy Vauxhall car from the 1960s.

INDEX